关于价格和货币流通状况的历史

A History of Prices, and of the State of the Circulation

（英）托马斯·图克（Thomas Tooke）
（英）威廉·纽马奇（William Newmarch） 著

中国财富出版社

图书在版编目(CIP)数据

关于价格和货币流通状况的历史. 第一卷 = A History of Prices, and of the State of the Circulation Volume 1:英文 / (英)托马斯·图克(Thomas Tooke),(英)威廉·纽马奇(William Newmarch)著.—北京:中国财富出版社,2019.12

ISBN 978-7-5047-7104-9

Ⅰ.①关… Ⅱ.①托… ②威… Ⅲ.①经济史—英国—1793-1856—英文 Ⅳ.①F156.194.1

中国版本图书馆 CIP 数据核字(2019)第 270157 号

策划编辑 郭 莹 **责任编辑** 张冬梅 郭 莹
责任印制 尚立业 **责任校对** 卓闪闪 **责任发行** 白 昕

出版发行 中国财富出版社
社 址 北京市丰台区南四环西路 188 号 5 区 20 楼 **邮政编码** 100070
电 话 010-52227588 转 2098(发行部) 010-52227588 转 321(总编室)
010-52227588 转 100(读者服务部) 010-52227588 转 305(质检部)
网 址 http://www.cfpress.com.cn
经 销 新华书店
印 刷 北京九州迅驰传媒文化有限公司
书 号 ISBN 978-7-5047-7104-9/F·3131
开 本 710mm×1000mm 1/16 **版 次** 2020 年 8 月第 1 版
印 张 25.5 **印 次** 2020 年 8 月第 1 次印刷
字 数 355 千字 **定 价** 148.00 元

PREFACE

The present Work may, in some points of view, be considered as an enlargement and continuation of one which was published fifteen years ago under the title of "Thoughts and Details on the High and Low Prices of the Last Thirty Years," inasmuch as it embraces the same line of argument, and proposes to establish the same conclusions; but it is essentially different, both in its arrangement and in its details. The view now presented of the operation on prices of the more general causes, precedes instead of following, as in that work it did, the statements bearing upon the period more immediately under consideration: while the details are here placed in chronological order, and in historical connection, embracing a much wider collection of illustrative facts, more especially of those relating to the state of the circulation; with a continuation of the narrative of events in their relation to prices, and to the state of the circulation, in the fifteen years which have elapsed since the publication of the above-named Work. In fact, with the exception of a very small part, the whole of that which is now submitted to the public, has been written afresh, and has therefore every claim to be considered as a new Work.

London, *April* 28, 1838.

CONTENTS

PART Ⅱ ON THE EFFECT OF WAR

PART Ⅲ ON THE CURRENCY

INTRODUCTION

The high range of prices which prevailed in the closing years of the past, and in the earlier part of the present century, contrasted with the comparatively low range, observable in the period which has elapsed from 1819 to the present time, forms a very striking feature in the history of the agriculture and commerce of this country. The contrast thus presented involves fluctuations in the value of property so great as naturally to have excited, both from a sense of interest and from a feeling of rational curiosity, an anxious desire to obtain a satisfactory solution of phenomena so remarkable. Accordingly, publications without number or end have appeared, professing to explain the extraordinary variations of prices which have marked that eventful period. The explanations hitherto offered, whatever may have been the nature of the proofs and illustrations brought forward in support of them, resolve themselves mostly, if not wholly, into the assignment of one or other of two general causes; namely, the WAR and the CURRENCY.

The effect of war in raising the prices of articles directly taxed, has been generally admitted. But as the amount of taxes levied for defraying the expenses of the war continually (with the exception of the property tax, which avowedly did not act upon prices) undiminished down to the summer of 1822; and as the fall of prices of articles divested of duty, that of provisions especially, had then been as great, and to as low a point of depression as has, with trifling exceptions, been since witnessed; and moreover, as the very great reduction of duties of customs and excise, which has taken place since 1822, has not been attended with any corresponding fall of the prices of provisions, or of other articles divested of duty, the previous elevation of prices cannot be ascribed to the war, merely on the ground of its attendant taxation. ①It is, accordingly, to the war, not as having caused the taxes, but chiefly as having, by the enormous amount of the government expenditure defrayed by loans, caused a great and increasing demand for all the leading articles of consumption, that the remarkable elevation of prices has been ascribed by a theory which numbers among its supporters no mean authorities.

But the theory of war-demand, as having raised prices, and of the peace as having, by the consequent cessation of that demand, been necessarily followed by a fall of prices, is now rarely advanced. The preponderant, and almost exclusive theory, is that which refers all the phenomena of high prices from 1792 till 1819, and of the comparative low prices since 1819, to alterations in the system of our currency, holding all other circumstances that can have had any influence to be so subordinate as not to be worth mentioning.

These opinions, however ingeniously and plausibly advanced and

---

① The impediments to importation, and the consequently increased cost of foreign supplies, are occasionally referred to as accounting for some increase of price. But this effect of the war is slightly noticed, and laid little stress upon by any of the supporters of either of the theories of war-demand or of the currency.

maintained, admit, as I conceive, of being shown, by a careful examination of facts, to be wholly erroneous. The error, indeed, of the theory of war-demand, is no longer one which can be attended with any practical evil. The association of war with high prices, and supposed consequent prosperity, is not likely to exercise any influence on the foreign policy of our government. But there is constant danger from the prevalent theory of the currency.

Repeated attempts have, even down to recent periods, been made to induce the legislature to revise, with a view to alter and debase, the present standard of value; and such is the pertinacity with which the opinions in favour of debasement, or of a return to inconvertible paper are urged, and the weight of influence by which they are supported, that there is ground for apprehension lest, under the pressure of any temporary inconvenience, the legislature might be led to listen to some one or other of the multifarious schemes for the degradation of the currency which are always afloat.

The claims for revision, and the plans for alteration, all proceed on the assumption that the greater part, if not the whole, of the rise, and of the high range of prices observable during the interval in which cash payments were suspended, was distinctly caused by the restriction, and that the resumption of cash payments has been the main, if not the exclusive, cause of the subsequent fall of prices.

The persons maintaining this doctrine hold, as a settled article of their creed, that Mr. Ricardo, and the other promoters of the Act of 1819 for the resumption of cash payments, commonly called Peel's Bill, were manifestly in error when they contended that the utmost effect of that measure upon prices would not exceed 4 or 5 per cent, that being the difference which then existed between paper and gold; for, that in fact, the consequences of the passing of that bill have been felt in a general fall of prices to the extent of 30 and 40 per cent, and, according to some, even to the extent of 50 per cent.

Granting, for the sake of argument, that Mr. Ricardo and the other promoters of Peel's Bill were wrong, and that the whole of the fall of the prices of commodities and labour, and of property generally, had been clearly the *consequence*, and not merely *a sequence* of that measure, it would not follow that there would be any claim on grounds of justice, and still less on grounds of policy, to unsettle a settlement made so many years ago. But if it should be made to appear by the most extensive induction of facts, that Peel's Bill *did not*, as according to any correct mode of reasoning it *could not*, cause the fall of prices beyond the difference between paper and gold, there would cease to be even the shadow of a pretence for the clamour which has been raised, and so pertinaciously maintained, against that just, wise, and salutary measure.

It is of practical importance in this respect, as also with the object of forming a just estimate of many things otherwise inexplicable in the state of agriculture and trade, at the several periods of the interval under consideration, to take a more extended survey than has hitherto been attempted of facts bearing upon the question. To institute such a survey, and to endeavour by it to rescue from misconception and misrepresentation the most eventful and interesting periods in the history of the agriculture and commerce of this country, is the purpose of the present work.

It is perfectly possible, that a knowledge of the facts about to be stated may lead to conclusions different from those which I may think them calculated to establish. But it is quite certain that without a knowledge of those facts, not only as to their existence but as to the order of time in which they occurred, no correct estimates can be formed, no just conclusions drawn with reference to the questions under discussion; and it may not be assuming too much to add, that without a knowledge of the circumstances, which will be detailed in their connection with prices, no just conception can be formed of the nature and causes of the great vicissitudes which have marked the state of agriculture, of manufactures, and commerce in the long interval which is to come under examination.

The general description of the principal causes to which the phenomena of the high prices observable between 1792 and 1819, and the comparatively low prices from 1819 to the present time, will be found referable, according to my view of them, may be classed under the following heads:

1. The Variety of the Seasons.
2. The War.
3. The Currency.

There are, indeed, two other circumstances of a general character, which may be supposed to have influenced prices, viz., the increase of population, and the improvements in agriculture and manufactures. But as these circumstances have been uniform and progressive in their operation, although in opposite directions, they do not form any prominent part of the grounds on which the great *fluctuations* of prices can be accounted for.

In as far as the mere increase of population might be supposed to account for any part of the range of high prices of provisions, by the necessity of resorting for production to inferior soils, it must be admitted (the ratio of increase of population having been progressive) as a counteraction of any tendency to fall. And as the improvements in agriculture and manufactures, all tending greatly to reduce the cost of production, were in progress during the whole period, although not so rapidly in the earlier part of it, they must have operated as a corrective against so great an advance in price of those articles to which they applied, as might from the operation of other causes have been expected. This cause need therefore only be incidentally referred to, as accounting for the further fall of the particular commodities to which it is applicable, below the level to which they might otherwise have subsided.

The historical sketch which will be given in the course of this work, of the circumstances which may admit of being connected in the relation of cause and effect with prices, will afford the means of judging of the degree in which each, or any one or more, of the three general causes above stated may be supposed to have operated. But the conclusions to be drawn from a view of the facts as they occurred in connection with prices, during the period immediately under consideration, will derive additional force in as far as they may be found to be consistent with what might be inferred *à priori* from a reference to the mode and degree of influence of those general causes, and from experience of what has been their operation during intervals of some length anterior to 1793.

The course which it seems most expedient to adopt with this view is, in the first place, to consider the mode of operation of each of these causes, and the relative degree of importance to be attached to it on general grounds, illustrated by a reference to any observable influence exercised by it in some of the most prominent fluctuations of prices, antecedent to the period more immediately under examination, and then to proceed, with the inferences thus derived, to investigate the degree of influence that may be legitimately ascribed, separately or collectively, to these causes in the great variations of prices that have occurred since 1792.

PART I

ON THE EFFECT OF THE SEASONS

CHAPTER I
GENERAL VIEW OF THE SUBJECT

Nothing has struck me as being more strange in all the discussions and reasonings upon the subject of the high and low prices of the period under consideration, than the little importance which has been attached to the effects which a difference in the character of the seasons is calculated to occasion.

Individuals interested in the markets for agricultural produce are habitually alive to the prodigious influence of the weather, at particular periods, on the result of the harvest in point of quantity, and still more in point of exchangeable value; and yet the same individuals, when called upon to account for a range of high or low prices at an antecedent period, perfectly within their recollection, seem wholly to neglect or overlook the consideration of the possibility of any influence on an extended scale of that cause, to which in detail, or in accounting for the produce of any particular year, they cannot help attaching a weight preponderating over every other. The farmer naturally, and almost instinctively, watches, with painful anxiety, the several critical periods in the growth of the different descriptions of produce, and infers, according as appearances are decidedly unfavourable or propitious, and as they extend, or are supposed to extend, generally to the same descriptions of produce in other districts, the probability of a great alteration in the price: thus severe frost, or heavy rains at the blooming time, or unfavourable weather at harvest, or general indications of blight or mildew, or other extensive injury from some peculiarity in the atmosphere, lead him irresistbly to the conclusion that, supposing the same cause to apply to the greater part of the country, there must be a great rise in price, whatever may be the state of the currency, or the aspect of politics. If, on the contrary, after a year of bad produce and high prices, appearances are favourable for the growing crops; or if, after threatening indications of injury in the earlier stages of vegetation, the weather suddenly becomes propitious, all parties interested in the price immediately anticipate a fall, without refining upon the supposed agency of other causes.

Yet such being, in the minds of farmers and of persons interested in the corn trade, the paramount importance of the influence of particular seasons on the production of corn, it is not a little surprising, that among the numerous witnesses examined by the parliamentary committees on agricultural distress, there appears to have been, with a single exception, none who included in their consideration of the means of accounting for the prevalence of the high prices from 1793 to 1815, the possibility of a more than usually frequent recurrence of unfavourable seasons, which, combined with the impediments from the war to a foreign supply, might go far to explain the phenomena. The general impression has been, both among practical men and speculative writers, that although there were two instances of scarcities during the war, viz. 1794, 1795, and 1799, 1800, and one subsequently in 1816, there was nothing otherwise of deficiency from the season of more than usual occurrence, or such as to justify a higher than usual range of prices between 1793 and 1819.[①]

Even when incidentally admitting the effect of the more prominent scarcities, little if any notice is taken of the mode and degree in which deficient crops promoted, during their prevalence, the prosperity of the farmers and landlords, or of the inevitable effect of the transition from a long course of comparative dearth to abundance, in causing agricultural distress.

With a view to show that there is nothing unwarranted by experience, in the supposition of the more frequent recurrence of unfavourable seasons in intervals of twenty years or upwards, than in intervals of equal length immediately preceding or succeeding; or in the assignment of a succession of years of plenty, as a cause of suffering to farmers and landlords; I propose to adduce instances derived from antecedent periods in the history of our agriculture. In order, however, to judge of the degree in which the variations of the seasons, such as they will be shown to have been, are calculated to affect the prices of produce and the condition of the agricultural interests, it may be necessary to premise some general observations on the effects of quantity on price.

---

① The partizans of war-demand, limit their explanation of high prices to 1814, while those of the currency extend theirs to 1819.

CHAPTER II
EFFECTS OF QUANTITY ON PRICE

It is not uncommon to meet with persons, who, in reasoning upon prices of corn and other commodities, take for granted that the variations in price must be in exact or near proportion to the variations in the quantity which may, at different times, be actually in the market or in the country for sale; and who, if the variations in price do not correspond with the variations in quantity in a near proportion, infer that there must be something in the currency, or some unusual cause in operation, to account for what appears to them so anomalous an effect. Thus, the late Mr. Mushet, in a treatise on the currency, the object of which is to account for all the phenomena of prices by the state of the circulation, maintained, that such a fall of price as was in question could not be the effect of abundance if the currency remained unaltered, nor be productive of agricultural distress.

"Mr. Tooke has land too much stress upon this argument: the cheapness that would follow from increased production would come gradually upon the public; and, if the amount of currency remained the same, the fall in prices would be relative to their abundance. But that one, or even two, good harvests should cause a fall of price generally from 30 to 45 per cent, is giving more to the bounty of nature than I think will be found consistent with the fact. But admitting the fact, does it follow that this abundance should cause general distress, and reduce the agricultural community to the verge of ruin? Admitting the argument, that a productive harvest would cause a fall of price beyond the actual abundance, would the farmer have no recompense whatever from such abundance? Would such abundance render him incapable of paying for two or three years in succession more than two thirds or three fourths of his rent, when landholders were obliged to meet their tenants with a reduction to that extent, or have their farm thrown on their hands? I cannot contemplate such a state of things from bountiful harvests, even under the operation of our present coin laws. Nor am I aware that any evidence of such being the case, can be produced in the history of the agriculture of this country, unaccompanied with variations in the amount of the currency."

I have been the more induced to insert this quotation, because it was chiefly on the authority of Mr. Mushet's work that Mr. J. B. Say, the most distinguished of the French writers on Political Economy, expressed a most exaggerated opinion of the depreciation of the currency of this country; while, curiously enough, Mr. Say had occasion at the same time to notice variations of prices as great in France, which he accounted for upon very obvious grounds, without inferring any alteration of the value of money.

And more recently an opinion to the same effect has been stated by one of the most distinguished of the partisans of the doctrine of the paramount influence of the currency. Mr. E. S. Cayley, M. P., in his evidence before the Lords' Committee on agriculture, in 1836, said —

"It is one of the false notions entertained by political economists, that a bad harvest is an advantage. In all periods of history a good harvest was always considered as a blessing, good both for man and beast, for then there is plenty in the land. When there is a deficient crop, that increases the price, but not sufficiently to compensate for the loss of produce, but the increase of produce by a good crop in a proper state of things, more than counterbalances the fall of price."—*Report of Lords, Committee on Agricultural Distress*, 1836 p. 321.

But the history of our agriculture tends very clearly to prove that in all the signal instances of scarcity and abundance of the crops, the variations of price have been in a ratio much beyond the utmost computation of the difference of quantity, and that on every occasion of marked transition, from dearth to abundance there have been complaints of agricultural distress.

The fact that a small deficiency in the produce of corn, compared with the average rate of consumption, occasionally causes a rise in price very much beyond the ratio of the defect, is obvious upon the slightest reference to the history of prices at periods when nothing in the state of politics or of the currency could be suspected to have had any influence.

Some writers have attempted to deduce a strict rule of proportion between a given defect of the harvest, and the probable rise of price.

The rule of this kind that has been most commonly referred to, is one by Gregory King, which is introduced in the following passage by D'Avenant: —

"It is observed, that but one tenth the defect in the harvest may raise the price three tenths; and when we have but half our crop of wheat, which now and then happens, the remainder is spun out by thrift and good management, and eked out by the use of other grain: but this will not do for above one year, and would be a small help in the succession of two or three unseasonable harvests. For the scarcity even of one year is very destructive, in which many of the poorest sort perish, either for want of sufficient food, or by unwholesome diet.

"We take it, that a defect in the harvest may raise the price of corn in the following proportions: —

Defect.		Above the common rate.
1 tenth	raises the price	3 tenths
2 tenths		8 tenths
3 tenths		16 tenths
4 tenths		28 tenths
5 tenths		45 tenths

So that when corn rises to treble the common rate, it may be presumed that we want above one third of the common produce, and if we should want five tenths, or half the common produce, the price would rise to near five times the common rate."

It is perhaps superfluous to add, that no such strict rule can be deduced at the same time, there is some ground for supposing that the estimate is not very wide of the truth, from observation of the repeated occurrence of the fact, that the price of corn in this country has risen from 100 to 200 per cent, and upwards, when the utmost computed deficiency of the crops has not been more than between one sixth and one third below an average, and when that deficiency has been relieved by foreign supplies.

All that can be said, therefore, in general terms, is, that a decided deficiency of supply is commonly attended in the case of corn, more than in that of most other articles, with an advance in price very much beyond the degree of the deficiency. And the reason of the fact is as clear, upon a little reflection, as the fact itself is upon the slightest observation.

The process by which the rise beyond the proportion of defect takes place, is the struggle of every one to get his accustomed share of that which is necessary for his subsistence, and of which there is not enough or so much as usual for all. Supposing a given deficiency, the degree in which the money price may rise, will depend upon the extent of the pecuniary means of the lowest classes of the community. In countries where the pecuniary means of the lowest classes are limited to the power of obtaining a bare subsistence in ordinary times, as in Ireland, and on many parts of the Continent, and where neither the government, as in France, nor the poor laws and contributions by wealthy individuals, as in England, come in aid of those means, a proportion of the population, according to the degree of scarcity, must perish, or suffer diseases incidental to an insufficient supply of food, or to a substitution of inferior and unwholesome diet. And the increased competition of purchasers being thus limited to the classes above the lowest, the rise in price may not be very considerably beyond the defect of quantity. But in France, where it is a part of the general policy of the government to provide by the purchase of corn, in times of dearth, for the subsistence of the lowest classes, and particularly for that of the inhabitants of Paris; and in this country, where the poor laws create a fund for the maintenance of the lowest classes, at the expense of all the classes above them; where, moreover, the voluntary contributions of richer individuals swell that fund; it is clear that the competition of purchasers would be greatly increased, while the supply being limited, the price would rise very considerably beyond the ratio of the deficiency. The final effect of a rise in price so much beyond the defect of the crops, when that increased rise is produced by the causes mentioned, is to limit the consumption and to apportion the privations resulting from scarcity over a larger part of the population; thus dimmishing the severity of pressure upon the lowest class, and preventing or tending to prevent any part of it from perishing, as it might otherwise do, from actual want of food.

It is of the utmost importance to bear in mind the operation of the principle of the great increase of price beyond the degree of deficiency, with a view to account not only for the high range of prices, but, likewise, for the extraordinary prosperity which attended the agricultural interest[①] during the first half of the period that will come under consideration, and which cannot, in my opinion, be accounted for in any other way.

It is clearly through the medium of prices raised beyond the ratio of deficiency, that farmers gained such great profits pending the term of their leases, and that landlords obtained such greatly advanced rents at the granting of new leases.

If prices of produce had risen only in exact proportion to the deficiency of growth; thus, if in commonly good years, an acre of wheat produced 33 bushels, which sold for 6*s.* per bushel, or 9*l.* 18*s.*, but, in a bad season, produced only two thirds of a crop, or 22 bushels, which sold for 9*s.* the bushel, or 9*l.* 18*s.*, supposing the expenses of getting in the crops to be the same in both cases, the farmer would be neither gainer nor loser by the deficiency of his crops, that deficiency being here assumed to be general. The deficiency would be a general calamity, and farmers and landlords would bear their shares of it in their quality of consumers.

But, upon the principle here stated, the case would be widely different. In the event of a deficiency of one third of an average crop, a bushel of

① By *agricultural interest*, I mean exclusively farmers and landlords, and owners of tithes, who are alone benefited by an advance of price resulting from scarcity. The condition of the labouring classes, even of those employed in husbandry, is well known to be deteriorated in periods of dearth, as the wages of labour do not rise in full proportion to the advance in the price of provisions.

wheat might rise to 18*s*. and upwards.[①] Now, 22 bushels, at 18*s*. per bushel, would be worth 19*l*. 16*s*., whereas, the 33 bushels at 6*s*., were worth only 9*l*. 18*s*., making a clear profit to the grower of 100 per cent. This, of course, is an extreme case, and cannot, in general, be of long duration; it supposes no great surplus from former years, and no immediate prospect of adequate relief from importation. While the deficiency exists, however, whether in reality or only in apprehension, such, and still greater, may be the effect.

For the sake of illustration of the mode and degree in which a deficiency in the crops, compared with an average produce, is calculated to affect the condition of the agricultural interest, let us suppose that the average produce of corn in this country were 32 millions of quarters[②] of all kinds, which would sell at 40*s*. per quarter all round as a remunerative price, making an amount of 64,000,000*l*. to be distributed as wages, profit, and rent, including tithe; but by the occurrence of a bad crop, deficient one eighth, uncompensated by a surplus from the former season, the price advanced to 60*s*., there would then be 28 millions of quarters at 60*s*., making 84,000,000*l*. being a clear addition of 20,000,000*l*., to be distributed among the farmers and landlords, and receivers of tithe in kind, in the first instance. Eventually, increased wages would form some deduction, if the advance in price, from the continuance of deficiency,

---

① Considering the institutions of this country relative to the maintenance of the poor, if there should be a deficiency of the crops amounting to one third, *without any surplus from a former year, and without any chance of relief by importation*, the price might rise five, six, or even tenfold.

② It was computed by Dr. Colquhoun, that the consumption of all kinds of grain in this kingdom amounted, in 1812, to 35 millions of quarters, exclusive of seed. Mr. M'Culloch estimates that, in 1834, the consumption might be computed at 44 millions exclusive of seed, and 52 millions including seed.—See article, Corn Laws and Corn Trade, in his Commercial Dictionary.

lasted for more than one season, or if, by the recurrence of deficiency at short intervals, the advance were, on an average, in the same relative proportion. If the deficiency were one quarter, and the price were to rise, as it infallibly would, to at least double, the gain among those classes would be

32, 000, 000 of quarters at 40*s*. = 64, 000, 000*l*.

24, 000, 000 of quarters at 80*s*. = 96, 000, 000*l*.

There can be little doubt that, in such a state of things, the agricultural interest would enjoy, not only the appearance, but the reality of prosperity. But it is clear, that the increased income distributed among the agricultural interest must, with the exception of the increased expenses incurred by the landlords and farmers in their quality of consumers, be at the expense of the other orders of the community. The advocates, however, for the agricultural claims, which, if they were admitted and could be made operative to their full extent, would artificially perpetuate the effects that could otherwise arise only from the sterility of the soil or the unpropitiousness of the seasons, seem to confine their observation of the consequence of the high price of provisions to the direct and obvious advantages resulting from the increased sum to be distributed among the farmers and landlords; and infer that this increased sum is the creation of so much additional wealth. It was the same confinement of view to the increased sum which an advance in the price of corn occasioned to be distributed in the shape of profit and rent, that led the sect of economists in France, who considered the raw produce of the earth as the only source of wealth, to look upon every advance in the price of that produce as so much increase of national wealth.

While the fact, indeed, and the reason of the fact that, as relates to commodities generally, and to corn more especially, a deficiency of quantity produces a great relative advance in price, has been repeatedly noticed and variously illustrated by severalwriters; the converse of the proposition, viz. that an excess of quantity operates in depressing the prices of commodities generally, but of corn more especially, in a ratio much beyond the degree of that excess, was little noticed until the publication of the report of the Agricultural Committee in 1821, or, if casually noticed, was not applied systematically in accounting for instances of great depression of prices, and of consequent distress among those who felt the effects of that depression. In the report of that Committee, the principle which is here alluded to, and upon which I was particularly examined, is stated, and some of the consequences flowing from it are pointed out in the following passage: —

"The cause which produces this greater susceptibility in the corn market, cannot be better explained by your Committee, than in the following extract from the answer of one of the witnesses who was particularly examined to this point: — 'Why should a different principle apply to corn than to any other general production? Because a fall in the price of any other commodity, not of general necessity, brings the article within the reach of a greater number of individuals: whereas, in the case of corn, the average quantity is sufficient for the supply of every individual; all beyond that causes a depression of the market for a great length of time, and a succession of two or three abundant seasons, must evidently produce an enormously inconvenient accumulation.' — 'Is there not a greater consumption of corn when it is cheaper than when it is dear, as to quantity? There may, and doubtless must be, a greater consumption; but it is very evident that if the population was before adequately fed, the increased consumption, from abundance, can amount to little more than waste; and this would be in a very small proportion to the whole excess of a good harvest or two.'"

The report then proceeds to say: —

"In the substance of this reasoning your Committee entirely concur; and it appears to them that it cannot be called in question without denying either that corn is an article of general necessity and universal consumption among the population of this country, or that the demand is materially varied by the amount of the supply. This latter proposition, except within very narrow limits altogether drsproportioned to fluctuation in production, is not warranted by experience. The general truth, therefore, of the observation remains unaltered by any small degree of waste on the one side, or of economy on the other; neither of which are sufficient to counteract the effect which opinion and speculation must have upon price, when it is felt how little demand is increased by redundancy, or checked by scantiness of supply."

It has been chiefly a want of consideration of the magnitude of the excess or defect of the crops in particular seasons, and sometimes in a succession of seasons, beyond the average rate of consumption, that has led a large, and, probably the largest class of reasoners on the prices of corn to suppose that an increase of consumption, arising, whether from cheapness, or from increased employment of the working classes, in consequence of a flourishing as contrasted with a dull state of trade and manufacture, could form any considerable proportion to the excess of a superabundant harvest. [①] If it is considered that the produce of an ordinary crop of wheat in this country, at the commencement of the century, was estimated at nearly 9 millions of quarters, and is now variously computed at from 12 to 14 millions, and that the variations from season have been to the extent of one fourth, or upwards, in excess or defect, making in the earlier period a difference of upwards of 2 millions of quarters, and in the later of upwards of 3 millions above or below an average, and a difference of upwards of 4 millions in the one case, and of 6 millions in the other between a very deficient and a very abundant crop, — it may easily be imagined, that retrenchment on the one hand, and increased consumption, however wasteful, on the other, can make comparatively little impression on such enormous difference of supply: but more especially, when such difference of supply is extended to more than a single season.

It is not therefore to be wondered at, that a succession of seasons, of somewhat more than ordinary produce relatively to the usual rate of con sumption, should be attended with an extreme depression of price; and that the fall of prices, consequent upon such a succession of seasons of more than ordinary produce, must be very ruinous to farmers, who were under agreement to pay rents which had been calculated on-a higher range

---

① Of the little comparative influence of retrenchment on the one hand, or of increased consumption on the other, two striking instances may be adduced: —

In the parliamentary committee on the scarcity in 1800, the deficiency of the crop of wheat was estimated at about 2, 000, 000 quarters, and in the examination into the resources for meeting that deficiency, after allowing for importation, the use of substitutes for wheat, and the stoppage of the distilleries, the whole amount of *retrenchment*, reckoned upon as the consequence of the very high price, was taken at 300, 000 quarters. On the other hand, the more recent instance of the crop of 1834 proves, in a striking manner, the insignificant effect of extra consumption upon a productive harvest.

of prices. ①

It will accordingly be seen, on reference to former periods of our history, that there were very different proportions of favourable or unfavourable seasons, in periods of considerable length; and that on the transition from dearths of some continuance to abundance, there have been complaints, as in more modern times, of farmers ruined, and of rents unpaid.

① The effect of abundance In depressing the price of corn, although it must be much beyond the ratio of the excess, is not calculated to be in the same ratio as that of deficiency in raising the price. In the event of a superabundant harvest, a part more or less of the excess may, according to the opinion and the capital, or credit of the farmer, be held over. If, however, the recurrence of propitious seasons should be such as to render the accumulation manifestly and inconveniently large, the subsequent depression would be the greater, in proportion to the previous resistance to a fall, and the only remedy would be an exportation at ruinously low rates, and eventually a diminished cultivation. As a general position, therefore, it may safely be laid down that an excess of the supply of corn is attended with a fall of price much beyond the ratio of excess; and that the larger quantity consequently will yield a less sum of money than the smaller quantity.

CHAPTER Ⅲ
ON THE CHARACTER OF THE SEASONS AND THE STATE OF PRICES, AND THE CONDITION OF THE AGRICULTURAL INTERESTS PREVIOUS TO 1793

SECTION 1 *Period ending in 1692*

Of the character of the seasons, such as it is to be inferred from the state of prices down to the latter part of the 17th century, a concise, and, as it appears to me, a correct view, is taken in the following extract from an article in the Quarterly Review, No. 57, which contains a critique on a former work of mine, from the pen, I have reason to believe, of the late Mr. Malthus: —

"In that very valuable table of prices collected by Sir Frederick Morton Eden, in his work on the Poor, periods of high and low prices are to be found, of considerable duration, for which it would be very difficult to give any other adequate solution, than the comparative abundance or scantiness of the supplies of corn, arising from the number of favourable or unfavourable seasons included in such periods.

"After the great plague, which occurred about the middle of the reign of Edward Ⅲ., and gave occasion to the first attempt to regulate wages by law, one should naturally have expected that, owing to the great loss of people then sustained, corn would become cheaper rather than dearer;

instead of which it appears to have risen from about 5*s*. 4*d*. , the average of the first twenty-five years of the reign of Edward III. to 11*s*. 9*d*. , the average of the last twenty-six years, with very little difference in the quantity of silver contained in the same nominal sum. For this great rise of bullion prices, spreading itself over a period of twenty-six years, it would be scarcely possible to assign an adequate cause without resorting to a succession of unfavourable seasons. During the reigns of Richard II. and Henry Ⅳ. , a period of thirty-four years, the bullion price of corn seems to have fallen rather lower than it was in the first half of the reign of Edward Ⅲ. In the first twenty-three years it was 5*s*. 7*d*. , and in the last eleven years 6*s*. 1*d*. ; and as in the latter half of the reign of Edward Ⅲ. the pound of silver was coined into 25*s*. , and at the end of the reign of Henry IV. into 30*s*. , the bullion price of this period was rather below what it was in the first half of the reign of Edward Ⅲ. , and it certainly would be very difficult to explain the low prices of these thirty-four years, and the high prices of the preceding twenty-six, without the powerful operation of seasons. "

In 1444, other statutes regulating the price of labour were passed, probably owing to the high price of corn, which had risen on an average of the ten preceding years to 10*s*. 8*d*. , without any further alterations in the coin, and for this rise there seems to be no adequate cause, but a succession of comparatively scanty crops, particularly as after this period there was a continuance of low prices for above sixty years. The average price of wheat from 1444 to the end of the reign of Henry Ⅷ. in 1509, re-turned to about 6s. , while the pound of silver being coined into 1*l*. 17*s*. 6*d*. instead of 1*l*. 2*s*. 6*d*. , as at the time of passing the first statute of labourers in 1350, showed a very decided fall in the bullion price of wheat. This fall, however, was so considerable, and lasted for a very long period, that we cannot attribute it wholly to the seasons. Still less are we disposed to attribute it to the cause assigned by Adam Smith, a gradual rise in the value of silver, because, if we refer to his own criterion of value, *labour*, we shall find that while the bullion price of corn had been falling, the bullion price of labour had been rising, and consequently, silver had been diminishing, instead of increasing in value. These prices of corn and labour could only have arisen from a great and continued abundance of corn, which was evinced by the very large quantity of it awarded to the labourer; and this abundance was occasioned probably by the combined operations of favourable seasons with the introduction of a better system of agriculture, before the distribution of property and the habits of the labouring classes had been so far improved as to encourage a proportionate increase of their number.

"The rise in the price of corn during the course of the next century may, no doubt, be easily accounted for by the progress of population and the discovery of the American mines, without any aid from unfavourable seasons, although in fact such seasons did combine with the other causes just mentioned, in raising the price of wheat towards the end of the century from 1594 to 1598. The same cause unquestionably operated for twenty years about the middle of the subsequent century, from 1646 to 1665 inclusive, when the price of the quarter of wheat was 2*l*. 10*s*.— considerably higher than it was either in the earlier or later part of the century, and it is somewhat singular, that while during a considerable part of the civil wars between the houses of York and Lancaster, and subsequently, corn was remarkably cheap; during the civil wars under Charles I., and sometime subsequently, it was as remarkably clear — a pretty strong presumptive proof that the seasons had more to do with the prices in both cases than the civil wars."

The following extracts, from the Sloane MSS. in the British Museum, No. 4174, give a description of the effect, on the payment of rents, of a fall of prices, which occurred between 1617 and 1621, namely, from 43*s*. 3*d*. the quarter, of 8 bushels, to 27*s*. ①: —

"Mr. John Chamberlain to Sir Dudley Carleton.

"12 February, 1620.

"We are here in a strange state to complain of plenty; but so it is, that corn beareth so low a price that tenants and farmers are very backward to pay their rents, and in many places plead disability; for remedy whereof the council have written letters into every shire, and some say to every market-town, to provide a granary or storehouse, with a stock to buy corn, and keep it for a dear year. But though this be well advised, and make a fair show in speculation, yet the difficulties be so many, that it will not be so easy to put it into practice."

The following was written at the same period:

"England was never generally so poor since I was born as It is at this present; inasmuch that all complain they cannot receive their rents. Yet is there plenty of all things but money, which is so scant, that country people offer corn and cattle, or whatsoever they have else, in lieu of rent — but bring no money; and corn is at so easy rates as I never knew it to be at,

① The quotations of prices of wheat, until after 1792, will be confined to those of the Windsor market, as contained in the Eton tables for the Winchester quarter of 8 bushels. As the quality is supposed to be superior to middling wheat, it has been usual among writers on corn to deduct one ninth for the difference; but this I conceive is more than is warranted; and the quotations, therefore, stand as they are given in the Parliamentary Papers.

twenty or twenty-two pence a bushel, barley at nine pence, and yet no quantity will be taken at that price; so that for all the common opinion of the wealth of England, I fear, when it comes to the trial, it will prove as some merchants, who, having carried on a great show a long time, when they are called upon too fast by their creditors, be fain to play bankrupt."

And further: —

"Sir Symonds d'Ewes, in his unpublished diary, notices, in 1621, the excessive cheapness and plenty of wheat, the consequence of which was to reduce the price of lands from twenty years' purchase to sixteen or seventeen. ① The best wheat was then 2*s.* 8*d.* and 2*s.* 6*d.* the bushel, ordinary 2*s.*; barley and rye, 1*s.* 3*d.*.

"The farmers murmured; the poorer sort traversed the markets to find out the finest wheats, for none else would now serve their use, though before they were glad of the coarser rye-bread. This daintiness was soon after punished by the high prices of all sorts of grain every where, which never since abated."

Again, in 1670, prices having fallen on a comparison with those which had prevailed during about 20 years, namely, from 1646 to 1665, gave occasion to considerable suffering.

The distress complained of by the agricultural interest was the reason of a new corn bill, imposing duties on the importation amounting to a prohibition. The state of things after that act is thus described by Roger

① The fall in the price of land, as indicated by the reduced number of years' purchase, has evidently, in this case, been computed upon the rents which were *payable*, but *not paid*; and the uncertainty whether the low price of produce might not entail a fall of rent would naturally deter purchasers from giving so much for land as they would have done before the great reduction in the value of the produce.

Coke in his treatise, entitled "The Church and State are in equal Danger with Trade," published in 1671.

"The ends designed by the acts against the importation of Irish cattle, of raising the rents of the lands of England, are so far from being attained, that the contrary hath ensued. And here I wish a survey were taken how many thousand farms are thrown up since this act, how many thousand farms are abated, some above one sixth, others above one fourth, others above one third; some, I know, which after two years' lying waste, are abated one half.

In 1674 there was a considerable dearth. The price by the Eton Tables for Ladyday 1673, had been 35*s.* 6*d.*, but the harvest of 1673 having proved defective, the price on the Ladyday 1674 had risen to 64*s.* And the two years 1674 and 1675 are referred to as a period of great dearth. ① The harvests of 1677 and 1678 appear, by inference from the prices, likewise to have been defective. ② At Ladyday 1677, the pricehad been 30*s.* 3*d.*:

① *Comber, on National Subsistence*, p. 133.

② It may be a question how far quotations of price are admissible as evidence of the state of the seasons, when the degree in which price may be affected by the seasons is the very object of investigation. The answer is, that doubtless direct historical testimony would be better authority; but that, in the present case, the inference to be drawn from any great difference of price within short periods may be quite sufficient for practical purposes, when there is no direct description.

From an account in the Appendix of the prices of the Windsor market, from the Eton Tables, any very marked variation in the produce or promise of the season may be clearly inferred by a reference to the difference between the quotations of the spring and autumn, when nothing in the state of the currency, or any other important circumstance calculated to affect prices, is recorded to have occurred. The inference to this effect is strengthened by the accordance of direct notices of the state of the seasons, whenever they are given, with the indication conveyed by the variation between the Ladyday and Michaelmas prices. Hence, in the absence of any historical notice, it may be safely concluded, when no considerable difference is observable in the quotations from six months to six months and from year to year, that the seasons have preserved a general uniformity of character as to productiveness.

and at Michaelmas, 1678, 56*s*. 11*d*. On the average of seven years the price was from 1666 to 1672, both years included, 36*s*.; and from 1673 to 1679, 46*s*. being a rise of nearly 30 per cent.

This comparative high range of prices had probably, the tendency to encourage and extend tillage, the effects of which seem to have been developed by a succession, in the following *twelve years*, of favourable seasons and very low prices, with the exception only of one year, viz. 1684, in which, judging by a reference to the price, there seems to have been a somewhat deficient crop.

The low range of prices in the six years ending in 1691, is more especially remarkable, the average for those years being only 29*s*. 5*d*.; but if we take only the four years ending in 1691, the average price will be found to be still lower, viz. 27*s*. 7*d*., or a fall of upwards of 40 per cent, compared with the *average* of the seven years ending in 1679; this price too being for a quality better than middling.

The state of the currency, instead of accounting for this low price, adds to the grounds for wonder at its being so low. The silver, which was then the only current coin, had, during some years before this time, been undergoing a progressive deterioration, and had probably, at the revolution in 1688, reached nearly to its most degraded state, inasmuch as it was, very soon after that event, that the attention of Government was drawn to the magnitude of the evil, and the necessity of a remedy by recoinage. The deterioration of the coin, previous to the recoinage, was estimated, by Mr. Lownds, at 25 per cent①; but

① Silver was then the only current coin by which prices were determined. The guinea commonly exchanging at that time for 30*s*. of the worn and clipt silver. In 1695 the common price of silver bullion was 6*s*. 5*d*. an ounce, being 1*s*. 5*d*. or nearly 25 per cent above the Mint price.

supposing the degradation, in 1688, to have been only to the extent of 20 per cent, it would bring the price in money of full weight, on the *average* of the four years ending in 1691, to 22*s*.: and, applying the same deduction to the lowest quotation by the Eton Tables of that period, viz. at Michaelmas 1688, 21*s*. 4*d*., the price in silver coin of standard weight would be reduced to 17*s*. 1*d*. for the Winchester quarter of wheat, of better than the average quality. That there is no material error in this very low quotation of the Windsor market is proved by a similar low quotation of the Oxford market in Mr. Lloyd's tables, viz. 21*s*. 11*d*., at Michaelmas 1688. It is impossible to assign these extremely low rates to any other cause than that of an inconvenient accumulation arising from a succession of favourable seasons, operating upon a state of tillage, extended, doubtless, by the comparatively high prices which had prevailed some time before.

Dr. Adam Smith, who notices the very low price of this period, seems inclined to consider it as an indication of, and resulting from, an increase in the value of silver. For, according to his view, the utmost effect of the discovery and working of the American mines, in reducing the value of silver, had been completed between 1630 and 1640, or about 1636. But supposing that there had been better grounds than there now appear to have been for the opinion entertained by Dr. Smith, of a tendency to a rise in the value of silver, this cause must necessarily have been extremely slow in its operation, and could most assuredly not account for so low a price as that of the four years ending in 1691, viz. 27*s*. 7*d*.; or, allowing for the deterioration of the coin, 22*s*. 1*d*., being the lowest at which it had ever been since 1595; long before the American mines could possibly have produced their full effect.

The bounty system[①] to which, by its advocates, the low prices of corn in the first sixty-five years of the last century were ascribed, cannot in any way be brought to explain the low rate now under consideration. The measure was not adopted till 1688; and whatever might be its ultimate effect in encouraging an extended tillage, and thus *eventually* reducing the price, the first operation of it would be, as it was intended that it should be, a forced exportation, and a consequent immediate relief to the growers and dealers from the weight of accumulated stock with which they were oppressed. Accordingly, the markets did recover in a slight degree, after the passing of that measure, although they continued at a low range till 1692.[②] But if neither the supposed increase of the value of silver, nor the operation of the bounty can by possibility be assigned as the causes of that low range of prices, as little can anything be found in the state of politics or trade to account for it.

A fall of the price of wheat to 29*s*. had taken place after the harvest of 1687, when the country was in a state of perfect political tranquillity: and it does not appear that the revolution in 1688 had any effect in deranging the markets for provisions. If, from such a cause, they had been particularly depressed, the rebound, when the extraordinary cause of depression was removed, would have been proportionably great; whereas the quotation at Ladyday 1689, of the Windsor market, was 23*s*. 1*d*., and

---

① By 1 William and Mary, a bounty was granted, of 5*s*. per quarter, on the exportation of wheat, when the price did not exceed 48*s*. 2*s*. 6*d*. per quarter on barley and malt, when not exceeding 24*s*.; and 3*s*. 6*d*. per quarter on rye, when not exceeding 32*s*.. A bounty of 2*s*. 6*d*. per quarter was subsequently given upon the exportation of oats and oatmeal, when the price of the former did not exceed 15*s*. per quarter. Importation continued to be regulated by the act of 1670.

② Indeed it must be perfectly clear, that the prices in the three years following 1688, low as they were, would have been still lower but for the bounty on exportation.

of the Oxford market 25*s*. 6*d*. And at the end of two years after the revolution, viz . at Ladyday 1691, wheat in the Windsor market was only 29*s*. —the silver coin being then at nearly its lowest point of degradation. There appears, therefore, no ground of inference that any part of the depression of prices so remarkable between 1685 and 1692, can be referred to the state of politics in that interval: and as to any influence from the state of trade, there is no reason whatever for ascribing to it a depressing effect on the price of provisions, unless an improving and flourishing state of it is calculated to have that effect. The Board of Trade represented in 1697: "We have made inquiry into the state of trade in general, from the year 1670 to the present time; and from the best calculations we can make, by the duties paid at the Custom House, we are of opinion, that trade in general did considerably increase from the end of the Dutch war in 1673 to 1689, when the late war began."—*Chalmers's Estimate*, p. 47.

It is indeed manifestly impossible to discover any cause for the remarkably low prices from 1685 to 1692①, but that of a succession of favourable seasons, acting upon a probably extended cultivation. Of the agricultural distress, resulting from such seasons, a sufficient proof is furnished by the enactment of the celebrated measure of the bounty; the real object of which was, although professing to have in view the encouragement of tillage, to relieve the landed interest from the pressure of

① In a publication, entitled as General Chronological History of the Air, Weather, &c. , by Dr. Short, 1749, is the following quotation from a diary of the Rev, S. Say, of St. James's, Westminster:— "In the latter end of the reign of King James, and the beginning of the reign of King William, the seasons were kindly to the fruits of the earth; in 1688, wheat was sold in Norwich at 2*s*. per bushel, and in 1691 for about 2*s*. 6*d*. . "

distress arising from low prices.

SECTION 2 *1693 to 1714*

But if the low prices immediately antecedent to 1693 are, chiefly by inference (irresistible as the grounds for such inference are) referable to the state of the seasons, there is direct evidence of the influence of that cause in the remarkably elevated range of prices in the following seven years, which are traditionally known as the barren years at the close of the seventeenth century. ①

Of these seasons there are various notices to be collected from publications relating to that period. Among them are the following: —

"1692. Great rains in autumn; an earthquake was felt in England, and in most parts of Europe."

"1693. A very wet summer; this unseasonable weather extended to France, where numbers perished for want, notwithstanding they imported much corn from Sweden and Denmark. In Kent, turnips made a considerable share of bread for the people."

---

① In *The Farmers Magazine for January* 1800, is a passage in which the editors, after noticing the importance of a register of the seasons, add, "Such a register will not only inform the present generation, but must also prove very interesting to posterity. We need hardly say, that if similar information could be procured concerning the causes which occasioned the scanty crops at the end of the seventeenth century, traditionally called the *barren years*, it would be considered as a particular obligation." And Mr. M'Culloch, in his very elaborate work, "A Statistical Account of the British Empire," adverting to the scarcities with which Scotland has occasionally been visited, observes, that, "Those from 1693 to 1700, emphatically termed the 'seven ill years,' were particularly severe. During the 'seven ill years,' the distress was so great that several extensive parishes in Aberdeenshire, and other parts of the country, were nearly depopulated, and some farms remained unoccupied for several years afterwards."—Vol. i. p. 424.

"1694. A very wet summer."

"1695. Many of the Scotch are driven into Ireland by the excessive price of corn."

"1696. A very wet summer. A great want of money in specie, but this was soon remedied by the new coin coming out."① "1698. A very wet summer. Great complaints are made of the dearness of provisions and decay of trade."

"These cold and wet seasons lasted more than seven years; the dismal effects of famine were felt in most parts of Europe." *An Inquiry into the Prices of Wheat, Malt, and occasionally of other Provisions, as Sold in England from the Year* 1000 *to the Year* 1765. (Folio, published for T.

---

① The state of the weather in 1697 is not noticed in this publication, but it is noticed in the following description, extracted from a "Syllabus of the general State of Air, Health, and Seasons," by Thomas Short, M. D..

"1697. From January 17. to February 11., a hard frost. A cold north wind all March, and to April 11. July 16. and 17., frost and mildew: calm to August 10.. By constant daily rains growing corn sprouted in the ear; then came good harvest weather."

"1698. January had much snow, and deep drifts. February was a cold cloudy month; 14 inches deep snow on the 26th, ice 4 inches thick. April 22., a deep snow. May 3., a general deep snow; and to June 18., very rainy. The 16th of June, in a warm rich soil, was the first wheatear seen near London. The backwardest spring in forty-seven years. The four months, to the end of August, had scarce two days together without rain (except from July 18th to the 26th). The wettest season known. Whole fields of corn spoilt, even in Kent, much more in the north. Horses were turned into the pease and barley. The earliest wheat had not been cut till the middle of September. In Kent, September the 29th, bailey standing uncut there; much lay in the swath till December; that which was brought in was soaked with wet, and almost useless. Much corn in the north ungot at Christmas; and, in Scotland, they were throng reaping in January, and beating the deep snow off it as they leaped the poor green empty crop. Bread, made of wheat, was got; would not stick together, but fell in pieces, and tasted as sweet as if made of malt. The seedtime was so wet, that there was hardly above half a crop sown this year."

"1699. Now begins the first of several hot summers. June and July were so hot, that wheat began to be cut the 1st of August; and though there was but half a crop sown, yet it fell from 9*s*. and 10*s*. a bushel to a reasonable price; and continued so for several years."

Longman, 1768.)

The scarcity resulting from such seasons is noticed by Dr. Adam Smith, in the following terms: "The scarcity which prevailed in England from 1693 to 1699, both inclusive, though no doubt principally owing to the badness of the seasons, and therefore extending through a considerable part of Europe, must have been somewhat enhanced by the bounty. In 1699, accordingly, the further exportation of corn was prohibited for nine months." As the price, on the average, was above that up to which the bounty was payable, it does not appear how that measure could have enhanced the price, and I quote the passage merely as evidence of the notoriety of the fact of the prevalence of scarcity through the greater part of Europe during an interval of about seven years.

The relatively high prices of that period cannot, indeed, be satisfactorily accounted for in any other way. The bounty must, on the grounds which I have stated, have been wholly inoperative to that effect; or, rather, in as far as it was calculated to have the effect ascribed to it of forcing a surplus produce, it might, when the exportation was prohibited, have had a temporary effect in a contrary direction, viz. of preventing the rise to so great an extent as might otherwise have taken place.

Of the inveterate tendency which exists to refer every instance of relatively high prices of corn to the currency, however palpably attributable to other causes, there cannot be a stronger instance than that among speakers in parliament, and among writers out of it, whenever reference has been made to the prices of corn in the closing years of the seventeenth century, it seems to have been taken for granted that they were exclusively the result of the deteriorated state of the coin.

The assignment of this cause for the great rise of prices in the closing years of the seventeenth century, is at the outset negatived by a very obvious and simple consideration. The silver coins were, in 1691, at, as nearly as might be, their greatest debasement; and it is the rise from that period of nearly 100 per cent which is to be accounted for. It would be extravagant to suppose that the further deterioration, till the calling in of the bad coin in 1695, could have been such as to produce any sensible effect on prices.

In the course of the years 1694 and 1695, measures had been taken for a new coinage; and the effect of these measures, while they were in progress, was to occasion great scarcity of circulating medium, by the inducement to hoard or to export the more perfect pieces, and to reject the imperfect. In 1695 a proclamation was issued, prohibiting the currency of the clipped money. In the early part of 1696, being the interval between the crying down of the old, and the issuing of the new coin, the scarcity of money seems to have been severely felt, as appears by the following extracts from Evelyn's Memoirs.

"June 11 1696. Want of current money to carry on the smallest concerns, even for daily provisions in the markets. Guineas lowered to 22*s.*, and great sums daily transported to Holland, where it yields more, with other treasure sent to pay the armies, and nothing considerable coined of the new, and now only current stamp, cause such a scarcity, that tumults are every day feared, nobody paying or receiving: so imprudent was the late parliament to condemn the old, though clipped and corrupted, till they had provided supplies. To this, add the fraud of the bankers and goldsmiths, who, having gotten immense riches by extortion, keep up their treasure in expectation of enhancing its value."

Nothing can indicate more strongly than this description the great stagnation of the circulation, and the consequent enhancement of the value of the circulating medium①; and it is probable, therefore, that prices, high as they were from deficiency of supply arising out of the seasons, would have been still higher in the interval immediately preceding 1696, if the contraction of the circulation had not been greater② with a debased, than it subsequently was with a more perfect coin. In 1696 the new coin began to appear, and, in the course of the two following years, the reformation of the currency was completed; but it was precisely in this interval, viz. from 1696 to 1699, both years included (the two last being years of peace), that prices reached their greatest height. The comparison of the prices of wheat in the four years ending in 1691, when the coin was deteriorated by at least 20 per cent, with the price in the four years ending in 1699, when the coin was restored to its full standard value, will stand thus:

	s.	*d.*
4 years ending 1691 – – –	27	7
4 years ending 1699 – – –	56	6

A further presumption, if any were wanting, against the supposition of the currency having had any influence in this high range of prices, is derived from the circumstance that a still greater proportionate rise, in the same period, occurred in France.

With regard to the hypothesis of war having occasioned these high prices, it is to be observed, that the prices continued low during the first

① Mr. Huskisson, in his speech in June, 1822, on Mr Western's motion, quoted from Archdeacon Cove's publication of the correspondence between king William and the duke of Shrewsbury several particulars which fully confirm this statement of the scarcity of money and general stagnation which prevailed in 1696.

② The depression of the exchange immediately previous to 1696, to the extent of nearly 25 per cent, was the effect of the large foreign expenditure. But that depression could, of course, not have taken place if the coin had been perfect.

two years of the war, viz. from 1689 to 1692, and that nearly the highest prices, viz. in 1698 and 1699, were after the conclusion of peace.

Upon the cessation of the long period of dearth, in the closing years of the seventeenth century, the fall of prices was rapid.

The price, after harvest, at Michaelmas 1700, had fallen to 33*s*. 9*d*., and, after the harvest of 1702, to 25*s*. 6*d*. This fall of *upwards of 50 per cent* took place, notwithstanding a renewal of the war with France in the year before, and notwithstanding the full operation of the bounty on exportation. The fall being so great, it might naturally be supposed that rents which had probably been regulated with some reference to the previous long range of high prices, could not easily be paid, and there happens to be testimony that rents were not paid. Evelyn, in his Diary, January, 1703, writes: "Corn and provisions so cheap, that the farmers are unable to pay their rents."

The harvest of 1703 seems to have been unfavourable, as the price of wheat rose by Ladyday following to nearly double of what it had been in the preceding spring, viz.

Per Winchester Quarter.

		s.	*d*.
1703	Ladyday – – –	26	8
	Mrchaelmas – – –	37	4
1704	Ladyday – – –	51	7

At Michaelmas, 1704, it fell to 30*s*. 10*d*., indicating that the crops of that year had proved abundant; and, from that time (the government expenditure, be it remarked, arising from the war being then on a very large scale) till 1708, it continued at a low range, viz. from 23*s*. 1*d*. to 27*s*. 3*d*. The following is a notice of this period, extracted from the work which I have already quoted: —

"1706. — Historians take notice that about this time the kingdom was blessed with plenty, that the people cheerfully contributed to the expense of the war."

The same author proceeds to say:

"1708.① —A hard frost, which brought on a prodigious scarcity of provisions, more in France than in England. In general the summer was cold and wet.

"1709. —The queen, in her speech to parliament, complains of coin being exported at such high prices as distressed the poor. Exportation prohibited for one year. There fell this year rain to the depth of 26 $\frac{1}{2}$ inches. I think the mean depth of rain falling in England is 19 $\frac{1}{2}$ inches.

"1710. — Exportation prohibited for one year."

The effect of this variation of the seasons on prices is strikingly exemplified in the following quotations: —

① The winter of 1708-1709 is one of the most memorable of any in the last century for severity and duration. The instances of extreme and prolonged frost were the subject of observations interchanged among all the scientific societies of Europe. In this country, and throughout the greater part of the Continent, the frost began in October, and continued with few intermissions into a very advanced period of the spring. The summer following was cold and wet. And the dearth with which Europe was visited in 1709, as the consequence of the severe winter, and the cold and wet summer, appears to have been very severe and very general. Dr. Short gives a detailed account, too long for extract, of this season; but he notices one circumstance, which is worth recording, of the effects of the cold backward spring, following so severe a winter, on the wheat crop: "Wheat over the kingdom," he says, "was generally destroyed on the northeast side of the furrows." This is precisely similar to the effects ascribed by Mr. Burke, in his publication entitled "Thoughts and Details on Scarcity," to the cold east winds in June, 1795.

	s.	d.
1708 Ladyday – – –	27	3
Michaelmas – – –	46	3
1709 Ladyday – – –	57	6
Michaelmas – – –	81	9
1710 Ladyday – – –	81	9

Being a rise of 200 per cent in two years. We were then indeed at war, as we had, however, been during the previous low prices; but as if to negative the possibility of ascribing the rise in this instance to extra demand or consumption arising from the war, it so happens that the price fell again, in 1712, to 33*s*. 9*d*. Nay, even further to prove how independent of the war the fluctuation was, the price having continued at about 30*s*. the quarter till the peace of Utrecht, in 1713, immediately after that event, rose (at Michaelmas, 1713) to 56*s*. 11*d*. or 70 per cent. During all these fluctuations, the silver coins were in an undeteriorated state. There had been some variations in the value at which the gold passed, but these did not affect prices which were estimated in silver.

A comparison with the prices in France may again be resorted to, as showing, by a coincidence of the fluctuations, that they were produced by causes common to both countries, and not by any peculiarity in the currency of this country. Indeed, whether by reference to that comparison, or by an inspection of the difference between the Ladyday and Michaelmas quotation of either the Eton or the Oxford tables, there can be no doubt but that there was, on the continent of Europe as well as in this country, a considerable proportion of deficient harvests in the seven years ending in 1715, as compared with the preceding seven years.

And taking the whole period from 1692 to 1715, embracing an interval of twenty-three years, it will be seen that by direct evidence for the greater part, and by irresistible inference for the rest, there are not fewer than eleven of these twenty-three seasons of more or less deficient produce.

It is to be borne in mind, that in the period here referred to, the bounty on exportation had been in full operation, and that previously to the institution of it, the growth of corn had, in ordinary seasons, been such as afforded some surplus for exportation. Upon the occurrence, therefore, of years of scarcity, the portion of land cultivated beyond that which in ordinary years was sufficient to supply our own ordinary consumption, would be available (especially when enforced by a prohibition of export) in lieu of what, under opposite cricumstances, would be the necessity for an increased importation. So that, if from 1693 to 1715 we had been in the habit of requiring an annual foreign supply of corn, the prices would have been higher by at least the ordinary charges of importation, and during the time of war by the extra charges incidental to the difference in ordinary wars. But as it was, the average prices of seven consecutive years of that period were upwards of 80 pen cent higher than those of the seven years immediately preceding, and this obviously by the mere effect of the seasons. If, then, to the prices of the seven years ending in 1699, were added such extraordinary charges as formed the condition of a foreign supply during the latter period of last war, the average of those seven years would be much higher relatively to the interval of seven years ending in 1692, than the average from 1807 to 1814, relatively to the seven years ending in 1792.

SECTION 3 *1715 to 1765*

But if the period of twenty-three years, ending in 1715, be remarkable for a high range of prices of corn, compared with the period immediately preceding, there is still more ground for remark in the very low comparative range of prices observable in the 50 years following 1715.

The average of 23 years, ending in 1715, is, by the Eton tables, 45*s*. 8*d*. ; while of the 50 years following 1715, it is 34*s*. 11*d*. In order to obviate any question as to the accuracy of these quotations, they may be compared with those of the Oxford tables, which have been collected with great care by Mr. Lloyd; and allowing for the usual difference of markets, it will be found that they lead to the same comparative results. ①

In this long interval of 50 years, there appear to have been only five

---

① C. Smith, the author of the tracts on the Corn Trade, published in 1765, bears the following testimony to the accuracy of the Windsor prices, Referring to a speech addressed by the Procureur-general to the parliament of Britany in France, on the 20th August, 1764, wherein he has occasion to state that the usual price of wheat throughout Europe was reckoned to be twenty livres the septier, Mr. Smith adds the following remarks: —

"Equal to 33*s*. $6\frac{1}{2}d$. the London quarter. Now, it appears that the average price for the last 79 years, viz. 1686 to 1765, hath been 33*s*. $2\frac{1}{2}d$. at Windsor, that is, 4*d*. below the general market of Europe: whereas before for 91 years it was 38*s*. $\frac{8}{9}d$. that is, 4*s*. 6*d*. above the said general price. And that these Windsor prices are more to be depended on than could at first be known, is proved, not only by the said average price of Europe, but also by the average price at London from 1740 to 1764, being found, on inquiry, to have been only 6*d*. per quarter less; and by the average of all the wheat bought at the victualling offices at London, Dover, Portsmouth, and Plymouth, for the last 20 years, ending February 18. 1765, as appears by an account laid before parliament, being only 32*s*. $6\frac{1}{2}d$. , that is, 10*d*. above the Windsor price for the same time; and this last sum will amount to about 2 per cent, discount on the bills, but we cannot well call it less than 5 per cent, and then it will be found to have been 6*d*. below the Windsor, and to agree with the London price."

It is to be observed, that C. Smith, in his quotation of the Windsor prices of wheat, from the Eton tables, makes a deduction, not only of one ninth for the reduction from the 9 gallon measure to the Winchester measure of 8 gallons, but of one ninth more for the difference of quality above middling wheat.

seasons winch, whether by inference from prices, or by historical notice, could be considered as of a marked deficiency of produce, or in any way approaching to what could be designated as seasons of scarcity. These were 1727 and 1728; 1740; 1756 and 1757.

It may be a question whether the year 1725 should not be included among the seasons of marked deficiency inasmuch as the Michaelmas price rose nearly 12*s*., namely, from 37*s*. to 49*s*., above that of Ladyday. But the price gave way in the spring following; and as the quantity of wheat exported was about 200,000 quarters, that of the preceding year having been still greater, besides about 300,000 quarters of malt, there is every reason to believe that the advance of price which was of very short duration, must have arisen mainly, if not exclusively, from the demand for exportation.

If the harvest of 1725 is not to be considered by inference from the price to have been deficient, there being no historical notice to that effect, it would appear that there was not a single season of marked deficiency of produce from 1715 to 1727.

From 1727 to 1729, was a period of some, though not of a severe, degree of dearth. It is noticed historically, and is further proved by the circumstance, that whereas for thirty years before 1727, and for thirty years after 1729, there had been a balance of export of wheat, there was in 1728 a balance of import of 70,757 quarters, and in 1729 of 21,322 quarters.

The price of wheat which had been at Ladyday, 1727, 32*s*. 11*d*. rose at Michaelmas to 41*s*. 9*d*., and at Ladyday, 1728, to 49*s*. 2*d*.. Referring to this period is the following passage, in "An Inquiry on National Subsistence," by W. T. Comber: —

"We learn from contemporary authority that the scarcity was owing to much rain which had fallen that year, and that the months of March,

April, May, June, and part of August of the following year, were also rainy. This occasioned wheat to rise from 4*s*. per bushel to 8*s*.. But the spring and summer of 1729 being remarkably dry, the harvest was abundant, and the prices of next year were only 28*s*. 4*d*.."

Low as the prices had been in the absence of seasons of scarcity from 1715 to 1727, they were still lower in the twelve following years, from 1729 to 1740. There does not indeed appear to have been in that interval a single season in which either from prices or from historical reference, any deficiency of produce can be inferred. The writer last quoted, observes—

"The average of 1731, 1732, and 1733, was only 22*s*., in the latter of which years the amount of all grain exported exceeded 697,000 quarters, of which 427,000 were wheat: 498,000 quarters of wheat were exported the next year, the price being 30*s*.. The average annual exportation of all grain for the ten years from 1731 to 1740, inclusive, was 527,000 quarters, and of wheat 290,000; and the average bounty 103,000*l*. per annum. The average price of this period was 29*s*., but in the concluding year it was 39*s*.."

The great fall of prices in 1731, 1732, and 1733, following the slight dearth of 1727 and 1728, was, as might be expected, productive of great agricultural distress. The following extract describes it in terms which might be supposed to have emanated from the late Mr. Webb Hall's Committee, or from the Agricultural Associations of a more recent period: —

"The interest of our British landholders has been declining several years last past, it has been a general observation, that rents have been sinking, and tenants unable to make as good payments as formerly, even in counties where there is the greatest circulation of money, the maritime ones, and those near the capital cities of the kingdom. As this is too well known to be their case, they deserve the attention and favour of our legislature: it is proper they should make a tolerable interest of their money, as well as adventurers in other businesses, which few of them do, who have not enjoyed their bargains twenty years, or a longer time, for lands are much dearer now. Wheat this year and last never mounted in some of the extreme parts of the kingdom, to above three shillings and eight pence per Winchester; barley is now sold in the West of England for two shillings per Winchester bushel. Prices are often higher fifty miles round London than elsewhere, which induces several great men to think that countrymen live better than they really do. Country measures (which are frequently larger than the Winchester or legal bushels) contribute farther to such mistakes. Before they can pay their rents, wheat of middling goodness ought, I think, to sell for about four shillings and three pence per Winchester, not in a few places, but throughout the kingdom; barley for 2*s*. 6*d*., peas, 2*s*. 3*d*., and oats 1*s*. 6*d*. per Winchester. I know in former times less prices were sufficient; but as circumstances alter, the same thing is altered: corn farms (iron, timber, harvest people, and servants, being much dearer than heretofore) will not yield sufficient profit to the occupiers of them, unless they can have such prices, particularly as cattle, pigs, sheep, butter, and cheese, are now one third part cheaper than formerly, and what is called a living price.

"The flourishing condition of the landed interest supports all trade, most trades now (except those which supply luxury, those of gold and silversmiths, lacemen, vintners, painters, dealers in silks, velvets, and high priced cloths) are in apparent decay; which is not only proved by the general declarations of tradesmen, but by too many instances of bankruptcy amongst them. I wish I could say the present times are not the worst. Our exports are, perhaps, as great as formerly; whence, then, all this complaint? Our farmers are worse customers than formerly, necessity has compelled them to more carefulness and frugality in laying out their money, than they were accustomed to do in better times." (The Landholder's Companion, or Ways and Means to raise the Value of Land, by William Allen, Esq. of Fobstone, in Pembrokeshire, 1734.)

As further proofs of the complaints of distress, and of rents ill paid, as attending the low prices of corn, are the following extracts. In a publication by the elder Lord Lyttleton, "Considerations on the Present State of Affairs" (1738), he says, "In most parts of England, gentlemen's rents are so ill paid, and the weight of taxes lies so heavy on them, that those who have nothing from the court can scarce support their families." And Arthur Young quotes a writer who, in 1739, speaks of the landholder as being in such a bad state, that he asks, "What must have become of them if it had not been for a demand from abroad?" —*Farmer Restored*, p. 14.

The winter of 1739-1740 was one of extraordinary severity and duration. It forms one of the three most memorable winters of last century, the other two being those of 1708-1709, and 1794-1795. A great number of interesting details of the phenomena attending it are recorded in contemporary publications. As in the case of the other two remarkably severe and long winters, it was followed by a very deficient harvest. The price consequently, which had been in the Windsor market at Ladyday, 1739, 31*s.* 5*d.*, rose at Ladyday following, 1740, to 41*s.* 9*d.*, and at Michaelmas to 56*s.*. ① This, and a corresponding high price of other

① The price in the Oxford market, at Michaelmas, 1710, was 59*s.*; at Michaelmas, 1738, it had been 20*s.* 2*d.*, the rise, therefore, upon the latter price was nearly 200 per cent.

provisions, was felt after so long a period of cheapness as one of great dearth. The exportation was prohibited for one year. This prohibition of export, combined with a favourable harvest in the following year, had the effect of reducing the price at Michaelmas, 1741, to 32*s*.. The dearth in this instance, accordingly, was confined to a single year; and it was followed by an uninterrupted succession of ten good and abundant seasons; namely, from 1741 to 1751.

The testimony to this effect rests on unexceptionable authority. The author of the celebrated Corn Tracts①, who is often quoted by Dr. Adam Smith, and who has furnished materials and facts for the great bulk of succeeding writers on the subject of corn, expressly says, "We had ten as good years as ever were known in succession, from 1741 to 1751."

In addition to this testimony as to the general character attaching to the term from 1741 to 1751, I have met with casual descriptions of particular years; and the following extracts from the letters of Mr. Peter Collinson②, a celebrated botanist, to Linnaeus, containing those descriptions, may not be uninteresting, at the same time that they will tend to form something like a standard of what may be considered as a fine season, to which to refer a comparison of the seasons of more recent occurrence, as well as of those from 1793 to 1813.

London, Jan. 18. 1743. O. S.

"We have now a wonderful fine season, that makes our spring flowers come forth. I am sure you would be delighted to see my windows filled with

---

① These (of which the first edition appeared in 1758) were published anonymously, but have been generally ascribed to Mr. Charles Smith.

② A selection of the correspondence of Linnaeus and other Naturalists, by Sir Jas. Edw. Smith, M. D., F. R. S., &c. 1821.

six pots of flowers, which the gardener has sent me to town[①], viz. great plenty of aconites, white and green hellebore, double hepatica crocus, polyanthus, periwinkle, lauristinus, vernal red cyclamen, single anemonies, and snowdrops. None of these were brought forward by any art, but entirely owing to the temperature of the season, though some seasons I have known things forwarder than now."

London, Oct. 26. 1747, O. S.

"My garden is in great beauty, for we have had no frost; a long, dry, warm summer, and autumn grapes very ripe.

"The vineyards turn to good profit, much wine being made this year in England."

London, Oct. 3. 1748, O. S.

"We have had a fine summer. Great plenty of all sorts of fruits and grain, and a very delightful autumn. It is now as warm as summer, no bearing of fires. My orange trees are yet abroad. My vineyard grapes are very ripe; a considerable quantity of wine will be made in England this year. We have not had one frosty morning this autumn. Marvel of Peru, double-flowered nasturtium, and all other annuals are not touched. My garden makes a fine show."

May 8. 1749.

"How the winter has been in Sweden I do not know, but at London the like warmth and mildness were never remembered. Our autumn was long, warm, and dry, with a few slight frosts before Christmas; but we have had since fine, warm, dry weather, and no frosts or snow. Our gardens were in great beauty in January and February: almonds, apricots, and peaches in

① Mr. Collinson's country house was at Mill Hill, in Middlesex.

blossom. Feb. 23. I went into the country. The elm hedges had small leaves, standard plums, almonds, and crocuses in full blossom; gooseberries showing their fruit. In short, it would be endless to talk to you of the wonders of this season. March 5. The fig in my London garden had small leaves when peas and beans under south walls were in blossom."

The exuberant abundance, resulting from seasons of which these letters afford a few specimens, is moreover referred to in several pamphlets, to which the dearths of 1756 and 1757, and of some subsequent periods gave rise. But the most unequivocal proof of the exuberance of the produce of such a succession of plentiful seasons, is afforded by a reference to the exportations of grain in the concluding years of that series. ①

---

① With reference to the ten years from 1741 to 1750, Dr. Adam Smith, after describing them as years of extraordinary plenty, and as attended with a remarkably low price, proceeds to observe, "Between 1741 and 1750, however, the bounty must have hindered the price of corn from falling so low in the home market as it naturally would have done. During these ten years the quantity of grain of all sorts exported, it appears from the Custom House books, amounted to no less than 8, 029, 156 quarters. The bounty paid for this amounted to 1, 514, 962*l.* 17*s.* 4 $\frac{1}{2}$*d.*. In 1749, Mr. Pelham, at that time prime minister, observed to the House of Commons, that for the three years preceding, a very extraordinary sum had been paid as bounty for the exportation of corn. He had good reason to make this observation; and in the following year he might have had still better. In that single year the bounty paid amounted to no less than 324, 176*l.* 10*s.* 6*d.*. It is unnecessary to obsserve how much this forced exportation must have raised the price of corn above what it otherwise would have been in the home market." — *Wealth of Nations*.

Agreeing as I do with Dr. Smith in his objection to the bounty as a measure of legislation, I must be allowed to differ from him in the opinion which he expresses of its operation in the present instance. As the price of wheat was falling coincidently with the enormous exportation of the three concluding years of the series, viz.

Years.	Wheat	Barley, Malt, and Rye	Total
1748	543, 387	530, 830	1, 074, 217
1749	629, 049	515, 684	1, 144, 733
1750	947, 602	658, 588	1, 606, 190

From what the author of the Corn Tracts states, the seasons from 1752 to 1755 seem to have been of doubtful produce; for his words are, after mentioning the ten good years in succession, "Nay, if the common opinion is right, we have had sixteen. "But we may conclude, that if not decidedly abundant, they were not deficient in any considerable degree; for there was a large export in some of those years, a great want of corn being experienced in the south of Europe in that interval, and the prices at home were not raised very materially by

---

In 1718 – 32*s*. 10 $\frac{1}{2}$*d*. per quarter.

1749 – 32*s*. 10 $\frac{1}{2}$*d*. do.

1750 – 2S*s*. 10 $\frac{3}{4}$*d*. do.

And as the very low price of this last year (being, moreover, low as it was, for a quality better than middling) coincided with the largest exportation of the whole period, it is difficult to conceive how it could be said to have raised the price. The utmost that can be said by the objectors to the bounty, of its operation in this instance is, that it may have prevented the price from falling so much as it might other wise have done. But the advocates for that measure might contend, and with apparent reason, that but for the relief afforded by the bounty to the glowers they must have reduced the cultivation, and thus have raised the price. In truth, the operation of the bounty appears to have been during this interval rather than that of counteracting the discouragement to cultivation from prices so very low as those which were the effect of a series of plentiful years than of raising the price, and of thus, according to the received notion, inducing a resort to fresh land at an increased cost of production.

that export.

I have been induced to trespass on the patience of my readers with so long a detail of the seasons in the interval from 1730 to 1755, because they present a series of twenty-six years, with the intervention of only one of a decidedly unfavourable character, viz. the winter of 1739 and 1740, followed by a bad harvest; and because the inferences from the fact are of importance as to the probable or possible effect of such a succession of favourable seasons on prices, independent of any alteration in the currency or in the financial measures of the government, and independent likewise of transitions from war to peace.

The degree of cheapness resulting from a succession of good seasons, or of seasons unmarked by the intervention of any one of great deficiency, is so curious as to be worth exhibiting more in detail than is usually done, as the tables containing average prices are generally confined to the quotations of wheat, and do not give the whole range of variations even of that single article. The following are the quotations of prices at Mark Lane and Bear Quay, for fifteen years, and they afford a confirmation in detail of the greatest depression having occurred during a period of war attended by a very large government expenditure defrayed by loans: —

January Prices of grain at Mark Lane and Bear Quay, extracted from the Appendix to Sir Frederick Morton Eden's work (page 80).

	Years.	Wheat.		Bailey.		Oats.	
		s.	s.	s.	s.	s.	s.
War.	1742	26 to	29	15 to	20	12 to	15
	1743	20	23	15	20	13	16
	1744	19	21	11	13	9	12
	1745	18	20	12	15	12	16
	1746	16	24	10	12	12	14
	1747	27	30	8	12	6 9d.	
	1748	26	28	13	14	9	12
	1749	27	32	17	18	14	16
	1750	24	29	14	17	12	14
	1751	24	27	14	17	13	14
	1752	33	34	17	19	12 6d.	16
	1753	29	33	17	18	10 6d.	12
	1754	27	33	17	19	12 6d.	13
War.	1755	24	26	12	14	10	13
	1756	22	26	11	15	12	13

And the average price by the Eton tables for wheat of better than average quality, for the ten years from 1742 to 1751, was 29*s*. 2 $\frac{1}{2}$*d*. .

The harvest of 1756 proved greatly deficient, as well in this country, as through the greater part of Europe. In Smith's Corn Tracts is the following description of it: —

"The last season of 1756 from its beginning was extremely unfavourable, thousands of acres remained unsown, and the bad condition in which many more were sown rendered them incapable of producing a good crop, although favourable weather had followed. It is certain that the weather, during the spring, summer, and harvest, was generally unfavourable, great quantities of grain perished by the rains and winds, and most of what remained proved defective, both in quantity and substance, by its not duly ripening.

The scarcity thence arising was attended with a very considerable advance of price, and with severe suffering among the lower classes, which is thus noticed in the work before quoted: —

"1756. Many insurrections in England, on account of the scarcity of corn, and the high prices of provisions. The king expresses to the parliament his concern for the sufferings of the poor, and the disturbances to which they have given rise, and exhorts them to consider of proper measures to prevent the like mischiefs hereafter. The exportation of corn prohibited from Christmas."

It may be worth while to break the course of this description of the seasons, in order to show the prodigious effect on price of one season of decided scarcity, when, from previous exportation or scanty crops, there was no considerable old stock. The quotations of wheat in Mark Lane, in 1756, before the deficiency of the harvest of that year had been ascertained, were 22*s*. to 26*s*..

In January, 1757, the price rose to				–	49*s*. to	50*s*.
February	–	–	–	–	47*s*.	51*s*.
March	–	–	–	–	46*s*.	54*s*.
April	–	–	–	–		64*s*.
May	–	–	–	–		64*s*.
June	–	–	–	–	67*s*.	72*s*.

The harvest of 1757 appears to have been deficient, although not in the same degree. It is probable, from the subjoined extract of Collinson's letters, that the extreme heat of the summer of 1757 may have rendered the crops light.

December 25 and 27. 1757.

"The extraordinary heat of our summer has ripened all sorts of fruit to perfection. In two gardens I saw this year pomegranates against south walls, without any art, ripened beyond what can be imagined in so northern a climate, they look extremely beautiful, and are of the size of some brought from abroad. Our autumn has been long, dry, and warm, and so continues; for a few slight frosts have not stripped the garden of flowers at Christmas day. The winter season has not closed before the spring flowers begin, for there are plenty of polyanthus, narcissus, pansies, and sweet violets."

The six succeeding seasons, viz. from 1758 to 1763, both years included, seem to have been favourable: the particular character of some of them is noticed in Collinson's letters.

July 25. 1759.

"We had the mildest winter ever known. Our spring was early and very agreeable, and our summer was the finest and warmest since 1750. Great plenty of all sorts of grain and fruits. New Wheat, of this year's produce, has been the 21st inst. at market."

London, Sept. 2. 1762.

"We have had a delightful warm summer, all the fruits of the earth very good and in great plenty."

"The season of 1763 is thus noticed by Collinson: —

London, Sept. 15. 1763.

Almost every day rain since the middle of July, the spring and summer very dry to that time. Very great plenty of grass, and all sorts of corn, but the weather unkindly for the harvest."

Of the succeeding season I find no direct notice by Collinson. As the price rose at Michaelmas, 1764, to 44*s.* 5*d.*, a high price at that time, the harvest of that year may be suspected to have been unfavourable, at the same time, as there was a large export, it is possible that the advanced price may in some measure have been occasioned by an unusual demand for corn abroad. ①

Mr. Collinson gives the following description of the season of 1765: —

London, Sept. 17. 1765.

"You, my dear friend, surprise me with telling me of your cold and wet summer, whereas our summer has been as much in the extreme the other way. For all May, June, and July were excessively hot and dry; but six or seven rainy days in three months, so that all our grass fields look like the sun-burnt countries of Spain and Africa. The beginning of August we had some fine rains, but they did not recover our usual verdure, since to the present writing, hot and dry weather, not a drop of rain for fourteen days. Our hay is very short, and oats and barley a middling crop; but of wheat, which we most wanted, good Providence has favoured us with a plentiful crop and a good harvest, which began two weeks sooner than in common years."

After this fine, though not very productive season, there was a series of

---

① In the chronological table of prices, and of the events connected with them, in the work before referred to, is the following passage: —"1764. The king reminds his parliament of the high prices of corn, occasioned by the exportation of it. The parliament finds the price of beef to be 3d. per 1b. to the vendor. Beef, mutton, and veal, at Exeter, 4*d.* to $4\frac{1}{2}$*d.*."

N. B. In the same work, under the date 1724, beef, mutton, veal, and pork, are stated to have been at $1\frac{3}{4}$*d.* per lb. at Exeter.

The exportations in the six years following 1758, were considerable, although they exhibit a decided falling off, as compared with the ten years ending in 1750.

Years	Wheat.	Other Grain.
1759	226, 426 qrs.	233, 556 qrs.
1760	390, 710	313, 903
1761	440, 746	437, 359
1762	294, 500	415, 081
1763	427, 074	218, 482

nearly ten years, marked by a very frequent recurrence of unpropitious seasons: and as henceforward a new epoch commenced in the corn trade of this country, characterised by a range of relatively high prices, and accompanied by a change from a balance of export to a balance of import of grain, it may be worth while to pause here for the purpose of considering some of the phenomena presented by the period ending in 1765.

All the writers who have turned their attention to the subject of the prices of corn, have been struck with the circumstance of the cheapness of the period from 1700 to 1765①, but more especially in the interval between 1715 and 1765, compared with the average price of the preceding century, and have endeavoured variously to account for that circumstance. The pamphlets with which the press teemed, upon the change from low to high prices, referred all the phenomena of the fluctuation, according as it suited the views of the writers, to the operation of the bounty on exportation. The question respecting the effects of the bounty seems, indeed, to have given rise to almost as much controversy at that time as the question of the effects of the bank restriction has since done.

The advocates for the bounty contended, that the cheapness of corn was wholly attributable to that measure, while, upon every occurrence of a season of dearth, the scarcity and consequent high price was by the

---

① "In the sixty-four first years of the present century, the average price of the quarter of nine bushels of the best wheat, at Windsor market, appear by the accounts of Eton College to have been 2*l.* 0*s.* 6 $\frac{10}{12}$*d.*, which is about ten shillings and six pence, or more than five and twenty per cent cheaper than it had been during the sixteen years preceding 1636; when the discovery of the abundant mines of America may be supposed to have produced its full effect, and about one shilling cheaper than it had been in the twenty-six years preceding 1620, before that discovery can be supposed to have produced its full effect. According to this account, the average price of middle wheat comes out to have been about thirty-two shillings the quarter of eight bushels."

adversaries of the bounty referred to the excess of exportation which had been thus artificially encouraged.

It is not my intention to enter upon a discussion of the principle and policy of the bounty on the exportation of corn; I have only the following short remarks to make upon it, as connected with its effects on prices between 1715 and 1765.

For the reasons already given a few pages back, while there appear to be no sufficient grounds for the opinion of Dr. Adam Smith, that the bounty had the effect of raising the price in that interval there seems to be as little ground for ascribing to that measure such encouragement to an extension of cultivation, as to have had the effect of sensibly reducing the price. But there is a further difficulty in ascribing to the bounty the remarkable cheapness of that period, compared with the period immediately preceding, or succeeding, and that is, that a similar degree of relative cheapness prevailed in France, as will appear by the following statement, extracted from, the Marquis Garnier's translation of Smith's "Wealth of Nations."

Prices of the Septier of Wheat in France, Pans Measure: —

Years			Francs	Cents
1706	to	1715	29	5
1716		1725	17	1
1726		1735	15	46
1736		1745	18	80
1756		1765	17	64
1766		1775	28	5

This degree of cheapness, be it observed, took place under a system of corn laws, the very reverse of that which prevailed in this country, the exportation thence being absolutely prohibited. Accordingly, while the low prices in this country were, by the advocates for the bounty, ascribed to our *encouragement* of exportation, a similar depression of prices in France was, by most French writers, attributed to the *discouragement* of exportation, and to the occasional encouragement of importation. So strong was the impression there that the low prices were occasioned by the restrictive regulations which prohibited, not only the exportation to foreign countries, but the free circulation from province to province, that in 1763 the government of France was induced to issue a declaration, allowing the free circulation of grain in the interior, and an edict in the following year granting a general liberty of export as well as of import, subject only to modification as to the price at which the export was to cease, viz. 12 livres 10 sous the quintal, equal to about 48*s*. the Winchester quarter. It might fairly then be asked, whether effects so exactly similar in the two countries can with any appearance of truth be ascribed to systems so exactly opposite.

Dr. Adam Smith has a remark to the same effect in the following passage: —

"In France, till 1764, the exportation of grain was by law prohibited; and it is somewhat difficult to suppose, that nearly the same diminution of price which took place in one country, notwithstanding this prohibition, should in another be owing to the extraordinary encouragement given to exportation." — Vol. i. chap. xi.

There is reason to believe, that in France the same prevalence of favourable seasons, or rather, the comparative exemption from years of dearth, was experienced, although with some considerable exceptions, during the fifty years which are marked by such relative cheapness.

On the prevalence of a general similarity of seasons, allowing for differences of climate on the Continent of Europe within a certain latitude, are the following remarks, in the justness of which I concur, in a work entitled, "On the Present State of England," by J. Lowe. 1823.

"Hardly aware of the similarity of temperature prevailing throughout what may be called the corn country of Europe, we mean Great Britain, Ireland, the north of France, the Netherlands, Denmark, the north-west of Germany, and, in some measure, Poland, and the north-east of Germany. All this tract is situated between the 45th and 55th degrees of latitude, and subject, in a considerable degree, to the prevalence of similar winds. Neither the superabundance of rain which we experience in one summer, or its deficiency in another, are by any means confined to Great Britain and Ireland; while in winter both the intensity and duration of frost are always greater on the continent. Exceptions certainly exist in particular tracts; but in support of our general argument, we have merely to recall to those of our readers who are of an age to recollect the early part of the war, or who have attended to registers of temperature, the more remarkable seasons of the present age; thus, in 1794, the spring was prematurely warm on the continent, as in England; there, as with us, the summer of 1798 was dry, and that of 1799 wet; again, in 1811 the harvest was deficient throughout, the northwest of Europe generally, from one and the same cause, blight; while that of 1816 was still more generally deficient, from rain and want of warmth. In regard to a more remote period, we mean the 17th and 18th centuries generally, if the temperature has not been so accurately noted, we find, from the coincidence in prices, that it is highly probable that there prevailed a great similarity in the weather of the continent; thus, in France, the latter years of the 17th century, the seasons of 1708 and 1709, as well as several of the seasons between 1764 and 1773, were as unpropitious, and attended with as great an advance of price, as in England." (Page 149)

One of the most remarkable circumstances attending the state of things here described is, that while the price of corn had fallen so considerably, as we have seen, on a comparison with the preceding century, the price of labour in this country had risen.

Dr. Adam Smith, referring to this period, observes: —

"The money price of labour in Great Britain has risen during the present century. This, however, seems to be the effect, not so much of any diminution in the value of silver in the European market, as of an increase in the demand for labour in Great Britain, arising from the great, and almost universal, prosperity of the country. with the average money price of corn. Both in the last century and the present, the day wages of common labour are said to have been pretty uniformly about the twentieth part of the average price of the septier of wheat, a measure which contains a little more than four Winchester bushels. In Great Britain, the real recompense of labour, it has already been shown the real quantities of the necessaries and conveniences of life which are given to the labourer, has increased considerably during the course of the present century. The rise in its money price seems to have been the effect, not of any diminution of the value of silver in the general market of Europe, but of a rise in the real price of labour in the particular market of Great Britain, owing to the peculiarly happy circumstances of the country." — *Wealth of Nations*, vol. 1. chap. xi.

According to Arthur Young, the average price of wheat was, for the whole of the 17th century, 38*s*. 2*d*. per Winchester quarter; and for the 66 years from 1701 to 1766, 32*s*. 1*d*., being a fall of 16 per cent; while the price of agricultural labour, which, on the average of the 17th century had been $10\frac{1}{4}d.$ per day, was, for 66 years ending in 1766, 12*d.*, or a rise of 16 per cent.

The fact, indeed, of a rise of money wages in this country, coincidently with a fall in the price of corn during the long interval in question, rests on unquestionable authorities.

Dr. Adam Smith, in the passage quoted, considers the advance in the rate of wages as the consequence of an increased demand for labour, and the decline in the price of corn as a consequence of an increased value of silver. The utmost effect of the supplies of gold and silver since the discovery of the American mines had, in his opinion, (founded, as it should seem, chiefly, if not entirely, on the price of corn) been felt somewhat before the middle of the 17th century. Who had made great researches on the subject, seem disposed to concur in the opinion entertained by Adam Smith, that, considering the price of wheat for a series of years of some length as the best measure of value, a rise in the value of silver was to be inferred by the fall in the price of wheat during the first 65 years of the last century. But without going into the general question of a measure of value, or of the connection between the price of corn and the price of labour, it may now be, it is to be presumed, considered as a conceded point, although still not without difficulty, that the money price of common day labour is a better criterion than corn, of the value of the precious metals.

According to this criterion, combined with the circumstance that many other important articles of consumption besides corn had risen, there can be little hesitation in coming to the conclusion, that the value of the precious metals was undergoing some depreciation through the whole of the 65 years of last century, during which there had been so marked a fall in the price of provisions. And the fall and the low range of the price of corn, while money was undergoing, however slowly, a depreciation, prove how powerful must have been the depressing circumstances operating upon the price of corn, to be sufficient, not only to prevent a rise corresponding with the diminished value of silver, but to cause a tendency in an opposite direction. The tendency to a decline of prices through so large a portion of last century occurred too, notwithstanding an increase, although slow, of the population, and a change which was in progress to the use of a higher diet.

It will appear by a reference to the following division of this work, "On the Effect of War on Prices," that whatever may have been the influence of war in other periods of our history, it had no effect of raising prices during the intervals in which it prevailed in the period under consideration: and that the longer intervals of peace, during which the prices were higher than during the wars, cannot therefore be adduced as among the means of accounting for the low prices from 1700 to 1765.①

The profound internal tranquillity which this country enjoyed during that interval (for the attempts in 1715 and 1745 in favour of the Stuart family were too feeble and too short-lived to be worth mentioning, as affecting the

① This exception is readily acconnted for, partly by the effects of the war in which we were then engaged with France, and partly, as far, at least, as regards the amount of tonnage, by the prohibition against the export of corn, a prohibition which was in force during a part of that periond, and which, of course, while it lasted, worval cause a diminution of the tonnage usually employed in the transport of grain. The shipping required for the export of corn in the middle of last centary must have formed no inconsiderable proportion of the whole of the to unage employed in the trade of the kingdom.

general state of internal peace and security), may be considered as having had some influence when compared with the 17th century.

The civil wars which prevailed near the middle of the 17th century might, doubtless, be supposed to have interfered in some degree with tillage, although, for the reasons already stated, it should seem that the high prices of that interval were more owing to the seasons than to the civil war; and this is the more probable, because the same relatively high prices prevailed in France during the middle of the 17th century as in this country. But admitting the disturbed state of the country to have contributed to the high range of prices which prevailed during the civil wars, these were at an end before 1650. And during the concluding 50 years of the 17th century, there was no such interruption of internal peace as could be supposed to interfere with the operations of husbandry, or the general inducements to cultivation.

If, then, the fall of prices in question cannot be accounted for by our corn laws, nor by the price of labour, nor by the state of the country in respect of population, of trade, of war or peace, or internal tranquillity, nor by any supposed increase of the value of silver, we have to seek for some cause more distinctly affecting the production of corn.

It is universally admitted, however, that no single cause affects the production of corn in respect of quantity from year to year, so much as the difference of the seasons; and the variation of price from this cause, is, as we have had occasion to observe, in a ratio much beyond the difference of quantity. The only difficulty therefore which attends the supposition of the seasons having had the principal influence in producing the cheapness of provisions in the period alluded to of last century, is in the length of time to which the operation of that cause is assigned. It has been assumed, most arbitrarily, that the differences of seasons, in their influence on the production of corn, must be equalised within certain periods, limited to suit some particular conclusion.

If the fact of such comparative exemption be allowed, there can be no difficulty in considering it as sufficient to account for the greatest part, if not for the whole, of the relative cheapness of that period. If in the 50 years, instead of only 5 years of recorded scarcity, there had been upwards of 20 years, it is perfectly clear that the produce must have been much less, and the price much higher. The difference in respect of the quantity of produce, is equivalent to a difference in the average fertility of the soil during the period. A comparative frequent recurrence of bad seasons affords a less produce for the same labour and capital, and therefore resolves itself, during the preponderance of that description of seasons, into an increased cost of production.

The comparative exemption from adverse seasons would consequently be equivalent, during the period to which it applied, to a diminished cost of production; and would thus, with the aid of the bounty, prevent the throwing of land out of cultivation, or even might admit of an extended tillage, notwithstanding the fall and low range of prices observable in this period. ①

This long period of great abundance, and consequent cheapness of the prices of provisions, was one which appears to have been attended with a

① There is at the same time a consideration which may have some weight in aid of the influence of a series of plentiful years in reducing the cost of production, and thus admitting of keeping up or extending the cultivation — I mean the very low rate of interest which prevailed through the reigns of George I. and II, and which would render the outlay of capital on land remunerative with smaller returns, than when the rate of interest was, as it had previously and has since been, so much higher.

great improvement in the condition and habits of the great bulk of the population. In the passage already quoted from Adam Smith, he refers to "the peculiarly happy circumstances of the country" during that period, and Mr. Hallam, in his "Constitutional History," describes the reign of George II. as "the most prosperous period that England had ever experienced." The author of the Corn Tracts, writing in 1765, observes, that "bread made of wheat is become more generally the food of the labouring people." This resort to a higher diet is a most indisputable sign of the improvement of their condition. The great command which the labouring classes possessed over the necessaries of life during that interval, might, according to the received theory of population, be expected to have been attended with an accelerated ratio of increase of numbers. But, according to the best evidence of the progress of population in this country, the ratio of increase during the long interval under consideration, was much slower than it has been since, under circumstances of diminished command of necessaries by the labouring classes. Mr. Malthus seems to have been struck by the apparent anomaly, and gives the following explanation of it in his work entitled, "Principles of Political Economy, considered with a View to their practical Application,":—

"It is well known that during this period the price of corn fell considerably, while the wages of labour are stated to have risen. During the last forty years of the 17th century, and the first twenty years of the 18th, the average price of corn was such, as, compared with the wages of labour, would enable the labourer to purchase with a day's earnings two thirds of a peek of wheat. From 1720 to 1750 the price of wheat had fallen, while wages had risen; instead of two thirds, the labourer could purchase the whole of a peck of wheat with a day's labour.

This great increase of command over the necessaries of life did not, however, produce a proportionate increase of population. It found the people of this country living under an excellent government, and enjoying all the advantages of civil and political liberty in an unusual degree. The lower classes of people had been in the habit of being respected, both by the laws and the higher orders of then fellow-citizens, and had learned, in consequence, to respect themselves: and the result was, that, instead of an increase of population exclusively, a considerable portion of their increased real wages was expended in a marked improvement of the quality of the food consumed, and a decided elevation in the standard of their comforts and conveniences."

The solution here given is apparently just. But the fact itself speaks volumes against the theory by which the partisans, whether of depreciation or of corn monopoly, seek to connect a high price of provisions with a state of public prosperity; and it equally militates against the theory of demand, which, as will be seen in the next section, attempts to explain the sudden rise of prices following this long interval of cheapness, by the hypothesis of a sudden increase of consumption.

SECTION 4 *1765 to 1775*

The change which dates from 1765 in the prices of provisions from cheapness to dearth, and in the corn trade from a regular exportation to a preponderance of importation, has been the subject of general remark, and has given rise, as usual, on occasions of great change, to controversy as to the causes of it. The same change from cheapness to dearth occurred coincidently through the rest of Europe; and this dearness, like the preceding cheapness, was referred to the most contradictory causes. In France it was ascribed to the recent permission of export, at the same time that, in this country, it was attributed to the occasional prohibitions of export and suspensions of the restrictions of import, such prohibitions and suspensions being argued to operate as a discouragement of tillage; not to mention the clamours which were then universally prevalent against the supposed improper practices of farmers, millers, and bakers, in raising and keeping up prices.

The most plausible of the reasons among the numerous ones which have been advanced for the great rise was the supposition of a fall in the value of silver. A considerable increase in the produce of the American mines is noticed by Humboldt and other writers, to have taken place in the middle of last century, and more especially about the year 1770. But the influence of this cause, if to be traced at all, which appears to be doubtful, must have been very gradual, and scarcely perceptible; and it could not come into operation at all so as to affect prices in Europe, till after all the phenomena of the high prices now under consideration had occurred; at any rate, it would not account for so sudden a rise as took place in 1766, and still less would it account for so great and sudden a transition from a large export to a large import of grain, as took place between 1765 and 1775.

But another mode of accounting for the phenomena in question has of late years become more general. The very able and well-informed writer of an article in the supplement to the "Encyclopædia Britannica" on the Corn Laws and the Corn Trade, gives the following explanation of the change: —

" After the peace of Paris in 1763, the national improvement was prodigiously accelerated. The extension of industry caused by the acquisition of new branches of commerce, by the increase of our colonial possessions, and, perhaps, more than all the rest, by the introduction of improved machinery into the cotton manufactories, was followed by a sudden increase of the population, and, as importation was prohibited, by a corresponding rise of prices."

And the late Sir Edward West, the distinguished author of an "Essay on the Application of Capital to Land," in a subsequent "Essay on the Price of Corn," referring to the rise of price between 1765 and 1775, says: —

"The true cause of this rise of price, in all probability, was the increasing population, and the increased cost of providing the additional produce for that increasing population, according to the principle which I have endeavoured to explain in my former publication. This opinion is confirmed by the fact of the very great increase of the population between the years 1760 and 1780. On reference to Mr. Rickman's Preliminary Observations to the Population Abstract, it will be found that the population increased at a rate far more rapid during this interval than at any former period. At about the same period, too—namely, between 1766 and 1773, our imports of corn began to exceed our exports, and we have since been a regularly importing instead of an exporting country."

The opinion to this effect has become very general, constituting a theory which refers the principal phenomena of the prices of corn to difference of demand or consumption, neglecting or treating as subordinate any variations of supply; but it is a theory which will be found to be constructed on a supposition of facts which did not exist, and to be irreconcileable with those which will be shown to have existed in the clear relation of cause and effect.

That a prosperous state of manufactures and trade, and a generally flourishing condition of the country, accompanied by an increasing population employed at full and increasing wages, would have a tendency to increase the consumption, and that the effect of a continued increase of consumption, under a given state of supply, would be to raise prices, diminishing the exportable surplus in the first instance, and forcing eventually a resort to fresh soils at an increased cost, or to an importation in as far as permitted, may readily be allowed.

But an increase of population, even in its most accelerated progress, and allowing for the utmost possible difference between a full and restricted consumption, cannot operate *persaltum*. And supposing even that the assumed increase of consumption had not been accompanied and in a great degree compensated by a coincident improvement and extension of cultivation, it would not account for the enormous difference between an export in 1763 and 1764 of 820,000 quarters of wheat, and an import in 1767 and 1768 of 830,000 quarters; the whole annual consumption of wheat at that period not being estimated at more than about 4,000,000 of quarters. Still less would it account for so great and sudden an increase of price, as from 33*s*. $2\frac{1}{4}$*d*. at Ladyday, 1763, to 58*s*. 8*d*. at Michaelmas, 1767.

There is, however, reason to believe that there was not only no increase of consumption to account for that rise of price and transition from export to import, but also the rise of price was required to limit, and did limit, the consumption below its former rate, and was further required to induce a foreign supply to make good the deficiencies of our own growth.

The reason for supposing that the consumption was diminished instead of having been increased, compared with what it had been in the period immediately preceding, is, that the rise of wages did not precede, but follow, very inadequately, the rise in the price of provisions.

Arthur Young[1] states, as the general result of the information obtained by him in his extensive agricultural tour in 1767, 1768, and 1770, that the mean rate of wages for the whole year was 7*s.* $4\frac{1}{4}$*d.* per week. Taking an average of the five years, from 1766 to 1770 inclusive, the price of the quarter of wheat was 47*s.* 8*d.*, or nearly 48*s.*, which would be 6*s.* the bushel, and 1*s.* 6*d.* the peck. At these prices of labour and wheat, the earnings of the labourer would be somewhat under five sixths of a peck. Now, in 1763, and for 30 years before, his wages had been 7*s.*[2] a week, and the average price of wheat in the 5 years ending in 1763 being 33*s.* $1\frac{1}{2}$*d.*, his daily earnings would be equal to very nearly a peck of wheat. And if the price of wheat be taken at the average of 20 years preceding 1755, it would appear that he then earned somewhat upwards of a peck. It is difficult, therefore, to conceive that earning so much less wheat in 1767, he should have consumed more in 1763. But if, from diminished command of necessaries, the inference were not clear against the supposition of an increased consumption, there is sufficient presumption, from the contrast between the contented state of the population in the interval from 1720 to 1755, and the disturbed and insurrectionary state of it between 1765 and 1775, of their being fully fed in the former interval, and underfed in the latter.

There is, moreover, a further objection to the theory which supposes a

① *Annals of Agriculture*, No. 271. p. 215.

② *Malthus*, *Political Economy*, p. 279. *Arthur Young*, *Progressive Value of Money*, p. 90.

direct and observable influence of the alternations of prosperous or declining trade, on the prices of provisions, that the supposed coincidence is, as will be seen, not borne out by facts.

Dr. Adam Smith, in the following passage, refers, in my opinion, to the right cause. At the same time I would observe upon this passage, that inasmuch as the ten or twelve bad seasons accounted, in his opinion, for the range of high prices without inferring a diminished value of silver, the ten years of extraordinary plenty, to which he refers, might be considered as accounting for the low prices without inferring as he has done an increased value of silver.

"The high price of corn during these ten or twelve years past, indeed, has occasioned a suspicion that the real value of silver still continues to fall in the European market. This high price of corn, however, seems evidently to have been the effect of the extraordinary unfavourableness of the seasons, and ought therefore to be regarded not as a permanent, but as a transitory and occasional event. The seasons for these ten or twelve years past have been unfavourable through the greater part of Europe; and the disorders of Poland have very much increased the scarcity in all those countries, which in dear years used to be supplied from that market. So long a course of bad seasons, though not a very common event, is by no means a singular one, and whoever has inquired much into the history of the prices of corn in former times will be at no loss to recollect several other examples of the same kind. Ten years of extraordinary scarcity, besides, are not more wonderful than ten years of extraordinary plenty. The low price of corn from 1741 to 1750, both inclusive, may very well be set in opposition to its high price during the last eight or ten years." (Vol. 1. p. 310. 3rd ed.)

Of the prevalence of a series of bad seasons, or, at least, of the very frequent recurrence of them in this country, and in a still greater degree, perhaps, in the rest of Europe, in the interval between 1764 and 1775, there can be no reasonable doubt.

The price rose considerably after the harvest of 1704, viz. to 44*s*. 5*d*. at Michaelmas, and 49*s*. 9*d*. at Ladyday following. This rise might be occasioned by a moderate degree of deficiency, there being, probably, little or no surplus in consequence of the very large exportation, which, in 1764, amounted to no less than 396, 857 quarters of wheat. The season of 1766, and some of the effects of the deficient crops of the harvest of that year, are thus described by Collinson: —

London, September 25. 1766.

"We have had a most uncommon rainy summer, which was no way propitious to the growth of wheat, but it pleased Providence to send us the finest hot and dry harvest ever known, yet the warm constant rains drew up the wheat so much to stalk, that the ears are very light. I hope there will be sufficient to support the nation, now we have prudently stopped the exportation; for so great are the wants, and the demand for foreign markets was so great and so pressing, that it advanced the price so considerably as to occasion insurrections in many parts of the kingdom, to stop by force the corn from being exported, but now a proclamation is come out to prevent it, I hope all will be quiet again."

The letters of Collinson are discontinued after the winter of that year; but the following details, extracted from the Annual Register, will, it is presumed, afford sufficient evidence of severe and long-continued dearths: —

In 1766, the quartern loaf in London was, at one time, as high as 1*s*. 6*d*.. Addresses were sent from different parts of the kingdom, stating the general distress of the people. A proclamation was issued in September to suspend the exportation, and enforce the laws against forestallers and regraters; and the speech from the throne on the meeting of parliament in November of that year began in the following terms: —

"The high price of wheat, and the defective produce of that grain last harvest, together with the extraordinary demands for the same from foreign parts, have principally determined me to call you thus early together, that I might have the sense of parliament as soon as conveniently might be, on a matter so important, and particularly affecting the poorer sort of my subjects."

The harvest of 1767 appears to have been deficient in a still greater degree.① The price at Michaelmas, 1767, rose to 58*s*. 8*d*.; and although the exportation was prohibited for another year, it continued high till the following harvest, which, with that of 1769, may be inferred to have been of ordinary produce, inasmuch as the prices gradually gave way, and in the latter year got down to 40*s*.. But although the privilege of export under a bounty was restored, the exportation was trifling.

The five years from 1770 to 1774, both years included, were attended with unproductive harvests. The dearth arising from them caused considerable distress, and consequent commotions among the people, and uneasiness on the part of government. In the year 1770, an act passed,

---

① Such was the severity of the sufferings of the people from the dearth of provisions, that serious disturbances broke out, and prevailed with greater or less violence over the greater part of the kingdom. Much mischief was done; and many lives were lost in different places. The military were called out, and the gaols filled with prisoners, for the trial of whom a special commission was issued.

The king in his speech on the meeting of parliament in November, 1767, referred to the continued scarcity in the following terms: —

"Among the objects of a domestic nature, none can demand more speedy, or serious attention, than what regards the high price of corn, which neither the salutary laws passed in the last session of parliament, nor the produce of the late harvest, have been able so far to reduce as to give sufficient relief to the distresses of the poorer sort of my people."

empowering justices, at the quarter sessions, to order returns of the prices of grain; and the returns thus obtained formed the materials for the average prices, thenceforward periodically published. The exportation was again prohibited in that and the following year.[①] In 1772, importation was allowed duty free, to the 1st of May, 1773. In 1773, the city of London offered a bounty of 4*s*. for 20,000 quarters of wheat, to be imported between March and June.

These were all indications of scarcity, and of alarm arising from it, not to be mistaken.

Mr. Arbuthnot, a contemporary writer, remarked, in 1773, "that we have had five successive bad crops, and this last more generally than any of the former; it had been nearly the same all over Europe; and, therefore, till there was a plentiful year, corn could not be cheap." He concerved that no effectual measure could be taken to prevent the recurrence of scarcity till this event happened, and till wheat was nearly the same price all over Europe.

It is said by this author, that by accounts laid before parliament at this time, the yearly produce of wheat alone was calculated to be four millions of quarters, which he believed to be short of the reality.[②]

It was in consequence of this state of things that the opponents of the

---

① "The lord mayor ordered the meal weighers to stick up in a conspicuous place, in the corn market, in Mark Lane, the quantities and prices of wheat sold, and the names of the buyers."—*Comber on National Subsistence*, p. 167.

The following extract from the Annual Register will show that the scarcity extended to Ireland: —

Dublin, May 4. 1771.

"We have cause of complaint of the dearness of provisions as well as the English, prime pieces of beef and mutton are here 6*d*. per pound, lamb 8*d*., veal 7*d*., and butter 10*d*.."

② *Comber*, p. 168.

corn law, as it then existed, succeeded in carrying a fresh act in 1773, by which importation was allowed at a duty of 6*d*. per quarter, when the price of wheat was at, or above, 48*s*. per quarter, and the bounty and exportation together were to cease when the price was at, or above, 44*s* The importation and exportation, and bounty for other grain, in their relative proportions to wheat.

The year 1774① was equally adverse with the preceding season. And

---

① In the Transactions of the Royal Society, vol lxxvi. p. 240., is a paper entitled "On the Variations of the Seasons, from Observations at London by Mr. Barker." And as it refers to the period now under consideration, a copy of it is here inserted.

"*On the Variations of the Seasons*"

"Measuring the rain for a few years will not show completely the general quantity of rain which falls in any place; for there is a very great difference at different periods of time. If I had measured the rain at London only in the four years, 1740, 1741, 1742, 1743, the mean would have been found to be only $16\frac{1}{2}$ inches in the year, yet they were not at all complained of as dry summers. 1740 was cold and dry till July 30., 1741 was cold and dry; the summer was hot, dry, and burning till the beginning of September; then ten days wet, and very warm again, being the finest autumn for grass ever known. 1742 was a showery summer, and 1743 wet in the middle, but then the winters were dry, so that the quantity of rain on the whole was small 1741 to 1750, the mean was $18\frac{1}{2}$ inches. 1741 and 1750 were hot, dry and burning; 1750, being the hottest year I have known. The intermediate years were neither very wet nor very dry; and this was the most plentiful and cheapest time for corn of any ten years I remember, for grain oftener fails in England from too much wet than from too little. 1751 to 1760, the mean year was $22\frac{1}{8}$. 1760 was hot, dry, and burning; but several of the summers were wet, and not so plentiful. Three wet summers together — 1754, 1755, and 1756 — were a time of scarcity, and we have had more failing crops since that time than before it. From 1761 to 1770 there was $23\frac{1}{4}$ in a year. 1762 was hot, dry, and burning, and 1765 was cold and dry; but several years were wet—1763 and 1768 remarkably so, and of those ten several had failing crops, and some had great snows. There was a great change of the seasons at 1763; for I have had more rain since that time than I had before it, in the proportion of five to four. From 1770 to 1780 there was at a mean 26 inches. 1771 was dry, and 1778 and 1779 were hot, yet not without fits of rain; and most of the other years were wet, and some great snows. 1773, 1774, and 1775 were so wet that there came 32 inches in a year, which is nearly

indisputable proofs exist of the scarcity arising from that and the preceding season, inasmuch as the importations were, in

Years.			Qrs. of Wheat.	Including all other Grain.
1774	–	–	269, 235	803, 844
1775	–	–	544, 644	1, 039, 122

When these quantities, and the equally large importations of 1767 and 1768, are considered with reference to the total estimated produce at that period, and with reference also to the very large surplus which the seasons immediately preceding had yielded for exportation at low prices, some conception may be formed of the enormous difference of the productiveness of the crops; but the conception would be inadequate, unless allowance were made for an excess above an average in the one case much beyond the mere quantity exported, and in the other for a deficiency greater than the quantity imported.

The average price from the Eton tables of ten years, from 1755 to 1764, was 37*s.* 6*d.* ; and of ten years, from 1765 to 1774, was 51*s.* ; being a rise of upwards of 35 per cent; but the ten years ending in 1764 comprise two seasons, viz. , 1756 and 1757, of bad, and one, viz. , 1664, of indifferent produce. If we compare the ten years ending in 1774 with a series of ten good seasons, such as from 1742 to 1751, the difference will be more striking: —

---

double what there was from 1740 to 1743. In twelve months from October, 1773, to September, 1774, there came 39. 390 inches of rain, which is a Lancashire year. And in one month, September, 1774, there was 8 inches; this was in bailey and pease harvest, and for three weeks together not a load could be caried. By the above state of the case it appeals that for four successive periods of ten years, the quantity of rain has been increasing each time. " (*Philosophical Transactions*, vol. lxxv. p. 240.)

And in another paper Mr. Barker writes: —

"In four years, 1740, 1741, 1742, 1743, there came about 66. 361 inches of rain. In the four years, 1772, 1773, 1774, 1775, there was 124. 957 inches of rain, which is nearly twice as much. "

	s.	d.
10 years, ending 1751, average	29	2
10 years, ending 1774	51	0

The advance therefore in the ten years ending 1774 was 75 per cent upon the price for the ten years ending in 1751①; the cheap period, be it observed, embracing five years of war, accompanied by large loans, while the dear period was one of universal peace. It may be worth while too, with a view of having some notion, however imperfect, of the difference of produce in these two periods, to contrast the aggregate quantity exported in the one with the balance of importation in the other.

Years.		Wheat.	Grain of all Kinds.
		Balance of Exports.	
1742 to 1751	– –	4, 700, 509qrs.	8, 869, 190qrs.
		Balance of Imports.	
1766 to 1775	– –	1, 363, 149qrs.	3, 782, 734qrs.

It is true that the population had increased greatly during the interval; but so likewise had the extent of cultivation. The numbers of acts of inclosure had been,

In the reign of George I.	– – – –	16
George II.	– – – –	226
And in the first fifteen years of George III., viz. from 1760 to 1775	– – – – –	734

The probability, therefore, is that the increased extent of cultivation had nearly, if not quite, kept pace with the increase of the population: besides

① It is probable that if in the period of dearth from 1765 to 1775, the practice had prevailed which was introduced twenty years later, of making up for deficiency of wages by parish allowance, the prices would have been still higher.

that there is every reason to believe that improvements in the mode of cultivation, although not so great as those which have been strikingly observable of late years, must have been more or less in progress during the above-mentioned period.

The whole interval from 1765 to 1775, in which there was such a frequent recurrence of seasons of scarcity in this country, was marked by dearths of equal, if not greater severity, on the continent of Europe. Reference to the inclemency of some of the winters, and to the cold, wet, and stormy character of the summers, are to be met with in the published correspondence of several French writers of that period. But it will be sufficient for the present purpose to refer to the following passages from the "Annual Register:" —

"1767. The irregularity and inclemency of the seasons for some years past in different parts of Europe has occasioned an uncertainty and great deficiency in the crops of several countries, by which the poor have suffered great distresses. The Ecclesiastical State, and some other parts of Italy, have been severely affected by this calamity. England, which usually supplied its neighbours with such immense quantities of grain, and allowed a considerable bounty on the exportation of it, has been a sufferer from the same cause, and it has required the utmost attention of the legislature to guard against and prevent the dreadful consequences attending it.

"1768. The badness of the late harvest in France had occasioned provisions of all sorts to bear an immoderate price; and corn, in particular, was not only very deal, but, in general, very bad, and the bread, consequently, disagreeable and unwholesome. The distresses of the people were excessive, and their complaints and murmurings became universal. In such situations, all the world fancy themselves ingenious in finding out the causes of public calamities; and if any novelties have been introduced, they always come in for a great share of popular odium. It was upon this occasion; and, without any regard to the influence of seasons, or to the will of Heaven, the miseries of the people were attributed to the edicts which the king had passed some time ago, for the free importation and exportation of corn in all the ports, and an unlimited circulation of it through all the interior parts of the kingdom.

"1770. A scarcity of provisions prevailed in France. The distresses of the people were this year so excessive, that it is said 4000 persons perished by famine in Limousin and Marche only, and in Normandy, the most fruitful province of France, barley bread sold at above 2*d*. a pound. This misery produced numberless riots and insurrections in different parts, in which much mischief was done, and many lives lost."

"Berlin, April 13. 1771. The present severity and extreme rigour of the weather is so very remarkable, that the oldest people here do not remember to have seen or heard the like; for it still continues to freeze every night as in the middle of winter, and a great quantity of snow lies on the ground, which so distresses the poor inhabitants of the country, that the most melancholy accounts are daily received of the misery and wretchedness occasioned by this dreadful calamity."

"Frankfort, April 7. 1771. The want of provisions is very great, both here and in the circle of Swabra. Our magistrates distribute bread to the poor gratis, and those of Nuremberg do the same. In Bavaria, bread is at an excessive high price."

"1773. The dearth which has so long afflicted different parts of Europe has this year been grievously felt in several countries. Germany, Bohemia, and Sweden have presented scenes of the greatest calamity, and multitudes have perished in that miserable extremity of wanting the plainest and most common necessaries of life. France, though in a lesser degree, has been a considerable sharer in this misfortune; and the distresses of the people have occasioned riots and disturbances in several of the provinces. Nor has the taking off of the bounty on exportation in England, with all the other measures that have been adopted to answer the same purpose, been sufficient to remedy the evils proceeding from inclement skies, and unusual seasons."

"1775. The distresses of the people, owing to the scarcity and dearness of coin in France, threw that kingdom into an uncommon state of disturbance and commotion during a great part of the spring and summer. Bread in several places could not be procured for money, and the beggars are said to have refused the latter, whilst they rent the air with cries for the former; so that gold was no longer a security against want. This distress was the more irremediable, as other nations were not abundantly supplied. The scarcity of corn in England not only cut off that resource, but also diverted a still greater by the immense quantities which it drew from the American colonies." (After enumerating instances of violence, the account proceeds.) "In the mean time no means were left untried by the government, either to quell these disturbances, or to alleviate their cause. Troops were stationed to protect the markets, and the roads sand rivers by which they were supplied, great companies of the burghers were aimed for the same purpose. The king granted a considerable bounty on the importation of corn. The public disorders, notwithstanding all these measures, increased to so alarming a degree, as at length to excite apprehensions of a general insurrection, and to make it appear necessary to call in the troops from the frontiers to the centre of the kingdom; so that the Isle of France, with some other of the interior provinces, were, in a manner, surrounded and intersected with lines of armed men. It at length pleased Providence that a most plentiful harvest removed the distresses of the people, both in France and most other parts of Europe."

SECTION 5 *1775 to 1793*

The seasons immediately following that of 1774, and comprised within the interval terminating in 1792, appear to have been irregular, but not characterised by such a preponderance of the proportion of inclement and unproductive seasons as occurred between 1765 and 1774.

The harvest of 1775 is described at the close of the extracts from the "Annual Register" which have been referred to, as having been plentiful in France and most other parts of Europe. And accordingly, immediately after the harvest, the price which at Ladyday, 1775, had been 59*s.* $1\frac{1}{4}$*d.*, fell to 43*s.* 7*d.* at Michaelmas, and continued at about that rate till the harvest of 1777, when the price rose to 51*s.* 7*d.*. In the mean time there had been a balance of export in 1776 of about 200,000 quarters of wheat; while in 1777 there was an importation of a like quantity.

The seasons of 1778 and 1779 were favourable, and were followed by a considerable fall of prices, the decline having been from 51*s.* 7*d.*, the quotation of the Windsor market at Michaelmas 1777, to 35*s.* 7*d.* at Michaelmas 1779.

In the "Farmer's Magazine," vol. ii. p. 139., is the following reference to the season of 1779: —

"Suppose a season of great fertility, such as the ever memorable year 1779. when the crop was one fourth above a medium crop."

This transition to abundance, after a long period of dearth, was attended, as is usual on such occasions, with stagnation and declining prices, and a general depression of the landed interest, or what is more familiarly known under the designation of "agricultural distress."

In the "Annals of Agriculture", is the following description in the extract of a letter written by Arthur Young, in 1780, of the fall of prices and consequent distress at the period referred to: —

"In the years 1776, 1777, prices fell considerably, and, in 1779, so low, that very general complaints have been heard of ruined farmers, and distressed landlords; and at the time I am now writing, the fact holds that there is a considerable fall in all products, and great numbers of farmers ruined. I have the prices of wool for forty years now before me, and that which from 1758 to 1767 was from 18*s.* to 21*s.* a tod, is for 1779 only 12*s.*, and was in 1778 but 14*s.*. We must go back to 1754 to find a year so low as the last. Wheat and all sorts of grain are greatly fallen."

The decline of prices here noticed has, by the theory which accounted for the previous rise as the effect of an increased consumption arising from a prosperous state of trade, been ascribed to a diminished consumption occasioned by a dull and declining trade. But as the state of trade, judging not only from exports and imports, but from the best authenticated contemporary accounts, was still declining in the three following years, being the concluding ones of the American war, viz. from 1780 to 1784, the supposed diminished consumption ought to have had the effect of further depressing, or, at all events, of keeping down the price, instead of which there was a considerable rise. For instance —

				s.	*d.*
1779	–	–	–	36	3
1780	–	–	–	43	$1\frac{1}{4}$
1781	–	–	–	52	5

Of the seasons of 1780 and 1781, I have not met with any particular notice ①; but that of 1782 is recorded as having been very unfavourable.

In Scotland the weather during the whole year was as inclement as the season of 1799 afterwards proved to be; and in the "Farmers' Magazine" for 1800, there is a minute description of the similarity in point of weather of those two years. In the rest of the island there was a deficiency of produce, although not to so great a degree as in Scotland. A winter of great severity followed, prices rose considerably, and a large importation of corn took place in 1783.

As an example of the great and sudden alteration of prices occasionally arising from the occurrence of even a single bad season, when there is not, as there appears not to have been in this instance, a large stock on hand, I subjoin an extract from the "Annals of Agriculture", of a communication from Mr. William Pitt, dated Pendeford, April 4. 1785, entitled.

"CONTRASTS."

The following contrast of effects arising from dissimilar seasons, now so recent, may perhaps appeal striking in some future succession of regular

① As far as can be inferred from a reference to the Ladyday and Michaelmas prices, it should seem that the produce of 1780 must have been considered to be deficient, inasmuch as the price of wheat, which, at Ladyday 1780, had been 38*s.* 3*d.*, rose, at Michaelmas, to 48*s.*, and at Ladyday, 1781, to 56*s.* 11*d.*. The price declined near 10*s.* the quarter after the harvest of 1781, which may therefore be presumed to have been considered as moderately good.

seasons, and, as it will not take up much room, may be worth preserving from oblivion, by registering it in the Annals of Agriculture. I doubt not but yourself and many others can recollect circumstances more remarkable: the following have come under my own immediate observation: —

Winter succeeding the Harvest of 1781.	£	s.	d.	Winter succeeding the Harvest of 1782.	£	s.	d.
Barley of the best quality sold in the markets of Staffordshire, our customary bushel of 9 $\frac{1}{2}$ gallons, down to	0	2	9	Bailey of the same quality sold in the same markets, same measure, common price, per bushel, 7*s.* to	0	7	2
Wheat, immediately after the harvest, clean for seed, the above measure per bushel-	0	5	0	Wheat of the best quality, same measure, per bushel, 10*s.* to	0	10	6

Spring, 1782.	£	s.	d.	Spring, 1783.	£	s.	d.
Bought sixty bushels of Dutch oats for seed, delivered at home, per bushel –	0	1	8	Sold out of the product oats that had lain a month in the wet, and so damaged in the stack by rain during making and carrying in bad order, that they moulded and grew together, per bushel	0	3	6
A friend of mine sold clover seed of a good quality at the common market price, which was per cwt.	1	11	6	Bought again cloverseed of the same quality for his own sowing, at per cwt.	5	10	0
1782.				1784.			
Bought Worcestershire hops, of excellent quality, at per cwt. –	2	2	0	Hops inferior in quality to the opposite, bought at per cwt. –	5	12	0

The season of 1783, although not so unfavourable as the preceding, seems not to have been a productive one. It was followed by two severe winters; and the spring and summer of 1784 were cold and ungenial.

The effect of so frequent a recurrence of winters of great severity was felt in a comparative scarcity and high price of animal food; and this description of dearth induced the Corporation of London, in 1786, to appoint a committee for the purpose of inquiring into the causes of the high price of provisions. The first resolution of the committee in their report is sagely couched in the following terms: —

"Resolved, That it appears to your committee, from the three different papers mentioned in the evidence of Mr. Montague, principal clerk in the Chamberlain's office, and Mr. Tomlinson, receiver of the tolls in Smithfield market, containing an account of the number of cattle and sheep brought into the said market during the last thirty-six years, that from the year 1732 to 1778, the same bad annually increased in a very considerable degree; and that there has been a greater increase from 1778 to 1783; but the decrease that has happened during the years 1784 and 1785, we are of opinion, from the evidence that has been laid before us, arises from the pernicious system of forestalling in the vicinity of this metropolis."

The committee likewise attacked the prevailing tendency to new enclosures, as one of the concurrent causes. I should not have noticed this strange document, but for the following information which the inquiry brought forth. The magistrates of Sunderland, in answer to the inquiries, write —

"For the last three years we have had two very dry summers, and three very severe winters, which caused much destruction among sheep and lambs in the spring, and occasioned a great consumption of all kinds of fodder, and even great quantities of oats were used after hay, straw, and turnips were eaten up."

There are other answers to a similar purport: I shall only further extract the concluding part of one from Arthur Young, dated August, 1786: —

"Last winter hay, straw, and fodder of all kinds were scarcer and dearer than ever known in this kingdom. Severe frosts destroyed the turnips and cattle of all kinds, and sheep suffered dreadfully; many died, and the rest were in ill plight to fatten early in this summer."

The seasons of 1785 and 1786 seem to have been attended with an ordinary produce of the wheat crops, and prices fell within the rate at which the bounty on exportation attached. There was accordingly a balance of export of wheat.

The average price of the Years			*s.*
1782, 1783, 1784	–	–	was 54
1785, 1786, 1787	–	–	44

Now it is very well known that there was an amazing burst of prosperity in the three latter, as compared with the three former years, which had been marked by great commercial and financial difficulties, and by a great contraction of the circulation, and yet, we see a fall in the price of 10*s*. per quarter in the latter period. This fall is readily ascribed to the difference of seasons; but had the effect of the seasons been reversed, the low prices of 1782, 1783, and 1784, would, according to the theory of demand, have been ascribed to the declining, and the high prices of 1785, 1786, and 1787, to the prosperous, state of trade, with just as much reason as their is for the supposition that the low prices of 1777, 1778, and 1779 were caused by the dull state of trade, as compared with the preceding period of high prices.

The winter of 1788-1789 was again a very severe one, and followed by a backward spring. The crops of 1789 were considered to be deficient in this country; and as they had failed in a still greater degree abroad, it was apprehended that an exportation, if allowed, might entail a dearth. There was consequently, after an inquiry by the Board of Trade, as to the result of the harvest of 1789, and upon information received of scarcity and very high prices abroad, as well as of a deficiency of our own crop of wheat, an order in council issued in December, 1789, prohibiting the export, and allowing importation duty free for a time limited. This order was confirmed by an act passed in the session of 1790.

As a consequence of the deficient harvest of 1789, the price which at Michaelmas, 1788, had been 48*s*. , rose at Michaelmas, 1789, to 57*s*. ; and had it not been for the prohibition of exportation, it would have risen much more, because in France the scarcity was such as to amount almost to a famine, and the government of that country, then under the administration of M. Necker, expended very large sums in procuring corn from abroad. In proof of the effect produced by those purchases on the general prices of Europe, of which those of Holland may be considered to have been at that time the best criterion, it may be observed, that the price of wheat at Amsterdam rose in 1789 to between 60*s*. and 70*s*. the quarter. Our bullion price accordingly was below the bullion prices of Europe in that year.

The summer of 1790 was wet, and the prices ranged high, so as to induce a large importation, the ports being open at the low duly of 6*d*. per quarter. At the close of the year the ports were shut to importation, but opened again in the spring following, thus affording a presumption that even with the aid of a considerable foreign supply, the produce of the preceding harvest had been below the consumption.

The season of 1791 is described in the "Annals of Agriculture", as one of the great abundance. And the produce of that harvest, following a large foreign supply, had the effect of reducing the price to 40*s.* 11*d.*, and thus of closing the ports, which remained shut through the following year. But the low price was productive, as usual, of complaint on the part of the landed interest, and was the occasion of a fresh corn bill. ①

The year 1792 is stated in the "Annals of Agriculture" to have been "remarkable for an extremely wet summer, by which the crop of wheat was much injured every where." This inferiority of the harvest, which raised the price at Michaelmas to 53*s.* 4*d.*, combined perhaps with apprehensions on political grounds, induced the government on the 9th of November, 1792, to issue an order in council, prohibiting exportation until the following spring; and subsequently parliament passed an act, *33 G. 3. c. 3.*, authorising the king in council to prohibit at any time during the session the exportation of all kinds of grain, and to permit the importation at the low duty.

On a review of the eighteen years from 1775 to 1793, it appears that, although not marked by any extraordinary inclemency of weather, or by a considerable degree of scarcity, as far at least as regards wheat, excepting from 1782 to 1784, the seasons were irregular, and that a large proportion of them were attended with harvests of scanty produce; not scanty merely with reference to an increasing rate of consumption, but scanty relatively to the average produce of a given extent of cultivation.

If compared with an equal number of years in the middle of the century, for instance, from 1730 to 1748, the preponderance of unfavourable seasons here

① By 31 G. 3. c. 30. from 15th of November, the former laws were repealed, and a new one enacted, by winch wheat was subject to a duty of 24*s.* 3*d.* if the puce was under 50*s.*; 2*s.* 6*d* at or above 50*s.* and under 54*s.*; 6*d.* at or above 54*s.*; and a bounty of 5*s.* on exportation at a price under 44*s.*. The duty and bounty on other gram, in the usual proportion.

described, between 1775 and 1793, is very great; there having been in the former series of eighteen years only one year of scarcity, or even of anything like deficient produce, while in the latter series there were several of acknowledged deficiency, namely, 1782, 1783, and 1784, 1789, 1790, and 1792, besides others, which, by inference from prices, and from the sudden transition from export to import, may be considered to have been defective. And it is difficult to resist the conclusion, that if there had been an equal exemption, not only in this country but throughout Europe, from adverse seasons in the latter, as in the former period, we should have witnessed, notwithstanding the increase of population, a much lower range of prices, and have continued, under the operation of the bounty, to have been an exporting country. The contrast in that case would have been still greater than it is between the prices of corn immediately before, and those subsequent to 1793. As it was, the irregularity of the seasons, and the more frequent recurrence of comparatively deficient crops in the last 35 years of the 18th century, appear to have compensated for the lower range of the first 65 years, and to have had the effect of raising the average price of the entire century to a level with the average price of the whole of the 17th century. The comparison of the average prices of wheat in the two centuries is thus given by Arthur Young: —

		l.	*s.*	*d.*	
17th century	– –	1	18	2	the Winchester quarter. ①
18th century	– –	1	18	7	

① The following is an extract from the passage in which the above statement of the averages is given: —

"By collecting the average prices of wheat for various periods, with all the attention in my power, I find the progress through four centuries has been the following. —

It would lead into too wide a field of discussion to enter upon the various questions which are suggested by this very remarkable coincidence of the price on a comparison of the two centuries. ① It is sufficient for the

---

		l.	*s.*	*d.*	
Average of the 13th century	–	1	2	9	per quarter.
14th century	–	1	6	0	
15th century	–	0	12	0	
16th century	–	1	3	8	

This result does not correspond with any general authority I have met with, which should not cause surprise, because the documents were equally unknown to Dr. Adam Smith, Sir George Shuckburgh, and probably to some other writers who have treated generally on the subject.

From 1595 we have fortunately a regular register of wheat at Windsor, but as the measure there is nine gallons, and the price minuted that of the best wheat in the market, the sums are reduced two ninths to bring them to the Winchester measure and average quality, until the year 1771, when Catherwood's tables for the average of the whole kingdom, by the authority of the Register Act, commenced; the price of this long period I have reduced to the following average. —

		l.	*s.*	*d.*
That of the 17th century was	– –	1	18	2
18th century	– – –	1	18	7

Being arise of only $\frac{1}{2}$*d.* per bushel.

The equality between these two centuries is one of the most remarkable circumstances to be met with in the economical history of this country. The average from 1701 to 1766, was 1*l.* 12*s.* 1*d.* , which is a fall of sixteen per cent below the price of the whole preceding century. The average of the 23 years from 1767 to 1789, both inclusive, was 2*l.* 5*s.* 3*d.* , from 1767 to 1800, being 34 years, the price was 2*l.* 10*s.* 6*d.*. — *Progressue Value of Money*, p. 75.

① Any attempt to explain that extraordinary fact would involve the necessity of a consideration of many points, upon which the means of information are wanting, such, for instance, as to how far the cost of production might not be in the course of progressive reduction, so as, with the aid of a more than ordinary exemption from seasons of scarcity, to countervail the continued depreciation which gold and silver appear to have been, however slowly, undergoing in the 18th century. The corn laws must be supposed to have had some operation, the precise nature of which it would be very difficult, if not impossible, to trace. At the same time, as the price in this country did not, during those two centuries, differ materially from the general prices of Europe, the presumption is, that the corn laws, although they might, and doubtless did, occasionally operate in aggravation of other causes of variation, must, in some instances, have operated in compensation, so that, however unjust and impolitic, however complex and absurd the system, its influence on prices is not very discernible down to the conclusion of the last century.

purpose of the present inquiry, that in the surveys which have been taken of series extending as far as 50 and 60① years each, compared with a series of an equal number of years immediately preceding or succeeding, during those two centimes, it has appeared that seasons of a favourable or unfavourable character have prevailed in a very different degree or frequency of occurrence in the respective series; and that there is nothing therefore at variance with experience derived from former periods of our history, in the assignment of a greater proportion of unfavourable seasons in the interval between 1792 and 1819, than in an equal interval anterior or subsequent to that period.

It is moreover to be borne in mind, in estimating the effects of a more than usually frequent recurrence of seasons of scarcity or plenty, that an enormous difference must be the result on prices, according as there may be more or less of impediments, whether from the corn laws, or from a state of war, to importation under deficiency, or to exportation of a surplus, of the home growth.

The corn laws were inoperative, or nearly so, between 1792 and 1815; but the war which prevailed during that interval operated most powerfully in aggravation of the influence of the seasons. The very great difference

① It is not essential to the purposes of the argument on the effect to be ascribed to a frequent recurrence of bad seasons in the interval between 1793 and 1818, to seek to establish the difference of frequency of recurrence of seasons of scarcity or abundance in series of more than twenty-four or twenty-five years. And to this extent, at least, it is to be presumed that the evidence adduced will have left little room for doubt. But the great difference which has been pointed out in the comparative productiveness arising apparently in a great measure from the exemption from bad seasons during an interval of fifty years, combined with the near approximation of the average prices of each of the two last centuries, may fairly justify a suspicion, if it does not go the length of authorising the conclusion, that a series of 100 years at least is reqursite to reduce to a fair average the inequalities of the seasons.

arising from the effects of the last war on the prices of corn will be exemplified in the period of high prices, which is about to come under examination. But before proceeding to the consideration of that period, it is desirable to obtain a clear view of the general effects of war on prices, and of the specific effects which may be ascribed to the last war.

PART II

ON THE EFFECT OF WAR

CHAPTER I
GENERAL VIEW OF THE SUBJECT

In estimating the manner and degree in which war and transition from war to peace may affect general prices, two distinct questions arise: the one is, how far the taxes requisite to defray the extraordinary expenses attending a state of war are calculated to raise prices; and the other is, whether the prices of commodities in general (including food and necessaries), independent of the degree in which they may be affected directly or indirectly by taxation, are liable to be influenced by war, and in what degree, through the medium of supply and demand.

CHAPTER II
EFFECTS OF TAXATION ON THE FLUCTUATION OF GENERAL PRICES

The effects of taxation on prices are liable to vary according to the mode in which the taxes are imposed.

An income or property tax, equally levied upon all classes, would not, in any way that I can conceive, tend to raise general prices.

Taxes levied upon particular commodities have, in general, the effect of raising the price of those commodities; and manufactured articles must be raised in price in some proportion to whatever tax may be imposed on the raw materials. But it does not seem to be a necessary consequence of taxes upon one set of commodities, that all other commodities, although untaxed, should be raised in price, while there are strong grounds of presumption that, under some circumstances, there might be an opposite tendency.

The conditions through which taxes upon one set of commodities are calculated to have an indirect or circuitous effect in raising the price of untaxed commodities, are, that the objects taxed should be the ingredients or the instruments of production; and that such taxes should not apply generally, and nearly equally, to all productions.

If the taxes be laid on the ingredients or instruments of production of some particular article and not of others, it is clear that such article must advance in price as the condition of continued supply; without such advance the article would not yield a profit equal to that derived from other productions, and it would, after some interval, cease to be produced in equal quantity, till the diminished supply should raise the price in some proportion to the tax.

But if taxes on the instruments of production, as on corn, or other necessaries of the labourer, or on the materials composing machinery and the implements of husbandry, apply equally, or nearly equally, to all branches of industry, they cannot have the effect of raising the price of the produce to which they are applied; for, provided the power of reproducing in general be not impaired, there will be no inducement to withdraw capital from one occupation and to transfer it to another. An advance of price is not, under such circumstances, a condition of continued supply.

In this country the taxes on the necessaries of the labourer, and on the instruments of production, do not apply exclusively to agriculture; they apply, at least in an equal, and probably in more than an equal, degree, to other branches of industry; and therefore, according to the principles here stated, they are not calculated to have the effect of raising the prices of agricultural produce, nor, in general, of raising the prices of other articles that are not the immediate objects of taxation.

It is not my intention, at present, to enter into a detailed statement of the grounds for this opinion, which would involve a discussion of the principles of taxation; a subject foreign to the purpose of this inquiry. It is sufficient to remark, in general terms, that if the level of the prices of articles not taxed, agircultural produce, for instance, were raised by the taxes laid on other articles, it would follow, that if the whole amount of taxation levied during a war were continued in peace, there would, as far as taxation is concerned, be no fall of prices in the transition from war to peace.

As, therefore, the whole amount of taxation (including land tax, tithe, and poor rate) down to the summer of 1822, was as great as during the war, with the exception of the income tax, the inference is, that in as far as untaxed commodities and labour were raised in price by that cause, the same cause, subsisting down to the summer of 1822, should have prevented prices from falling to the level to which they would otherwise have declined. And as the controversy has mainly turned upon the contrast between prices during the war and since the peace, till the close of 1822, the lowest point having been reached before any remission of taxation, the income tax excepted, we may fairly exclude the operation of taxes from among the causes of the fluctuations in the prices of untaxed commodities, such as agricultural produce, or of commodities divested of the taxes to which they may be liable on importation or consumption.

I shall therefore proceed to examine how far war, independent of taxation, may have contributed to the fluctuation of prices.

CHAPTER Ⅲ
EFFECT OF THE EXTRA DEMAND OR CONSUMPTION SUPPOSED TO ARISE OUT OF A STATE OF WAR IN GENERAL

Those persons who consider the range of high prices which prevailed from 1793 to 1814, as being fully accounted for by the war, independently of its attendant taxation, proceed on the assumed operation of the following causes: —

1. An extra demand or consumption arising out of a state of war in general.
2. The extra demand or consumption peculiarly characterising the last war.
3. The monopoly of trade enjoyed by this country.
4. The stimulus or excitement to increased population, production, and consumption, occasioned by the profuse government expenditure during the above period.

SECTION 1 *Extra demand or consumption arising out of a state of war in general*

The reasoning in support of the opinion, that the principal phenomena of high prices may be ascribed to the effects of war in general, through the medium of extra demand, independently of any reference to circumstances affecting the supply, may be stated in substance as follows: —

That the whole of the government expenditure for naval and military purposes may be regarded as creating a new source of demand for the articles constituting that expenditure, and consequently as tending to raise the price of such articles.

Not only the price of those commodities, which come directly under the description of naval and military stores, must experience an advance in consequence of the increased demand, but also the price of corn and other necessaries must likewise be affected in a considerable degree by the additional consumption occasioned by the maintenance of the men composing the fleets and armies.

Not only the demand for seamen and soldiers must tend directly to raise the rate of wages of that description of labourers from among whom these men are taken, and indirectly the rate of wages generally; but also the increased demand for various kinds of manufactured articles requisite for the equipment of fleets and armies, is calculated further to raise the rate of wages; and that this increased demand for labour, and the consequent advance of wages in general, naturally occasion increased population and increased consumption by the labouring classes.

Thus the government expenditure in all its ramifications is thought to extend the sphere and increase the activity of demand for necessaries, to operate directly or indirectly in promoting briskness of circulation, to vivify every branch of industry, and consequently to stimulate exertion to an increase of every kind of production.

The cessation, by the peace, of all such extra demand, the great customer war being withdrawn (when by the stimulus of previous high prices there was a general increase of production), would naturally, it is supposed, account for falling markets and consequent distress among the producing classes, and for reduced wages and diminished consumption; these leading, through a long course of suffering, to the only remedy, viz. a diminished production.

The fallacy of this doctrine, which represents a general elevation of prices, both of commodities and labour, to be a necessary consequence of a state of war, proceeds (and cannot otherwise than so proceed) on the supposition that the money expended by the government consists of funds distinct from and over and above any that before existed; whereas, it is perfectly demonstrable, that an expenditure by government, whether defrayed by immediate taxes to the whole amount, or by loan on the anticipation of taxes to be levied, is nothing but a change in the mode of laying out the same sum of money; and what is expended by government would and must have been laid out by individuals upon objects of consumption, productive or unproductive.

I am here supposing that, both on the part of government and on that of individuals, the habit of hoarding to any extent is out of the question. If government were in the practice of collecting a surplus revenue in coin in time of peace, and of accumulating it as treasure to be expended on the occurrence of a war, then indeed there would be a marked difference in general prices on the transition from peace to war; but even this addition to the circulating medium would be limited in its effect on prices to the time within which the treasure was in a course of progressive outlay, until its natural distribution into other countries was effected. A similar effect would follow, if individuals were in the habit of hoarding, and if, for the purposes of war, they were obliged to give up their hoards to the use of government. These suppositions, however, are quite foreign to the practice of the times which are under consideration.

But although, upon the breaking out of a war, there would not and could not be any increase in the total sum of demand (the quantum of the circulating medium remaining unaltered), there would be a disturbance of the proportion of the prices of commodities, relatively to each other, and also relatively to the price of labour. The articles which might suddenly be the objects of government demand would rise; but, on the other hand, those articles which would, but for the war, have been purchased by individuals, from the fund which is withdrawn from them, would experience an equivalent fall; in general, on such occasions, the demand by government, being sudden and on a large scale, for commodities of which the supply has not had time to accommodate itself to such extra demand, may produce a considerable rise in the price of such commodities; while the corresponding abstraction of demand being spread over an infinitely greater surface, would operate in a manner that might be hardly perceptible, but would not be the less real on the sum of general prices.

I have assumed that the quantity of money in circulation remains the same. If a state of war includes the supposition of an increase in the quantity of money, then indeed the case would be altered. But an increase of currency for government purposes must be either in coin, which can only be obtained by cheapness relatively to other countries, and consequently supposes the reverse of dearness, which is ascribed to war, or in paper, which involves the question of depreciation, and this will be separately considered. [1]

If the war supplies are raised within the year by direct taxation, that is, by an income or property tax, it is so perfectly clear, that whatever is expended by government must be exactly so much abstracted from what would otherwise have been the expenditure by individuals, and that there can consequently be no elevation of the aggregate of prices, whatever may be the disturbance of the relative value of commodities and labour among each other (the aggregate supply of these remaining the same), as to appear like a truism.

But it may be a question whether the raising of money by loan[2], the interest of which only is to be defrayed by direct taxation, might not enable

---

① It may be supposed that government might and did avail itself of its credit, in order to carry on its expenditure through that medium without requiring advances from capitalists, who would thus have their funds at liberty for their ordinary purposes, and thus the government expenditure might constitute an *additional* demand. But a slight consideration will show that such use of its credit by government cannot furnish any permanent addition to the means of purchase. If Exchequer, or Navy, or Victualling bills are issued in payment, these bills will occupy the money of the capitalists who buy them, as much as if the latter lent the same sum to government. Or if mere book credit were taken by government, the parties selling on such credit will have so much less money to go to market with. There is no doubt that a use of credit, whether by government or by individuals, is virtually, while in operation, equivalent, in its effect on prices, to money; but it its effect is to raise prices beyond the level which they could otherwise maintain, such effect would be felt in a depression of the exchange, and (if the paper were inconvertible) in a rise of the Mint price of gold above the market price, thus constituting that excess and consequent depreciation of the currency, which, as connected with general prices, forms a distinct branch of this inquiry.

② Dr. Chalmers, in his very elaborate work "On Political Economy, in connection with the Morals, State, and Prospects of Society", 1832, has done the honour to me of making some remarks on this part of my argument contained in a former work of mine. After having given it as his opinion that a government expenditure defrayed wholly by taxes would not have the effect of raising prices, except of the articles taxed, he proceeds to say, that "Mr. Tooke has not fully adverted to the distinction, in point of effect, between a war expenditure, that is defrayed wholly by taxes, and a war expenditure that is defrayed partly by loans." Dr. Chalmers agrees with me in considering that "the money which is in

government to buy to a greater amount than would be counterbalanced by the diminished power of individuals to purchase. A moment's consideration, however, will be sufficient to convince any one, that, there can be no rise of general prices in this case any more than in the former: the money advanced to government, would, but for such loan, have been laid out equally in purchases, though probably not of the same commodities, or would have been lent on private securities to such persons as would have laid it out in purchases. It is precisely of the nature of money advanced by way of mortgage to individuals; the lender would have, when he had advanced the money, just so much less to lay out as the borrower had more. It maybe said that the borrower might spend it on the maintenance of unproductive labour, whereas the lender might otherwise have laid it out reproductively: this might or might not be the case, and the difference might eventually affect the quantum of production; but we have supposed the aggregate supply to be undiminished by war; for how far it may be calculated to diminish supply is a separate question. All that is now contended for is, that there cannot, by the mere loan to government, be any addition to the total of demand for commodities, whatever might be the difference in the relative proportions of them. ①

---

the hands of capitalists is as much spent as would be the same money in the hands of government; and that, therefore, when transferred from the one to the other, there is no greater demand, I thereby created to hear on the general market, and so to raise prices. But," he adds, "it should be considered that though such a transference gives rise to no greater demand, it gives rise to a less supply, and that this will raise prices just as effectually." It will be seen, however, that I have not neglected this consideration, but have referred to it as a distinct branch of the argument, viz. the effect of war in diminishing or obstructing supply.

① The raising of the funds requisite for the purposes of the war, by loan, might be supposed to have the effect of temporarily affecting the channels of circulation. The amount advanced to government

In the case of indirect taxation, that is, of taxes on commodities, whether for defraying the whole expenditure or the mere interest of loans, the articles immediately taxed must, as I have already admitted, rise in price in some proportion to the tax: but a rise in price from this cause would be unconnected with any increased demand affecting commodities generally, as it is assumed by those who consider that the expenditure of government forms a fresh fund, whether arising from taxes or loans.

Viewed therefore upon general grounds, the conclusion appears to be irresistible, that the extra demand or consumption arising from government, expenditure cannot have the effect of raising the aggregate of prices; and this conclusion from general reasoning is fully borne out by a reference to experience of the effect of former wars upon prices.

It is of course to be understood that articles which are subject to a tax, such as malt, or to increased charges of importation, such as colonial and foreign produce, or to extra demand for naval and military stores, such as saltpetre and cordage, do not come into the comparison of general prices. With these exceptions it will appear, on reference to former periods of our

---

would be, it may be thought, collected from among large sums of monied capital, seeking investment, some of which might have lain dormant, waiting to be so called forth. And if, when paid into the Exchequer, or into the Bank, it were *immediately* distributed in payments by government, there might be a temporary briskness of demand upon the distribution through the minuter channels of the circulation of sums which were previously collected in masses. There does not appear to be much ground for the supposition, that any marked effect would be produced in this way, even admitting that it were consonant to the practice, which it is not. For, in point of fact, the payments by government were made, not suddenly, but distributed over intervals of some length. And so far from the distribution of the sums paid into the bank by the subscribers to the loans being immediate, they would, in some instances, have been inconveniently withheld from circulation, had it not been that the Bank, with a view to avoid such inconvenient contraction, used to make advances to the subscribers for a limited time for the amount of then subscriptions after the first payment.

history, that there is no observable coincidence of a rise of price during war, and a fall during peace. On the contrary, it so happens that, in the case of the agricultural produce of this country, there was for upwards of a hundred years previous to 1793 as low a range of prices during periods of war as during the intervals of peace. This has been eminently the case with respect to wheat, as will appear by the following statement of the Windsor prices from the Eton Tables: —

						£	s.	d.
1688	to	1697	10 years	War	–	2	2	$6\frac{3}{4}$
1698		1701	4	Peace	–	2	6	0
1702		1712	11	War	–	2	2	0
1713		1739	27	Peace	–	1	15	$10\frac{3}{4}$
1740		1748	9	War	–	1	11	$6\frac{1}{2}$
1749		1754	6	Peace	–	1	13	$11\frac{1}{2}$
1755		1762	8	War	–	1	17	$1\frac{3}{4}$
1763		1774	12	Peace	–	2	8	$11\frac{1}{2}$
1775		1782	8	War	–	2	6	$6\frac{1}{2}$
1783		1792	10	Peace	–	2	10	$2\frac{1}{2}$

A result nearly similar is observable in the price of meat, as may be seen by reference to Sir F. Morton Eden's work, entitled "State of the Poor", containing extracts from the Victualling Office prices. See also the prices of the Greenwich and Bethlem Hospital contracts, in the Appendix to the several Bullion and Agricultural Reports of the Lords and Commons, by all of which it will appear that the prices of meat and other provisions were as low in the periods of war as in those of peace, and in some instances lower. The Victualling Office returns are the more striking, because the demands for the navy must be supposed to be calculated to operate in a greater degree on this description of food than on corn.

The prices of wool would offer nearly the same result.

Other articles might be enumerated, as affording a similar conclusion.

Nor do the wages of labour appear to have been, in general, higher during war than in the intervals of peace: this will appear from the following extract from the Greenwich Hospital prices in the Appendix to the Commons' Report on the Resumption of Cash Payments.

		Carpenters per Day.		Bricklayers per Day.		Masons per Day.		Plumbers per Day.	
		s.	*d.*	*s.*	*d.*	*s.*	*d.*	*s.*	*d.*
Peace	1730	2	6	2	6	2	6	3	0
	1735	2	6	2	6	2	6	3	0
War	1740	2	6	2	6	2	8	3	0
	1745	2	6	2	6	2	8	3	6
Peace	1750	2	6	2	6	2	8	2	6
War	1755	2	6	2	6	2	8	2	6
	1760	2	6	2	6	2	8	2	6
Peace	1765	2	6	2	4	2	8	3	0
	1770	2	6	2	4	2	8	3	0
War	1775	2	6	2	4	2	10	3	0
	1780	2	6	2	4	2	10	3	0
Peace	1785	2	6	2	4	2	10	3	3
	1790	2	6	2	4	2	10	3	3

Here then, through the course of such a series of years, we have surely proof sufficient that it is not a *necessary* consequence of a state of war that the prices of labour① of agricultural produce, and other articles not taxed, or not the immediate objects of war consumption, should rise; for in fact they were lower, in the majority of instances, during the periods of war, than in the intervals of peace. That they should in some have been lower in war than in peace might, perhaps, to a certain extent, have been owing to a disturbance of the channels of circulation, and to an increase in

---

① It has been contended, that the government expenditure, by creating an extra demand for men for the army and navy, raised the general rate of wages; and that the rise of wages enabled the labouring classes to expend more money on the purchase of food and other necessaries. If the demand for men by government was not a *substitution* only for the demand which would otherwise have existed by individual employers, but constituted a clear *additional* demand for labour, the supply of it remaining the same, some rise in the general price of labour would be the consequence. It does not appear that, in the wars preceding the last, there was any sensible increase of wages; the probability, therefore, is, that the employment of men by the government of those times was merely substituted for what, but for the war, would have been their employment for other purposes. And the only ground for distinguishing the operation of the last war from former wars, in that respect, is the larger numbers, relatively to the population, who were employed by government in the last war. But, on the other hand, the vicissitudes of manufactures and commerce were, from the character of the last war, more frequent than in former wars; and, in many instances, the government demand did little more than absorb the numbers thus thrown out of employ. Mr. Mo Culloch in the following passage seems to consider that the demand for men by government is a mere substituted demand: —

"It has sometimes been stated that a loan occasions, while government is spending it, a greater demand for labour than it would have afforded had it continued in the possession of individuals. I confess, however, that I have not been able to discover any grounds for this opinion. If the government expend the loan in the purchase of military stores, they will not by doing so give any greater stimulus to labour than the capitalists, who have made the loan, would have given had they employed it to purchase raw or manufactured goods; and suppose government employed it in hiring soldiers and sailors, they will not thereby occasion a greater demand for labour than would have been occasioned by employing it to hire common labour. That there is frequently a very brisk demand for labour during periods of war is no doubt true; but we shall certainly find the cause of it in something else than the mere substitution of government employment for that afforded by individuals."—*Principles of Political Eronomy*, 2d cdit. p. 198.

the functions of money, while the principles and practice of banking and credit were so imperfectly understood. At the same time, there can be no doubt that the greater cheapness of the periods of war must have arisen mainly from their coincidence with more favourable seasons. Be this as it may, the fact itself of the relative cheapness of periods of war in the whole term is decisive against the effect ascribed to it, of raising the prices of provisions, and of commodities generally, independent of the degree in which they were taxed; and what, perhaps, is the most decisive consideration of all against the assumption of that preponderating influence, is that the period of the greatest cheapness in the whole term of 105 years, viz. the period between 1740 and 1748①, is precisely that of an uninterrupted and very large war expenditure, defrayed chiefly by loans. ②

SECTION 2 *Effect of the extra demand or consumption attributed specially to the last war*

So far as to the presumption of the effect of war generally, in raising prices: but it has been asked, "who, that contemplated the

① There is in this instance a specific cause of a reduction of the price in consequence of the war. As we had at that time a large exportable surplus of corn, chiefly destined for France, with which we were at that time at war, the increased freight and insurance would, if the demand from abroad were not so urgent as to compel the foreign buyer to pay those charges, fall on the exporter, and consequently form a deduction from the price.

② The government expenditure arising from the war of that period must be considered to have been very large, relatively to the ordinary peace establishment, and relatively likewise to the general level of the prices of commodities and labour. To contemporaries it appeared of extraordinary magnitude. Lord Bolingbroke says, "Our parliamentary aids, from the year 1740 exclusively, to the year 1748 inclusively, amount to 55, 522, 159*l.* 16*s.* 3*d.*; a sum that will appear to future generations, and is so almost to the present."—*Some Reflections on the present State of the Nation*, 1749, edit. 1773, vol. iv. p. 137.

character of the late war, that referred to the great military force which was employed in Europe, and to the consequent demand of all the great articles of consumption, could, for a moment, think of comparing the events of that war, and the state of things growing out of it, with the events and effects of former wars?"① Now, the obvious answer is, that as to this particular effect of war consumption upon prices, it is only a question of degree, whatever the difference of the nature of the contest may have been in other respects; and further, that, upon the general grounds before stated, the *extra* demand for such objects by the belligerent powers must be compensated, and probably more than compensated, by corresponding privations on the part of their subjects.

With regard to the alleged influence of war demand in raising the price of provisions, it must doubtless be admitted as operating in the immediate neighbourhood of large armies in a state of active military operations; for it is scarcely possible that the local supply can accommodate itself, except at a great advance of price, to sudden and casual a source of extra demand. But applying to this country the supposition of extra demand, arising out of a state of war, it is to be observed, that the quantity of food required for the maintenance of the soldiers and sailors composing the war establishment is not all so much beyond what would otherwise have been consumed. The only effectual addition of demand is for that part which is beyond what would have been the consumption of the same individuals in their former occupations②; but from this addition, small as it must be, compared with

① Lord Liverpool's Speech, 16th July, 1822.

② This additional consumption is hardly worth mentioning, for, take it at its utmost amount, it is a quantity quite insignificant compared with the difference between a good and a bad crop of wheat. — Suppose, for instance, that the extra consumption is four bushels of wheat per head for each (an

the mass over which it is distributed, is to be deducted that proportion which was supplied from the places abroad where our fleets and armies were occasionally stationed. Subject to these deductions, the mere extra quantity consumed by the army and navy must, when compared with the total production, be quite insignificant, and not calculated to have any perceptible influence on the price of the principal articles of food. ①

But, as consumption is the measure of the *extent* of demand ②, and as consumption has of late been considerably greater, and has increased at a

---

extravagant supposition) of the men composing the army and navy; suppose these to have amounted to 300, 000, there is an extra demand for 150, 000 quarters. While, between the limits of a bad harvest like 1816, which has been computed as low as 9, 000, 000 quarters, and an abundant one like 1820, which was supposed to have yielded 16, 000, 000, there is a difference of supply of 7, 000, 000 quarters.

① The insignificance of the extra consumption or waste of provisions by soldiers is expressly admitted by one of the ablest advocates for the doctrine of the great influence of a government expenditure defrayed by loans, on general prices. "That part of the loan which is distributed in pay to the troops is mostly expended in provisions for their maintenance. Probably a greater quantity may be consumed by them as soldiers than if they continued in their usual occupation: and this is much dwelt upon by some writers as the great cause of extra consumption during war; but I think more importance has been attached to this species of waste than can be justly ascribed to it." — *Observations on the Effects produced by the Expenditure of Government during the Restriction of Cash Payments, by William Blake, Esq. F. R. S.* page 69.

② This is the sense in which Mr. Ricardo uses the word demand, and he expressly objects to admit the use of the term when applied to a rise in the price of a commodity from an alteration in the value of money. "The demand for a commodity cannot be said to increase, if no additional quantity of it be purchased or consumed; and yet under such circumstances its money value may rise. Thus, if the value of money were to fall, the price of every commodity would rise, for each of the competitors would be willing to give more money than before on its purchase; but when its price rose 10 or 20 per cent if no more were bought than before, it would not, I apprehend, be admissible to say, that the variation in the price of the commodity was caused by the increased demand for it." — *Principles of Political Economy and Taxation*, 3rd edition, page 461.

There is another sense in which the word "demand" is frequently used, which is, in my opinion, inadmissible in a discussion of this kind; and that is, where it is applied to signify the increased eagerness or competition of buyers, and consequent advance of price, occasioned by the scarcity of any

more rapid rate than at any period of the war, it is incumbent on those who ascribe all the phenomena of high prices of provisions to war demand, to show why the smaller consumption during the war should be the cause of a rise of prices, while the greatly increased consumption since the peace should have been attended by a fall of prices. Considering the progressive increase of population, with the rapid improvement of our manufactures, which was going on down to the breaking out of the war, there is every reason to believe that, but for the war, there would have been a still greater demand for food and other necessaries than actually occurred; and that consequently, supposing the scarcity arising from the seasons, and the obstructions to importation, to have been the same in peace as in war, we should have had prices full as high, if not higher, less only the difference between paper and gold.

---

particular commodity, or, in other words, by an under supply of it relatively to the average rate of consumption.

The object of the present discussion is to determine whether the high prices during the war were occasioned by an extra consumption arising out of the war, that is, by a consumption beyond the average rate at which it was proceeding, independent of the war, or by an undersupply, compared with that average rate, it is, therefore, of the greatest practical importance to confine the use of the term, as to preserve the consideration of the alternative of these two causes, or of the proportion in which each operated, perfectly distinct. The advocates of the doctrine of war demand have not attended to this distinction; and to the neglect of it may be traced a good deal of the confusion and looseness of reasoning which pervades their arguments in support of that doctrine. If, in their use of the term, they actually mean an undersupply, relatively to what had been, independent of the war, the average rate of consumption, there is no difference between us, as it will be seen that I admit the influence of the late war in raising prices, by increasing the cost of production, and by obstructing and diminishing supply. But it is evident from the general tenor of their reasoning, however loosely expressed, that they do not understand the term, and that them, in fact, use it synonymously with consumption; for them, constantly refer to the war expenditure as having afforded the means of an extra consumption. It is in this sense, therefore, that I understand and use the term in its application to the question now under discussion.

There are particular articles of which the demand for naval and military purposes forms a proportion so large to the total supply, that no diminution of consumption by individuals can keep pace with the immediate increase of demand by government; and, consequently, the breaking out of a war tends to raise the price of such articles to a great relative height; but, even of such articles, if the consumption were not on a progressive scale of increase so rapid, that the supply, with all the encouragement of a relatively high price, could not keep pace with the demand, the tendency is (supposing no impediment, natural or artificial, to production or importation) to occasion such an increase of quantity, as to reduce the price to nearly the same level as that from which it had advanced. And accordingly it will be observed, by reference to the table of prices, that saltpetre, hemp, iron, &c., after advancing very considerably under the influence of a greatly extended demand for military and naval purposes, tended downwards again whenever that demand was not progressively and rapidly increasing. Any fluctuation independent of variations in the extent of government demand, may be clearly traced to the greater or less obstructions to supply.

SECTION 3 *On the effects of the monopoly of trade enjoyed by this country during the last war*

It has been contended that, admitting no influence by war demand upon prices, except of articles that are used as naval and military stores, there was a considerable effect produced on general prices by the monopoly which the war, as a consequence of our ascendency at sea, and of our exclusive possession of the East and West Indies, conferred on the trade of this country. As instances of the extent of the monopoly of trade which we thus enjoyed, we are referred to the number of British vessels, which were progressively increasing (and employed at advanced freights) with the continuance of the war; to the crowded state of the river and of the docks; to the consequently full employment of the various branches of industry connected with the building, repairing, and outfit of ships in the port of London, and in many of the outports; and, in short, to all the signs of great commercial activity.

A part of this description is true. Never before was the shipping of this country employed at higher freights; and scarcely a ship belonging to any other nation could sail without a licence from the government of this country. The whole of the exportable produce of the East and West Indies, and of a great part of South America, came to our ports; and no part of the continent of Europe could obtain a supply of coffee, sugar, and other colonial articles, or of the raw materials of some of their manufactures, except from this country. So far we may be said to have enjoyed the monopoly of trade; but the effects of this species of monopoly, in its supposed extension of our shipping and foreign commerce, have been greatly mistaken and overrated.

On a reference to the parliamentary returns, of the tonnage of British shipping, it will be seen that the rate of increase of it during the war was less than it had been during the immediately preceding years of peace, or than it has been since the termination of the war.

From the amount, however, of the tonnage registered during the war, ought to be deducted the ships which were engaged as transports, and which could not therefore be considered as forming a part of our mercantile marine. The shipping engaged as transports amounted to no less, on an average of the latter years of the war, than about 700 sail, registering nearly 200, 000 tons; which, deducted from the total amount of registered tonnage, leaves a greatly reduced quantity of shipping applicable to the purposes of trade during the war, compared with the subsequent years of peace. It is to be observed, too, that this smaller amount of shipping during the war was, in consequence of the detention of convoys — circuitous voyages, to elude the anticommercial decrees of the enemy — occasional embargoes, and other causes of delay even in our own or friendly ports — incapable of carrying on nearly so much trade then, as it would at present, more especially since the introduction of steam navigation. The difference hence arising, in the number of voyages performed by the same ship in a given time, will account in some degree for the different proportion of the tonnage cleared outwards, to the amount of registered tonnage at the several periods. The same circumstance, combined with the advanced cost of building materials and of stores, will account for the high freights which prevailed during the war.

It may be said that this reduced the employment of British shipping, for commercial purposes, was compensated by a greater employment of foreign ships during the war. True; but does not this circumstance militate with the received ideas of the nature of our boasted monopoly of trade? With regard to the crowded state of the river and of the docks during the war, it is sufficient to remark as a matter of notoriety, that the resort of shipping to the port of London has been much greater since the peace. And if the building of ships in the river has declined, it is because, in consequence of the greater expenses attending the river yards, a large proportion of that branch of business is transferred to the outports, and not because the annual amount of shipbuilding has diminished during the peace, on a comparison with the average of the war, as must be evident from the statements of the relative amount of tonnage at the several periods. The most rapid increase of shipbuilding, however, is that which has been going on in British America, in consequence of the great cheapness of the materials in that part of the world. ①

But what must be conclusive on this and all minor points referred to, in proof of the supposed effects of our monopoly of trade by the war, is that the aggregate amount of our foreign trade, which can alone be in question as affected by the monopoly, was not nearly so great during the war as it has been since the peace; and that the *rate* of increase was as great in the peace preceding 1793, as in the succeeding interval of war.

One of the effects of our monopoly of trade was an increase in the exports of foreign and colonial produce, the amount of which must previously have swelled the imports in a corresponding degree. In the interval, however, between 1807 and 1814, there was no corresponding export of the colonial produce compulsorily brought hither; as it was only in 1814 that an adequate vent could be found, on the opening of the ports of the Continent by the peace, for the accumulation of sugar, coffee, & c. that had taken place in the preceding five years. The value of the colonial produce so accumulated could be little short of fifteen millions sterling.

But, granting the utmost that ever has been claimed (upon very insufficient grounds) for the effects of the monopoly arising out of the war,

---

① Ships built in that quarter are, as may easily be supposed, from the nature of the timber, less durable, and of an inferior description in every other respect to those built in this country. The regulation of the timber duties, acting as a premium for dry rot, and yielding in impolicy and injustice to our corn laws only, is calculated greatly to increase the proportion of that inferior, and in every way objectionable class of shipping.

in extending the shipping and trade of this country, it still remains to connect the description of monopoly with the high prices ascribed to it. Now it so happens, that not an article which was the subject of monopoly was, as far as I am aware, at a higher price in this country than it would have been under the most free competition. While that monopoly was most strict, viz. in 1811 and 1812, prices of sugar, coffee, dye-woods, spices, and some descriptions of manufacture, which were the objects of our exclusive trade, were precisely those which, if a deduction be made for the difference between paper and gold, were more depressed than they ever were before or have been since. And it was only in *the almost certain prospect of peace*, and consequently of the *near termination of the monopoly*, that the prices of those commodities experienced any decided advance, viz. in 1813 and 1814.

Dr. Johnson defines the word "Monopoly" as "the exclusive privilege of selling": but, if the thing to be sold exists, and is offered for sale in as unlimited a quantity as it would have been without that privilege, what is the use of it to the party invested with it? If, when the French and Dutch colonies in the East and West Indies were ceded to this country, their produce had been suppressed or destroyed, and their cultivation prohibited, then indeed there would have been something substantial in our monopoly, as far at least as related to price; and the planters, or the proprietors of the produce of our old colonies, would have derived from that circumstance a decided benefit. Instead of which, by a large outlay of British capital, the French West Indian islands, and the Dutch settlements of Demerara and Surinam in the West, and Java in the East, were rendered more productive than they ever before had been. The collective and increased produce from all these sources, when poured into this country, while the export to the Continent was restricted, occasioned the real depression attending a glut; the very opposite state to that which is commonly supposed to be the consequence of a monopoly. The very high prices of colonial produce in 1813 and 1814 were, as I have already shown, in great part the result of ill-judged speculations on *the prospect of peace*; and those prices were not realised by the exporters in the eventual returns; but even supposing them to have been realised, they were so transitory, as not to afford a compensation for the long previous depression; and they cannot at any rate be considered as the result of monopoly arising out of the war, seeing that they were only the consequence of the opening of the new markets by a peace.

SECTION 4 *Effects of the stimulus or excitement supposed to have been occasioned by the government expenditure during the last war*

The advocates of the theory which accounts for the high prices observable during the late war, by the excitement supposed to arise from the profuse government expenditure, assume implictly that the operation of that cause was distinctly marked by an unusually rapid increase of population①,

① "These peculiarities (that is, of the late war) were the *unusually rapid increase of the population*," &c. — *Quarterly Review*, No 57. p. 222.

"It may still most safely he said, that in no twenty-two years of our history, of which we have authentic accounts, has there ever been so rapid an increase of production and consumption, both in respect of quantity and value, as in the twenty-two years ending with 1814." — *Ibid.* p. 229.

"The population increased with extraordinary rapidity, *which necessarily implies such a rise in the money price of labour, as, combined with more general employment, and other advantages in the purchase of clothing and foreign commodities, would enable the labouring classes to bring up larger families than before*" — *Ibid.* p. 233.

production, and consumption; and that the transition from war to peace occasioned the fall of prices, not by an increased supply and diminished cost of production since the peace, relatively to the same or an increased rate of consumption, but by a diminution of demand or consumption, relatively to the same or a diminished extent of supply.

Some distinguished writers, too, have supposed that the greater part of the period of the war was marked by an active and flourishing state of our manufactures, and that, this was a cause of an increased demand for, and price of, agricultural produce. Thus, in the article before quoted of the Quarterly Review, No. 57., ascribed to the pen of an eminent writer, is the following passage: — "It is undeniable, that during the greater part of that period (from 1793 to 1814) the trade of the country was in a state of unexampled prosperity." And Sir Edward West, in his very able treatise

---

"Examine the evidence of Alderman Rothwell, Mr. Rous, and various other witnesses, who all agree *that during the war there were both greater production and greater consumption.*" — *Observations on the Effects of the Expenditure of Government*, p. 67.

"There cannot be a doubt *that during the war more produce was raised, and more work done.*" — *Ibid.* p. 72.

"It is to be observed, too, that though in the first instance the demand might be for the materials of war, *it would gradually extend to almost every commodity ordinarily consumed by man.*" — *Ibid.* p. 76.

"The low prices (1822) are not confined to corn alone: it is well known that *manufactures are less in quantity, and less in price also.*"—*Ibid* p. 93.

"The *excitement* was not confined to manufactures. It extended to the producers of the raw materials in every branch of employment. The mines of copper, lead, tin, iron, coals, were all in activity."—*Ibid*, p. 89.

"It appears to me, that in whatever degree minor circumstances may have cooperated, the great and mighty source of the distresses felt by all classes of producers has been the transition that took place at the termination of the war; not the transition from war to peace, in the usual acceptation of those terms, not the transition that arises from the diversion of capital from one employment to another employment; not the transition from the waste occasioned by the extra consumption of troops, either at home or engaged in actual warfare; but the transition from an immense, unremitting, protracted, effectual demand for almost every article of consumption to a comparative cessation of that demand." — *Ibid* p. 88.

on the price of corn and the wages of labour, builds the greater part of his theory on this foundation.

It may be observed, however, that the principal arguments in favour of this theory were brought forward in publications and speeches of some years back, when the transition from war to peace was comparatively recent, and when many otherwise well informed persons entertained the belief that there was a retarded rate of population, and less consumed, and less produced, and less trade, after the peace, than there had been during the war. The assumption to this effect is essential to the theory of the stimulus of war demand; the stimulus being distinctly inferred from the assumed increase of population, production, and consumption during the war, as compared with the period which had elapsed after the peace; and if the facts tallied with the theory, the conclusion would be inevitable, that the state of war was more favourable than the state of peace to the progress of population and wealth. A hypothesis so utterly irreconcileable with any reasoning upon the general effects of war, or with any experience of the effects of former wars, might naturally raise doubts, whether it was possible that it could be sustained by facts. But whatever question there might be when those theories were broached, and in some degree of vogue, the statistical information since collected, has proved incontestibly, that there is not the shadow of a foundation in fact, for the assumptions on which the theory proceeds. To enter into a detailed proof to this effect would be at present work of superogation, and would needlessly swell this branch of the subject to a disproportionate extent; inasmuch as an easy reference may be had to indisputable evidence[1] of the progress of population, production, and consumption, by which it appears that these were in a *greatly accelerated ratio* from 1814 to the present time, as compared with the long interval of war.

If, then, an increased rate of production and consumption be going on at the end of two and twenty years of peace, such an effect must be referred to some other cause than the previous war expenditure; and some cause must be found for the fall of prices, other than a supposed diminution of demand from the cessation of that expenditure. What the cause or causes of the great variation of prices, beyond the difference between paper and gold, may have been, is what will be matter of further examination. In the mean time we may safely dismiss a hypothesis, which proceeds on the assumption of facts which never had any existence, which overlooks the most important of the facts that did occur, and is utterly irreconcileable with any rational or consistent explanation of the actual phenomena.

The only reason, indeed, for having entered into this examination, brief as it is, of the doctrine of the stimulus of war demand is, that the arguments in support of it have been advanced by very distinguished authorities; and that although the grounds on which that doctrine has been founded *fail in every part*, there is still a vague but strong impression in favour of it, by persons who, seeing the extravagance of the ultra currency doctrine, are not aware of any alternative but that of the hypothesis of increased consumption, to account for the high prices which prevailed during the war.

---

① See Tables of Revenue, Population, & c. from the statistical department of the Board of Trade, compiled under the superintendence of Mr. Porter, Statistical Account of the British Empire, by J. R M 'Culloch, Esq. , Progress of the Nation from the beginning of the 19th century to the present time, 1836, by G. R. Porter.

CHAPTER Ⅳ
EFFECTS OF WAR, AS OBSTRUCTING SUPPLY, AND INCREASING THE COST OF PRODUCTION

Enough has been said to prove that war cannot operate in raising general prices through the medium of increased demand; and that there is no sufficient ground for ascribing any effect in raising general prices to the monopoly of trade, or to the increased excitement and activity which characterized the last war.

The remaining question is, what effects are to be ascribed to war as regards supply? And the answer may be, in general terms, it is the tendency of war to diminish supply.

The mode in which war may be calculated to operate to this effect is, 1st, by a diminution of reproduction, and 2nd, by increased cost of production, and by impediments to commercial communication.

It will be readily admitted, that the immediate and obvious tendency of a state of war is to abstract a portion of the capital and labour, which would otherwise have been employed in reproduction; and if, from the course of military operations, or from arbitrary government exactions, an apprehension should be superadded of insecurity of property, there will be a further cause for diminished production; so that dearth and impoverishment are likely to be the consequences of a state of war in a country thus situated. In the early part of the war, the extensive military operations were calculated to diminish the produce of the Netherlands,

Germany, and Italy; and, at the same time, the political convulsions attending the revolutionary period might affect the extent and quality of the cultivation of the land in France. In the subsequent periods of the war the course of military operations can hardly have failed to diminish the produce of Poland, Prussia, Saxony, and Russia, as likewise of Spain, Portugal, and Italy. And while causes like these were, perhaps, operating in a diminished reproduction in some of the countries alluded to, there were circumstances arising out of the war, which, beyond all question, added greatly to the cost of production in this country; these were—

1. The increased rate of interest of money, which, more especially as regarded all outlay as fixed capital, formed an important element in the calculation of the price at which reproduction could be continued, or a new production afforded.

2. The increased rates of freight and insurance, which applied to the whole period of the war, but which in the last six years of it amounted (as will be seen when the period comes under consideration) to an enormous charge on all importations from the continent of Europe. And, although the greatest charge under this head applied to our foreign trade, there was also a great increase of freight and insurance attaching to our coasting trade, forming no inconsiderable item in the cost of all commodities, the more bulky ones especially, such as coin, coals, building materials, &c. conveyed coast-wise.

On the other hand, there may be, coincidently with a state of war in any particular country, circumstance arising from other causes calculated to counterbalance, and even to outweigh, the tendency in question: —

1. Increased activity, industry, and intelligence, in the mass of the population, so that the portion remaining, after the abstraction of labourers

for the purposes of war, may be able and willing to produce as much as, or even more than, was previously produced.

2. Increased disposition on the part of individuals to accumulate capital, so as to compensate for the war expenditure, without any diminution of the funds applicable to reproduction.

3. Improvements in agriculture and machinery, tending to increase reproduction with the same or less capital and labour.

4. Greater security of property relatively to other countries, thus inducing an influx of capital from abroad.

All these circumstances concurred in this country, during the whole of the last war, and the consequence was an increase of production and population *in spite of the opposite tendency arising out of a state of war*.

The effects, however, of the preponderating tendency of circumstances favourable to reproduction, as far as relates to agriculture, were repressed, or, at least, prevented from receiving their full development, by a course of seasons which were, as will be seen, more than usually improprtious.

Although the war cannot be said to have operated upon the supply of agricultural produce of our own growth and of other native commodities, sufficiently to outweigh the circumstances favourable to reproduction, it operated most powerfully in increasing the cost of production, and in obstructing the supply of such commodities as we stood in need of from abroad. It is, in fact, only with reference to the nature and degree of the impediments to commercial communications, that the last war, as far as relates to prices, is to be distinguished from former wars — coinciding as it did with a succession of seasons which made us dependent on other countries for an adequate supply of food.

Gigantic and terrific as that contest was, of which it has been truly said, that "compared with that crisis, there was nothing similar, unless it were that aera at which the irruption of the Barbarians subverted the Roman empire," the effect of it upon prices would have been very different, if, allowing the same scale of military and naval operations, and consequently of war expenditure, it had been divested of its anticommercial character; or if, possessing its anticommercial character, it had not occurred contemporaneously with years of scarcity in this country, approaching in some instances to famine.

But the extraordinary nature of the contest should be more especially borne in mind, as a caution against drawing any inference from average prices during last war. The prices were regulated by the increase, which was *enormous*, of the cost of production arising from the obstructions to commercial intercourse, which were *peculiar* to the last war, and not, in all human probability, likely ever again to occur.

PART III

ON THE CURRENCY

CHAPTER Ⅰ GENERAL VIEW OF THE SUBJECT

At the time when the paper system was at its height, when there was a great difference between paper and gold, it was confidently maintained by the advocates of that system (and these then included not only the government, but the great majority of persons, and more especially of the mercantile class, who took part in the discussions on the subject), that it was not the paper that was depreciated by abundance, but the gold that had become scarce, and consequently that no part of the advance of the price of commodities was attributable to the bank restriction. That doctrine seems now to be generally abandoned, and to have been replaced by one of an exactly opposite description.

So much of the discussions, which have arisen out of these opposing views, has turned on the word depreciation it has been used in senses so various, in some being a matter of mere definition, but in no agreed acceptation; in others, involving facts, or, rather, disputed assumptions of facts, leading to the most discordant conclusions, that it is impossible to advance a step, having for its object an explanation of the phenomena of prices dining the period under consideration, without feeling the necessity of attempting to clear the ground of this difficulty, which presents itself in limine; and the following explanations are offered accordingly: —

Depreciation of money, in its most extensive sense, is to be considered as signifying a diminished value, from increased quantity of money indicated by, and commensurate with, a general rise in the prices of commodities and labour. The term has not unfrequently been used to designate a rise of prices of some of the leading articles of consumption, without reference to the cause of the rise. But this use of it is evidently incorrect, and at any rate is inconveniently and unnecessarily ambiguous.

Depreciation, or diminished value of money, is, for the purposes, at least, of the present inquiry, to be understood as signifying an increased *price* of all objects measured in money, the alteration of price being assumed to have originated in an increase of the quantity of money, and to be confined to an alteration, exclusively on the side of the money; while the cost of production, and the supply relatively to the rate of consumption of commodities, are considered to be unaltered.

Depreciation of money may be either general, as applying to the world at large, or local, as applying to a particular country or state. When applied to the world at large, it is synonymous with a diminished value of gold and silver among all countries, which are in communication by international exchanges. This is the sense in which it has been used by the various authors, who have treated distinctly of the value of money, without reference to local currencies; and when it is said, that since the discovery of the American mines, the value of money has been diminished to one fourth, or one sixth; or, in other words, that prices have been raised by that event fourfold, or sixfold, it is meant that the rise of bullion prices to that extent has been general throughout the commercial world, according to certain laws, by which the distribution of the precious metals among different countries is regulated.

When applied to local currencies, the term depreciation of money has been used indiscriminately to signify a rise of prices, whether caused by a diminished value of the precious metals, or by a degradation of the standard, or by an excessive issue of paper.

If the value of a local currency is diminished by the same general causes only, which operate upon the value of money in the commercial world, it is hardly consistent with the correct use of language; and at any rate it is inconvenient to apply to such diminished value the term *depreciation of the currency*.

Depredation of the currency, as I conceive, must be, in strictness, understood to mean that state of it in which the coin is of less value in the market than, by the mint regulations, it purports to be, or in which the paper, if compulsorily current, is of less value than the coin in which it promises to be payable.

With regard to the term *depreciation*, *as applied to paper*, if bank promissory notes be issued in a deteriorated state of the coinage, and be really convertible on demand into the coin in which they purport to be payable, they cannot be said to be depreciated: the actual payment is equal to the promise to pay; the fault is in the coinage, not in the paper. There may, therefore, be a depreciation of the currency in which paper circulates, and an increase of the market price above the mint price of the metals, without any depreciation chargeable to the paper: such was the state of the currency in this country immediately previous to the great reformation of the gold coin in 1773.

But if the metallic part of the currency be really deteriorated, and if the paper, which purports to be payable on demand in that coin, be not so in fact, and cannot command as much gold or other commodities in this market *and* in foreign markets, as the same nominal amount in coin would do, the paper is depreciated, and the measure of its depreciation is the difference of the quantity of gold which the coin and the paper can respectively purchase.

In a perfect state of the coin, provided the exportation and melting of it be allowed, there cannot, it is evident, be an excess in the market price above the mint price of the metal, as measured in coin. It is possible, in such a case, that the coin may, even without a seignorage, be *more* valuable than bullion; but it is hardly conceivable that it should be less valuable: if, therefore, in a perfect state of the coin, there be in general circulation bank notes which, by law or custom, pass current in all transactions; and if, under these circumstances, the market price should be above the mint price of gold — the whole of the difference would constitute the exact measure of the depreciation of the paper.

Till, however, the act of of 1819, the gold coin, although not materially deteriorated, could not by law be exported or melted; if, therefore, there happened to be an extra demand for gold, for exportation or for consumption in domestic manufacture, the price of bullion might rise above the mint price by the amount of the risk of the penalty on the export or melting; and this difference might, for limited periods, exist in a purely metallic currency consisting, it is true of undeteriorated coin, but of coin rendered less valuable by being divested by law of some of the uses to which it might otherwise be applied. This difference has been variously estimated. In the treatise by Lord Liverpool "on the Coins of the Realm," one per cent is considered as the measure of the risk of exporting coin. In the evidence, however, before the Bullion Committee of 1810, it was stated, that the difference between the value of gold bullion that might be sworn off for exportation, and that of the gold produced, or supposed to be produced, from our own coin, amounted to between 3*s*. and 4*s*. per ounce.

As far, then, as this difference goes, an allowance may be made in deduction, under the circumstances supposed, from the excess of the market price above the mint price of gold, as a measure of the depreciation of bank notes previous to the passing of Peel's bill. And to this limited extent is there a difference in estimating the depreciation of bank notes, according as the standard is assumed to have been bullion or coin. ①

According to the foregoing explanation of the term depreciation, as applied to coin or paper, it is to be distinguished from a *diminished value* of the currency.

By *alterations in the value of the currency are* to be understood variations of the combined value of bullion and coin and paper, or, in other words, of the standard as well as of the coin and paper. For instance, if, while the market price of gold should be 10 per cent, above the mint price, indicating a depreciation of the paper, or coin, or both, to that extent, gold, or, in other words, the standard itself, should, from a great diminution of the produce of the mines, or from extended functions, (as for military purposes or hoarding, or for a circulation retarded by want of confidence and credit, or for a very general substitution of gold for paper) become more valuable by 10 per cent, then although the currency would, according to the definition, be depreciated to that extent, i. e. be less in price than it ought legally to be, yet, the standard itself being increased in value in the same degree, there would be no alteration in the *value of the currency*. On the other hand, if while paper and coin were depreciated by

① But it was not a difference to this limited extent that was involved in the controversy between the Bullion Committee of 1810 and then opponents, upon the question whether coin or bullion should be assumed as the standard by which the value of bank notes was to be measured.

excess or debasement 10 per cent, compared with *their* standard, and the standard itself *gold were*, whether from increased produce or diminished functions, reduced in value likewise 10 per cent, I should say that the alteration in the *value* of the currency generally was to the extent of 20 per cent. But if the metal of which the standard is composed were assumed to be of uniform value, the variations of the value of the currency would then, and then only, be measured by the degree of conformity of the paper or coin to its standard.

Of variations in the value of the standard itself there is no infallible criterion. Variations, therefore, in the value of the standard, if they occur, can only be inferred from variations of considerable extent and duration, in the bullion prices of commodities and labour, in cases in which these variations do not, according to the widest induction of facts, admit of being accounted for, by circumstances which may have influenced the prices of the commodities and labour in question, independently of the supposition of any alteration in the quantity or rate of circulation of the currency.① These definitions and the deductions from them will, probably, by those whose opinions I am about to examine, be admitted to prove the depreciation of the currency, during the bank restriction, to the extent for

① These definitions correspond with the sense in which Mr. Ricardo has used the terms "depreciation of the currency", and "value of the currency", and he fully and accurately defined and illustrated his meaning, in his speech on the 12th of June, 1822 on a motion of Mr. Western. The following is an extract from a printed copy of that speech:—"Now the whole difficulty, in reference to this part of his opinions, was as to the meaning of the word 'depreciation': it was quite evident that his opponents and himself attached a different sense to that word. He was quite sure that his opponents would admit the truth of such an inference. It was quite possible that, notwithstanding this depreciation, some of those general causes which operate on the value of gold bullion, such as war, or the mines from which gold is annually supplied becoming less productive, that gold might be so enhanced in value as to make the clipped sovereign comparatively of greater value in the market than it was before the reduction which I contend; but those persons maintain that the alterations in the value of our currency, that is, in the value of the metals as well as in the value of the paper measured by the metals, as a consequence of the suspension of cash payments, were greater than that can be inferred by a reference to those tests; that those tests may be allowed in proof of the minimum, but *not* of the maximum, of its effect on the prices of corn and other commodities. That in fact, though other causes may have concurred in producing the elevation of general prices in this country between 1797 and 1814, and the decline since that period; such other causes, whether in detail or collectively, sink into utter insignificance, compared with the *alterations in the system of our currency*. Now, as in one part of that period

---

in its weight. Would it not then be true that we should possess a depreciated currency, although it should be increased in value? The great mistake committed on this subject was in confounding the words 'depreciation', and 'diminution in value.' With reference to the currency, he had said, and he now repeated it, that the price of gold was the index of the depreciation of the currency, not the index of the value of the currency, and there he had been misunderstood. If, for instance, the standard of the currency remained at the same fixed value, and the coin was depreciated by clipping, or if the paper money were depreciated by the increase of its quantity 5 per cent, that fall, and no more, would constitute the alteration in the price of commodities, as affected by the depreciation of the currency. If the metal gold (the standard) continued of the same precise value, and it was required to restore the currency, depreciated 5 per cent, to par, it would be necessary only to raise its value 5 per cent, and no greater than that proportionate fall could take place in the price of commodities. In these cases he had supposed that gold always remain at the same fixed value, but had he ever said that there were not many causes which might operate on the value of gold as well as on the value of all other commodities? No, he had not, but just the contrary. No country that used the precious metals as a standard was exempted from variations in the prices of commodities, occasioned by a variation in the value of their standard. To such variations we had been subject before 1797, and must be subject to again, now that we have reverted to a metallic standard."

On this I have further to remark, that if the currency consisted exclusively of coin, and if that coin were reduced in value below its legal standard, whether, by increased alloy, or diminished weight, uncompensated by any principle of limitation of issue, the simplest term to apply to that state would be "debasement of the curiency."

the prices of necessaries, and of many other articles, advanced to the extent of from 50 to 100 per cent, and upwards, and have subsequently declined to, or below the level from which they had risen; and, as the average excess of the market price above the mint price of gold did not, in the first twelve years after the suspension of cash payments, exceed about 4 per cent, nor on the average of the succeeding five years about 20 per cent, we have to seek in the *mode of operation* of the bank restriction, and in the state of facts connected with prices of commodities, for all the excess of the alleged effect, beyond the mere difference between the paper and its standard.

CHAPTER Ⅱ
ARGUMENTS OF THOSE WHO ASCRIBE A GREATER EFFECT TO THE BANK RESTRICTION THAN THAT INDICATED BY THE DIFFERENCE BETWEEN THE MARKET PRICE AND THE MINT PRICE OF GOLD

The arguments in support of the opinion that the value of the currency was depreciated by the bank restriction, and enhanced by the resumption of cash payments, in a much greater degree than that indicated, at any time, by the difference between paper and gold, proceed upon the following grounds: —

1. That the banishment of the metals, gold principally, from the circulation of this country during the restriction, and the recall of them for the resumption, affected in a considerable degree of the value of gold and silver in the commercial world, diminishing their value during the former, and increasing it in the latter period.

2. That the compulsory paper system established by the bank restriction, had the effect of "*heightening*" all those expedients to which a prosperous state of society naturally gives birth, for economising the circulating medium, bringing the whole of it into activity, and multiplying it virtually by the substitution of credit for currency.

3. That the restriction was the cause of excessive issues from the Bank, a fact which is (assumed to be) hardly open to dispute, and that, if so, it must be charged with producing that excessive issue of country paper also which was an invariable concomitant of Bank of England paper.

4. That "the increase of prices was progressive from the year 1797 to 1814, subject only to such fluctuations as arise out of the nature of the respective commodities" and "that it was not accompanied by a growing difference in the value of bank paper and gold." "That the constant and invariable connexion of increase of price with the bank restriction, is a forcible proof of such a relation as that of cause and effect subsisting between the two phenomena;" and "that the near approach of the termination of that restriction has produced a fall of prices, greatly exceeding the difference between paper and gold; thus still further corroborating that connexion, and proving, almost demonstratively, that the prices from 1797 to 1814 were, to a certain degree, artificial; and that the comparison of paper with gold, during that period, did not afford a test of the real amount of the fall in the value of the currency."

This summary of the arguments in support of the doctrine of the indefinite depreciation of the currency caused by the bank restriction, is extracted from the Quarterly Review, vol. xviii., and was referred to in a former publication of mine, entitled "Thoughts and Details on High and Low Prices", as the ablest and most compendious exposition which had then appeared of that doctrine. And among the numberless publications and speeches in which the doctrine in question has been since asserted and maintained, there are none in which the supposed grounds for it, untenable as I consider them to be, are more fully and intelligibly stated. These arguments, therefore, as thus set forth, it is now proposed to examine under their several heads.

SECTION 1 *On the alleged effect of the bank restriction in depreciating the value of the precious metals*

The only ground that is at all intelligible for the opinion that the value of gold was depreciated during and by the restriction, and increased in value subsequently to and by the operation of Peel's bill, is that by which it is to be inferred,

"That the banishment of the metals, gold principally, from the circulation of this country during the restriction, and the recall of them for the resumption, affected in a considerable degree the value of gold and silver in the commercial world, diminishing their value during the former, and increasing it in the latter period."

Of this theory it is to be observed, in the first place, that the cause assigned is wholly inadequate to have produced any considerable effect on bullion prices, supposing it to have been uncompensated by circumstances of an opposite character; and in the next place, that, in point of fact, circumstances did occur of a description calculated, at least, to balance, if not to outweigh, the alleged effect; and lastly, that the periods of the highest prices on the Continent do not accord with those of the greatest disengagement of the metals from this country, or the periods of the lowest prices abroad, with the greatest influx of bullion into this country.

The amount of gold coin circulating in this country previously to 1797, has been variously estimated. Mr. Rose, in his speech on the bullion question, in 1811, entered into an elaborate statement, with a view to prove that the amount of gold coin in circulation, previous to the bank restriction, was at least forty millions.

The first Lord Liverpool, in his "Treatise on the Coins of the Realm," stated it at thirty millions. In the Lords' Bullion Report, 1819, page 11., the amount is assumed at twenty-five millions. Mr. Whitmore (Bullion Report, 1810, page 120.), and Mr. Harman (Commons' Report, 1819, page 40.), computed that it did not exceed twenty millions in the three years preceding the bank restriction.

Upon this last estimate, the writer of an able article in the Supplement to the "Encyclopedia Britannica", under the title of "Money", remarks, that though it is probably rather below the mark, there are good grounds for concluding, that it is the most accurate of any that have hitherto been framed, and that it has come as near the truth as is perhaps possible in such matters. Allowing, therefore, that this last sum is a little, or only a little, underrated, and that, consequently, the estimate in the Lords' Report is decidedly beyond the mark, a medium between these will leave about twenty-two millions and a half, as the utmost probable amount of gold coin in circulation previous to 1797.

That this estimate is not very wide of the truth, may be concluded from a reference to the amount of sovereigns issued by the bank from May, 1821, to the end of June, 1821. This comprises the interval from the first issue till the time when the circulation may be considered to have had as large an amount of gold, less the amount of country small notes, as it had before 1797. The amount issued within the above interval was,

In sovereigns and half-sovereigns,	16, 671, 030*l*.
To this add country small notes,	
a large estimate - - -	5, 500, 000
	22, 171, 030*l*.

There were considerable additional issues of sovereigns after June,

1821; but, as the exchanges then became adverse, those further issues were probably exported, or replaced only those which had been exported.

Assuming the amount to have been, on the grounds stated, at the utmost $22\frac{1}{2}$ millions, there is to be deducted the quantity that was hoarded in this country; an amount that must have been probably much larger than has commonly been supposed. There was scarcely an individual of a class above that which is limited to the means of bare subsistence, who had not a hoard, greater or less, of guineas that were put by as a provision against the various contingencies which were considered as endangering the value of paper, either in degree, as by depreciation, or totally, as by foreign invasion or domestic convulsion payments in specie, there was a near prospect of the complete restoration of the value and security of paper, large sums of guineas were poured into the hands of the London bankers, by their correspondents in the country, and by their customers in town. Those sums have been variously estimated: but, upon the whole, it is probable that an allowance of from four to five millions would be rather within than beyond the mark.

The following quotation from the evidence of Mr. Stuckey, an eminent banker in Somersetshire, given before the Lords' Committee of 1819, will serve as an instance of the extent of the practice of hoarding: —

"In 1817, we had a circulation of guineas, which we found very inconvenient. It cost us near 100*l*. to transmit gold and silver to London in the first six months of the year 1817. People were then in the habit of coming to our bank with guineas, requesting we would give our notes for them. I suppose they had been hoarded. I brought up 1000 guineas in May, 1817, and taking them to our London banker, they requested as a favour I would not leave them; they had lately sent in so many to the Bank of England, that they did not like to trouble them any more. Besides, the bank only took those which were quite full weight. The result was, that I took them to a dealer in coin, and sold them at 3*l.* 17*s.* 6*d.* per ounce."

Among other inducements to bring out hoards in 1816, one was, that light guineas, which had been previously of *more* value than those of full weight, from being legally saleable, were, in consequence of the fall in the market price of gold, becoming of *less* than the current value.

Mr. Huskisson expressed his opinion of the extent of the practice of hoarding, in the following passage of his pamphlet on the currency question, in 1810: —

"A great quantity of gold, which is now hoarded, would also make its appearance, if guineas were restored to their use and value as currency."

The treasure in the coffers of the Bank during the twelve years immediately following the restriction, was larger, too, than it had been on the average of the five years preceding that measure.

And, although guineas rarely appeared in circulation, yet there were cases of payment, for which they were reserved: Mr. Rose, in his speech on the bullion question, in 1811, supposed although as a high estimate, that three millions might then be still in circulation.

From these considerations it should seem, that a sum of from twelve to fifteen millions is an ample allowance for the quantity of gold which went to increase the mass of the precious metals in the rest of the world, and which, so far as it went, must have tended, *creteris paribus*, to diminish their value in the rest of the world.

In estimating what effect, *other things being the same*, the addition of twelve or fifteen millions to the circulation of the rest of the commercial world might have on general prices, or, in other words, on the value of the precious metals, as compared with coin and other commodities, it would be requisite to have some idea of the total amount of gold and silver existing in the world for the general purposes of use and ornament, viz. as coin, bullion, plate, and jewellery. By some authorities the total amount has been computed as high as two thousand millions. But Mr. Jacob, in his valuable work "On the Production and Consumption of the Precious Metals," computes, vol. ii. p. 347., the existing amount of coined and uncoined gold and silver in Europe and America, and Asia, about twelve hundred millions. And, as in his computations, he appears to be disposed in no case to overrate the production, while on every occasion he gives the utmost weight to the causes of increased consumption, that amount may safely be assumed as the lowest upon which the quantity disengaged, and resumed in consequence of the restriction and resumption of cash payments can have operated. There is little hazard, therefore, in assuming, that the addition or abstraction of from twelve to fifteen millions, *other things remaining the same*, would make little more than 1 per cent, and certainly not 2 per cent, difference in their value.

In this view of the utter inadequateness of the quantity of gold disengaged from, and eventually restored into, the circulation of this country, to have produced any sensible impression on the value of bullion, I have the concurrence of very eminent authorities. Mr. Malthus, in a publication entitled "On the Measure of Value", 1823, when referring to the fall in the price of labour, as indicating a greater difference than that between paper and gold, adds,

"This difference, of course, includes the effects which have been attributed to the purchases of the Bank, with a view to a return to cash payments, the amount of which separately it is scarcely possible to calculate; but I am inclined to agree with Mr. Tooke in thinking that it is not above one or two per cent."

"It is a lamentable proof of the public ignorance on these subjects, that the general fall of prices, or, in other words, the increasing difficulty of obtaining the precious metals, of which everyone is sensible should, by almost every one, be attributed to some causes of almost ridiculous inadequacy. It has been attributed to our return to a metallic currency, as if the subtraction of twenty millions of sovereigns, or less than four hundred thousand pounds troy of gold, from the ten millions of pounds troy of gold bullion coin, and plate, supposed to be in use throughout the world, that is, the removal of one twenty-fifth part, could sensibly affect the value of gold. It has been attributed even to the substitution of gold and silver for the three or four millions of one pound notes lately called in, as if the value of the two thousand millions sterling of gold and silver bullion, coin and plate, could be materially affected by the subtraction of less than one five-hundredth part of it." — *On the Cost of obtaining Money*, 1830, p. 21.

The arguments and authorities already adduced, show how insignificant this supposed influence must have been; but an important fact may here be referred to, as affording, by analogy, a strong confirmation of that conclusion. The fact alluded to, as bearing upon the question of the currency, was first noticed, as far as I am aware, by the late Lord King, in a publication which, at the time when it appeared, deservedly attracted great attention,

"On the supposition of the whole quantity of gold and silver remaining the same, they must, in a certain degree, be rendered cheap by every increase of paper currency. But as these metals are in universal request, and circulate more generally than any other articles of commerce, the effect thus produced cannot be partial, but must extend to all other countries, and it will, therefore, follow that the actual reduction in the value of gold and silver which is produced by the paper circulation of any particular country, is in the proportion of the amount of such circulation to the whole quantity of the precious metals applicable to the purposes of coinage and commerce throughout the world. It is probable that this proportion can never be very great, and experience seems to show that no considerable depreciation is ever produced in this manner."— *Thoughts on the Bank Restriction*, 1804.

The circumstance alluded to by Lord King, namely, the total absence of any observable effect on bullion prices, by the large amount of gold and silver displaced from circulation in France as coin by the assignats, in the early part of the revolution, appears to be quite decisive against the hypothesis of a considerable influence on the value of the metals, by the quantity disengaged from the circulation of this country. The amount of coin circulating in France, immediately previous to the revolution, has, by some authorities, been computed at nearly a hundred millions sterling; but according to Peuchet, whose estimate appears to be formed upon the best grounds, the amount was about seventy-four millions. Nearly the whole of this was banished from circulation, when the system of terror was at its height between 1790 and 1794. It is probable, that some portion of the coin displaced by the assignats, was retained in a dormant state in France; but there can be no doubt, that a considerable proportion must have been brought away, as being the most portable and valuable description of property, by the numerous emigrants from thence to the other parts of Europe, and chiefly to this country; besides that, the export of coin was a necessary effect of the great fall of the exchanges of France on other countries. Supposing that only about one half of the coin was exported from thence, it would amount to no less than about thirty-six millions of gold and silver, suddenly added to the circulation of the rest of the world, and in the first instance to that of the rest of Europe. If then, there was no distinctly perceptible increase of the bullion prices of commodities between 1790 and 1794, notwithstanding the addition of about forty millions from France to the rest of Europe, the effect of less than half that amount disengaged from the circulation of this country cannot but have been most insignificant. It must therefore be evident from these considerations that the utmost effect of the disengagement and reabsorption of gold and silver, by the circulation of this country, must have been hardly perceptible on prices, supposing other things to have remained the same.

But other things were *not* the same. For while, as a consequence of the bank restriction, about twelve or fifteen millions of our coin may be supposed to have gone abroad, there was, in consequence of the wars on the Continent, which were, with few intervals, coincident with the period referred to, a great and unusual demand for the precious metals. The military chests and the treasuries of the great belligerent powers, whose operations were on so vast a scale, necessarily absorbed a very large amount of specie. And it may be a question whether a still larger amount was not absorbed by the very extensive practice of hoarding which prevailed among the inhabitants of those states of the Continent which were either the seat of war, or which had issued paper to excess.

So striking were these circumstances, both separately and collectively considered, that they were, by the great majority of those who at that time look a part in the discussions on this subject, appealed to as very much outweighing the effect of the quantity of gold rendered available for the purposes of the Continent, by the substitution of paper in this country. It was, as has before been stated, the general answer to all charges against the conduct of the Bank, in suffering the depreciation of its notes, that gold had become scarce, and not paper overabundant: and it must be admitted, that there was ground for so much of the answer as went on a *primafacie* presumption that gold had become somewhat scarce relatively to a former period; or, that supposing the precious metals to have been otherwise of a given value, the obvious effect of the war, and of the peculiar circumstances attending it, was to enhance their value. Accordingly, the Bullion Report of 1810 (p. 2.), nearly at its outset states as follows:—"It will be found by the evidence, that the high price of gold is ascribed by most of the witnesses entirely to an alledged scarcity of the article, arising out of an unusual demand for it upon the Continent of Europe. This unusual demand for gold upon the Continent is described by some of them as being chiefly for the use of the French armies, though increased also by that state of alarm and failure of confidence which leads to the practice of hoarding."

It seems hardly possible to resist the conclusion that under these circumstances there must have been a greatly increased demand for the precious metals, and a consequently increased value of them during the war, *more than sufficient* to compensate for the utmost quantity spared from circulation as coin in this country, or even for the utmost rate of annual increase from the mines.

Much stress has been laid upon the circumstance of Russia, Austria, and the United States of America, having at the same time with this country substituted a paper for a metallic circulation, thereby further diminishing the value of the metals during the war and the restriction. But it will be found that the facts are erroneously assumed.

Russia had established a compulsory paper currency for many years before our bank restriction, and the circulation of that empire was as fully saturated with paper to the exclusion of the precious metals before the year 1797, as at any subsequent period. ①

Austria had but little of a pure metallic currency remaining in 1797. And that country being often the seat of war, the tendency among its inhabitants to hoard what gold and silver they could collect beyond their immediate necessities for expenditure, would probably more than compensate for the quantity liberated by paper issues from circulation as coin. The same remark applies to Prussia and the minor German States.

The United States of America never till recently possessed any large stock of the precious metals in circulation as coin. And it was not till 1812, after all the phenomena of high bullion prices had occurred, that there was any general suspension of payment by their banks.

It is clear, therefore, that no part of the high bullion prices during the war and the restriction can be accounted for by any increased quantity of the precious metals disengaged from the circulation of the countries just mentioned. If, however, there had been such increase, it might indeed have been an accessory circumstance in producing the depreciation of the metals which is alleged. But if a depreciation from this cause did occur, it has not and ought not to have any connexion

① But not only, however, did Russia not add to the mass of metals by disengagement from her circulation, but, in truth, she absorbed a considerable amount of bullion in 1812; for the fact is, and rather a curious one, that the value of the Russian paper money *increased* comcidently with the advance into that country of the French armies, insomuch that the exchange for the ruble, which, a few months before, had been 14*d*., lose, by the time they reached Moscow, to 24*d*.. Thus gold and silver formed the best then in great demand, from the fear that the French might cut off all farther supplies: accordingly, a good deal of specie was sent thither, and probably did not return from thence till between 1814 and 1816, when the exchange fell again below its former lowest level.

with the question, how far the bank restriction caused a diminution of the value of gold, or a rise of bullion prices beyond the difference between paper and gold in this country. As far as regards the disengagment, if such there had been, of the precious metals from other countries, coincidently with our bank restriction, there would equally, to whatever extent that cause might be supposed to operate, have been a rise of bullion prices if the paper of this country had continued to be convertible. ①

Whenever a reference has been made to the rise of bullion prices in other countries, prior to 1819, and to the subsequent fall, the only answer given has been that the alterations in our currency deranged the currencies of other countries. But we have never been told in what way our alterations produced that effect, with the single exception of the supposed influence of the quantity of gold disengaged from this country on the value of that metal in the rest of the world. ②

① The same observation applies to the effects of the varying produce of the mines of gold and silver. If the increased produce of the mines, anterior to 1819, was an element in the high range of prices, and if a diminished produce subsequently had been one of the causes of the lower range, these causes of variation of bullion prices must be viewed as totally distinct from those which can be imputed to alterations in the system of our currency. But in the opinions which prevail among the supporters of the ultra doctrine of depreciation, there is an extraordinary confusion of ideas in blending as the effects of the bank restriction, and of the resumption of cash payments, variations (greatly exaggerated, if existing at all) in the value of the metals, arising from causes avowedly distinct, by the very assignment of such causes, from the possibility of having been produced by the operation of the measures affecting exclusively the footing of the currency of this country.

② The influence here alluded to of our currency on the currencies abroad does not refer to the occasional fluctuations arising from speculations and operations on credit, and from the necessary reactions which communicate themselves to those countries abroad with which we are in commercial connection. The argument in the text is confined to a supposed influence, which applies to the whole period of the restriction in raising prices, and of each payments in reducing them.

Independently of the argument derived from the insufficiency of the cause assigned to have produced the alleged effect, it will be seen in the historical sketch which will be found in the further part of this work, that the great variations of bullion prices abroad do not correspond, in point of either time or magnitude, with the variations in the quantity of metals disengaged from use, and resumed as coin in this country.

This cause, therefore, namely, the quantity of bullion disengaged from circulation as coin by the suspension of cash payments in this country, and added to the general mass in the rest of the world, may be considered as wholly inadmissible in accounting for any part of the great elevation of prices observable at different periods during the restriction.

But if the addition to the general mass of the precious metals, by the substitution of paper for coin in this country, pending the bank restriction, cannot, on the grounds which I have stated, be fairly inferred to have produced, under any circumstances, a sensible effect on the value of those metals; and if there were circumstances such as those already mentioned, which were calculated, at least to compensate, if not to outweigh that effect: then it follows, by parity of reasoning, that the reabsorption, by the resumption of cash payments, of a similar amount of bullion to that which had before been spared, cannot have been attended with a greater effect in an opposite direction. This must be understood *mutatis mutandis*, viz. the disengagement of the sums employed for military purposes, and the return of security to commercial intercourse, renewing the facilities of circulation on the Continent, and diminishing the inducement to hoarding.

Having thus offered arguments, which to my mind are conclusive, against the presumption of any sensible effect from the alterations in the system of our currency, under the circumstances in which they took place, on the value of the precious metals in Europe, I shall proceed to examine what influence may be ascribed to the second class of circumstances, which, as a consequence of the bank restriction, are stated to have affected the value of the currency in this country, in a much greater degree than that indicated by the difference between paper and gold.

SECTION 2 *Effect of the bank restriction on the economised use of money*

The expedients for economising the use of the currency, although they date from a period long anterior to the bank restriction, and certainly had their origin in causes wholly distinct from it, did experience a considerable improvement about that time. But the economising practices which were then in progress, have not only subsisted in full force since the resumption of cash payments, but have experienced further improvements. Allowing, however, for the sake of argument, that the bank restriction was the cause of greater economy in the use of the currency, and that this greater economy was one of the causes of a diminution of the value of the currency, beyond the degree indicated by the difference between paper and gold, how happens it that, although all the refined machinery of the banking system subsists unimpaired, and is perhaps undergoing further improvements, it has no longer the depreciating effect ascribed to it?[1] Really, in order to have been good for anything in the argument which it was brought forward to support, this economy of the currency should have been proved, not only to have arisen from, but to have terminated with, the restriction: and it is proved to have done neither. On the contrary, while the prevailing complaint is of a tendency the very reverse of diminution in the value of the currency, it is notorious that circumstances are in progress calculated still further to economise the use of it. Not only are improvements daily taking place among the bankers, in their payments on the largest scale; not only is the practice of lodging money with a banker becoming more general, as including a large proportion of the smallest classes of tradesmen; but there is less detention in the very minutest channels of circulation, inasmuch as, by the institution of savings' banks, the most inconsiderable sums, which must, but for this mode of investment, have been dormant as petty hoards in the hands of mechanics and menial servants, have become, and are becoming daily, more available to swell the amount of currency applicable to general purposes.

So large is the aggregate saving of the use of bank notes and coin, from the foregoing causes, which have acquired their principal activity since the

---

① It was on the ground of the economised use of the currency that the Bullion Committee of 1810 endeavoured to account, consistently with their view, for the striking and lather puzzling fact of the very small numerical increase of bank notes to which they ascribed such depreciating effects Their inference, from the improvements referred to, might have been justified if it had been found that the price of gold had not fallen until the amount of bank notes had been reduced, as compared with that which had been pronounced to have been rendered excessive by those improvements. Whereas, while the economy in the use of the currency was undergoing progressive improvement, an increased amount of bank notes was found to be requisite for the transactions of the country, consistently with a fall of the market price of bullion to its mint price, and with a much greater fall in the prices of commodities.

termination of the bank restriction, and which have not yet apparently reached their utmost development; that, notwithstanding the extended functions of money consequent on an increased population, and on an enlarged scale of pecuniary transactions, it is perfectly conceivable that a smaller numerical amount of coin and bank notes is now requisite to circulate commodities at the same prices than before that period.

We may therefore safely dismiss the economised use of the currency from the list of causes concurring to produce the *diminution and subsequent increase* of the value of the precious metals, resulting from the restriction and resumption of cash payments by the bank.

SECTION 3 *Effect ascribed to the bank restriction of the substitution of credit for currency, and of the excessive issues of country paper*

The next effect ascribed to the bank restriction is "the multiplication of the circulating medium virtually by the substitution of credit for currency."

The manner in which the bank restriction is supposed to have produced these effects, is thus stated in the review already quoted: —

"In such a system, country banks find a less stock necessary to answer demands than they would keep if liable to pay in specie. In the former case, one in twenty is deemed sufficient, in the latter, one-fifth, or perhaps one-fourth, would be the safe proportion. The moral certainty that a banker feels, that he shall not be called upon to discount his own notes, is a strong temptation to issue them to the utmost practicable extent. He sets all the canvass his vessel will carry, more than in common prudence he would do if there were any apprehensions of a coming gale. But the bank restriction was a kind of security against all sudden and unexpected movements, a sort of monsoon, which, after passing one session of parliament, he was sure would continue to the next; and while that lasted, nothing was likely to happen that could disturb its course."

"All the merchants examined agree in stating, that country paper increased with the increase of bank paper. If, therefore, the bank restriction was the cause of excessive issues from the Bank — a fact which is at this time hardly open to dispute — it must be charged with producing that excessive issue of country paper also, which was an invariable concomitant, of the other."

"Now, it cannot be doubted that this hypothetical wealth was greatly augmented by the system of the bank restriction. If the Bank was always ready to discount bills upon real mercantile transactions; if country banks, in imitation of this example, did the same; not only were transactions entered into which, without such facility, never could have taken place, but numerous contracts were effected for which actual payment was not required at the time, and was, in fact, never made, other transaction in the mean time having taken place which either directly or indirectly had the effect of balancing these; thus performing, without regular book entries, the very office of a bank: the seller building as securely upon the credit of the buyer (a credit never actually put to the test), as upon his tangible property."

On this statement, which conveys the fullest view that I have met with of the specific manner in which the excessive issues of the Bank of England, asserted to have been caused by the restriction, are supposed to have swelled to a proportionate excess the whole of the circulating medium, the following observations occur: —

1. It is possible that the country bankers might habitually keep a somewhat smaller stock, or reserve, during the restriction than in a convertible state of the paper, and there might, to this extent, be some increased economy in the use of the currency, although hardly amounting to a set off against the progressive improvements which have since taken place. This effect, therefore, if it existed at all, must have been the most trifling imaginable.

2. A most erroneous impression is conveyed by the description in the foregoing extract, and is entertained very generally to this day, that during the restriction there was a sort of exemption from the penalties of overtrading; that bankers might issue *ad libitum*, and merchants trade to the utmost extent of their credit, without experiencing the usual penalties of loss and failure. The bank restriction is supposed to have operated as "a kind of security to the banker against all sudden and unexpected movements; a sort of monsoon, which, after passing one session of parliament, he was sure would continue to the next, and while that lasted, nothing was likely to happen that could disturb his course." But it did so happen, that his course was disturbed by exactly the same process as we have seen exemplified in more recent instances. The reaction from undue speculation seems to have been as inevitable during the restriction as before and since; witness the extensive failures in 1810 to 1812, and again, in 1814 to 1816, which will be more distinctly noticed hereafter. Of the latter it may be, as it has been said, although without the slighest foundation, that they were the consequence of preparations for cash payments; but neither this nor any other reason consistent with the currency theory, can be brought to account for the former.

3. The country bank paper is supposed to have increased with every increase of Bank of England paper, and an excessive issue of the one, to

have been an invariable concomitant of the other.

Of the amount of the country bank paper, it is impossible to give any accurate account. No materials whatever exist for the computation of it previous to 1804, when first a separation was made of the stamps for bankers' notes from those for bills of exchange and notes after date. In 1804, distinct stamps were issued for bankers' notes, which were not to be re-issued after three years from their date. Upon the stamps so issued, computations have been made, but they are the most vague and unsatisfactory imaginable, of the amount actually in circulation. These will occasionally be referred to hereafter. In the meanwhile it may be remarked of this portion of the circulating medium, that, supposing it to bear for local purposes a certain due proportion to the basis of the currency, the deviations from this, its due level, have been, not only during, but before and since the restriction, very considerable, expanding under circumstances, and in a state of opinion, favouring a rise of prices, and collapsing under the opposite circumstances; and these expansions and contractions have, in the majority of instances, not been preceded by any corresponding variations of the bank issues, although eventually they have come under the limitation and control of the bank regulation.

The same, and perhaps in a still greater degree, may be said of those other component parts of the circulating medium, bills of exchange, and book credits, to which allusion is made in the passages quoted from the review. The expansion and contraction of these and of country bank notes, are, as will be abundantly exemplified, the consequences, and not the causes, of a rise and fall of prices.

Credit, in its ordinary and legitimate application, forms one of the more important means of sparing the use of the currency, as well as of effecting the best and cheapest distribution of capital and revenue among the several orders of the community. But it is also a medium, which admits, during short intervals, of expansion, under the influence of the spirit of adventure, to an almost indefinite extent. Some striking instances of this expansiveness of the medium of credit will be exhibited in the following historical sketch. But it will be seen, that the susceptibility of expansion, and the consequent liability to collapse, have not been confined to the inconvertible state of our currency. And a reference, not only to the slate of the currency in this country anterior to the bank restriction, but to the currencies of the continental states of Europe, in which the basis of the currency has been purely metallic, will serve to show that a great abuse of credit has not been peculiar to an inconvertible currency. ①The Bank of

---

① The following notices, extracted from contemporary accounts, of considerable derangement of credit, in consequence of a previous undue extension of it among the principal commercial cities of the Continent of Europe, in the course of last century, may be considered as not altogether uninteresting or irrelevant to the subject under discussion:—

"Letter from the Bankers at Hamburgh to the Bankers at Amsterdam."

"Hamburgh, Aug. 4. 1763."

"This morning at eleven, when we were met to consider of the methods to be taken to assist the houses at this place that are tottering, we received a fatal express, with the terrible news, that you, the gentlemen of Amsterdam, would leave the Neufvilles to sink, by which we were all thunderstruck; never dreaming that so many men in their senses in your city could take such a step — a step which will infallibly plunge all Europe in an abyss of distress, if not remedied by you whilst it is still time. We therefore send this circular and general letter to you by an express, to exhort and conjure you, as soon as you receive this, to undertake still to support the Neufvilles, by furnishing what money they want, and giving them two or three persons of unquestionable probity and skill, for curators, that then affairs and their engagements may be concluded and terminated, without causing a general ruin, which will otherwise infallibly happen. If you do not, gentlemen, we hereby declare to you, that our resolution is taken, that is to say, that although we represent, a very respectable body of rich and respectable men, we have unanimously resolved to suspend our own payments as long as we shall judge it proper and necessary; and that we will not acquit them, or the counterprotests that shall come from you, or any whatever."

England, in the regulation of its issues of notes, which, during the restriction, constituted the basis of the currency, and into which, with

---

"This is the resolution which we have unanimously taken; and from which we will not depart, happen what will. The fate of the general commerce of all Europe is at present absolutely in your hands; determine, gentlemen, whether you should crush it totally, or support it. You are all too intelligent not to perceive, that by letting the whole machine fall to pieces, you will suffer heavy losses in all parts, which you may prevent to yourselves, and a thousand others, by assisting the Neufvilles to pay and wind up their affairs. Let us have your final resolution speedily, by express, for till that tune all will remain in suspense here, and none of us will pay one penny of the bills we have accepted till we know what you will do. Meanwhile, we have the honour to be, &c."

And they seem to have stopped accordingly, as such appears to be the allusion in the following extract from the Annual Register for 1763: —

"Aug. 29. 1763."

"There has been lately at Amsterdam, Hamburgh, and some other of the principal towns of Germany, a surprising number of bankruptcies. They began at Amsterdam about the 29th of July, by the bankruptcy of two brothers named Neufville, who failed for above 330, 000 guineas, and a Jew, who, a few days before, failed for between 30, 000 and 40, 000*l*. This was followed by a stoppage of payment by no less than eighteen houses in that city; and soon after by a much greater number at Hamburgh and other places, which put a stop to private credit, that no business was for some time transacted, but for ready money. But the Lombard houses at Amsterdam and Hamburgh, having supplied with large quantities of cash, such as could give real or personal security, enabled many, who must otherwise have stopped, to stand the run."

Another recorded instance of great derangement of credit occurred ten years later: —

"The great commercial failures, which threw such a damp last year upon all business in this country, arrived at their utmost extent about the beginning of the present in Holland, and were of so alarming a nature, and so extensive in then influence, as to threaten a mortal blow to all public and private credit throughout Europe. These failures were the effect of an artificial credit, and of great speculative dealings in trade, as well as in the public funds of diffident countries, and though attended with an immense loss to individuals, of not less, perhaps, than ten millions sterling, took nothing out of the general stock, neither money nor goods being thereby lessened."

the small and diminishing proportion of coin, all pecuniary engagements were, in the last resort, resolvable, controled and limited the other constituent elements of the circulating medium, exactly in the same way as a purely metallic basis controls and limits the convertible paper and the credit part of the circulation.

In the metallic currency of commercial communities, there are expansions and contractions of the circulation, without any corresponding movements of the metallic basis. But if from accidental circumstances there should coincidently with the tendency to speculation, through the means of credit, happen to be an enlargement of the metallic basis, an increased facility would arise, to the extension of the circulation, and to the spirit of speculation; and the converse would be the consequence of a contraction of the basis coinciding with a reaction from speculation and its attendant discredit.

So likewise in the regulation of the bank issues, if an undue enlargement of them happened to coincide with a tendency to an extension of the other constituent parts of the circulation, there would be a proportionate excess in the whole of the circulating medium. And the converse under the opposite circumstances.

If, therefore, the allegation of constant excess of issues by the Bank of England be substantiated, there can be no hesitation in admitting a corresponding excess in the whole of the circulation. It is proposed accordingly, to examine the grounds for that allegation upon which the question of depreciation beyond the difference between the paper and gold mainly turns. ①

SECTION 4 *On the alleged constant excess of issue by the bank of England, and thence of the whole of the circulating medium*

The charge of excess or overissues of paper from the Bank of England cannot but be admitted, if by that charge be meant only that during the restriction the issues were, for the most part, larger than could under the unusual circumstances operating on the exchanges, have been maintained under a convertible state of the currency. The issues were in that sense excessive, inasmuch as the amount exceeded that which was compatible with the maintenance of the value of the paper on a level with that of its standard. And as already noticed of the term *depreciation*, the measure of

① In the comparisons instituted for the purpose of judging of the relative quantities of money at different periods, it has been made a question whether the deposits in the hands of the bank should not be added to the amount of the circulation. The bank is doubtless as much liable to the payment of all the deposits, in gold if so required, as if the depositors were holders of bank notes. And it may be said, and truly said, that as the London bankers now are in the habit of lodging with the bank certain portions of their receives, instead of holding them, as they formerly did, in their own drawers in bank notes, so much of the amount under the head of deposits in the bank returns, should be considered as forming a part of the circulation. In fact, some part of the private deposits at the Bank, besides those of the London bankers, may come under the same description; because the common drawing accounts, it they had been kept with private hankers, would have added to their reserves, and would, consequently, have increased, in some degree, the bankers' deposits in the Bank of England. These are reasons for supposing that the same amount of bank notes issued is now much more effective than an equal amount formerly was, before the practice became so extended, that is, prior to 1825. And in comparing the quantity of money emanating from the Bank of England, it might depend upon the object for instituting the comparison, whether or not to blend the amount of the private deposits with the bank circulation. But, generally speaking, as it is the bank issues coming under the head of circulation, which enter more immediately into the money market, and thus influence, directly, the rate of interest, and, eventually and indirectly, the prices of commodities; and as it is the amount of the bank circulation, and not of its liabilities, which has been the standard chosen by the advocates of the ultra doctrine of depreciation, for the measure of the expansion and contraction of the currency, it will be chiefly to the circulation that in the following examination of the supposed influence of the bank restriction, reference will be made.

excess, in this case, would be the degree in which the value of the paper fell short of the value of the specific quantity of gold in which it purported to be payable. The charge of *excessive issue* being so confined, would be independent of any question whether the difference arose from an increase of the circulation, relatively to its functions, the value of gold being unaltered, or from an increased demand for gold, the quantity of money, or in other words, of the circulating medium being unaltered in its relation to the ordinary amount of revenue and trade, of commodities and labour, to be circulated.

But this is not the common acceptation of the term, nor evidently so intended in the argument under consideration. The restriction is supposed to have been the cause of a constant increase of the bank issues, and thence of the quantity of money, not only beyond that amount, which under the pressure of extraordinary foreign payments, could have been maintained consistently with the preservation of the par of the exchanges, and of the price of gold; but much beyond that which could have been maintained in an undisturbed state of politics and trade, and in the ordinary state of the balance of payments, without raising the price of gold, and, in a still greater degree, the prices of commodities and labour. The question is one of fact, determinable, however, only by presumptive evidence:—*Whether, in the altered proportions between money and the objects exchanged, by it, the variations of prices, consequent on those altered proportions, originated in, and were dependant upon, alterations in the quantity of money on the one hand, or in the cost of production, and the accidents affecting supply, on the other.*

Of the circumstances affecting the cost of production and the supply of the objects exchanged by money during the restriction, a historical sketch will hereafter be given.

We have had occasion to observe, that although the amount of Bank of England notes controlled and limited, in the long run, the other parts of the circulating medium, there might be, as indeed there have been, intervals of great divergence, which might equally occur for limited periods in a convertible state of the paper.

It may here be the place to remark, that, whether in a convertible or inconvertible state of the paper, there are, and must be, a variety of circumstances in constant operation to affect the numerical amount of the bank circulation, without justifying the inference of any corresponding alteration in the quantity of the circulating medium, or of its being in excess or defect, with reference to the revenue and commodities to be circulated by it. There is a constantly varying proportion of Bank of England notes, applicable to country payments compared with London payments; this was probably more than the case during subsequent to the restriction. And in cases of discredit of the country banks, sometimes only local, sometimes general, a sudden increase of Bank of England issues has taken place, in order merely to fill the temporary chasm of the country circulation. The amount too of London payments is liable to vary very considerably in short intervals. ① Sometimes the prompts for periodical sales coincide with the falling due of large acceptances in particular branches of trade. The payments passing between the receivers of the taxes

① Till within the last few years, there was, in the interval during which the books of the bank were shut, preparatory to the payment of dividends, a very considerable reduction of the amount of bank notes in circulation, and a corresponding increase immediately after the payment of the dividends. This cause of a periodical variation in the amount of the circulation, which was occasionally found to be inconvenient, has since been remedied by the practice adopted by the bank of making advances, by way of loan, on took and other approved securities, for the few weeks immediately precding the payment of the dividends.

and the exchequer, and between the exchequer and the Bank, influence the amount of notes issued by the Bank although they may not pass at all into the hands of the public. The same sum, circulating in times of confidence and speculation with rapidity from hand to hand, will perform a great many more exchanges, and act upon prices with much greater effect than a larger sum in periods of dulness and absence of grounds for speculation: or at times when alarm and want of confidence induce the bankers and possessors generally of monied capitals to increase their reserves, and to withhold their usual advances.

This would equally be the case if the currency were purely metallic; and for short periods, therefore, considerable variations of prices might take place consistently with a uniform amount of money, as, on the other hand, an undisturbed state of prices might prevail consistently with marked variations of the quantity of money.

But although for short intervals the variations of the Bank of England issues afford no certain criterion of the amount of the circulating medium, or of its being in excess or defect, yet for longer periods the regulation by the Bank of England of its issues during the restriction can be shown distinctly to have operated in limiting the other component parts of the circulation along with its own, in such a manner as that the whole quantity of money, or of the circulating medium, should seem not to have exceeded the amount which, but for the circumstances operating upon the exchanges, might have existed in a convertible state of the currency.

The circumstance here alluded to, the proofs of which will be brought forward hereafter, is that, while the amount of the bank issues was from 1797 to 1817 undergoing, with trifling exceptions, a progressive increase, *the exchanges upon every pause from the pressure of extraordinary foreign payments tended to a recovery* ①, and when the pressure had entirely ceased, the exchanges and the price of gold were restored to par, *while the bank circulation was larger in amount than at any preceding period*: thus affording the strongest presumption that the previous increase had not been the cause of the fall of the exchanges; and had not been greater than

---

① The authority of the opinions of Mr. Henry Thornton and Mr F. Horner may be adduced, in proof of the importance of the inference to be derived from the fact of a constant tendency of the exchanges to a recovery, upon every occasion of the restoration of the balance of foreign payments in our favour. Mr. Thornton, in his work on Paper Credit, has the following passage, in a note at page 236.—

"In general it may perhaps be assumed, that an excessive issue of paper has not been the leading cause of a fall in the exchange, *if it afterwards turns out that the exchange is able to recover itself without any material reduction of the quantity of paper.*" And at page 242., when referring to the difficulty of determining the effect of variation in the amount of Bank of England notes on prices, he proceeds to observe, "The perplexities of this subject, being such as I have now described, it naturally occurs to us to reason from the effect to the cause, and to infer a too great issue of paper, when we perceive that there is an excess of the market price above the mint price of gold. But this inference is one which should be very cautiously made, for it is to be borne in mind, that the excess may arise from other causes besides that of a too great emission of paper. A suspension of the foreign demand for British manufactures, or an increase of the British demand for foreign articles, circumstances which may arise when there is no increase of bank paper, are the much more frequent, as well as the more obvious, causes of a fall in our exchange, and therefore also of a high puce of bullion."

In a critique on Mr. Thornton's work, in the first number of the Edinburgh Review, Mr. Horner, the writer of the article, observes, "We have expressed ourselves with unfeigned doubt, with regard to the alleged dependence of the present rate of prices on the state of our paper currency, because it appears to us a problem of which a satisfactory solution has not yet been offered. According to that view of the question indeed, which seems to us the most correct, as well as the most simple, a sufficient answer will be assigned, in the excess of the market price of gold above its mint price shall be found to continue, notwithstanding the permanent restoration of the balance of trade to its accustomed preponderancy in our favour."

The foregoing extracts are from works of which the former was written in 1801, and the latter early in 1802, before either of the authors could have seen that without any diminution of the bank issues, the exchanges and the price of gold were reverting to their par value, when a fresh set of disturbing causes again deranged them.

would have been required if there had been no restriction, but also no extra foreign payments, in order to supply the extended functions of money incidental to an increased population, and to a vast extension of trade and revenue, and generally of pecuniary transactions; — or, in other words, that, in the divergence between the paper and the gold, it was the gold that, by increased demand departed from the paper, and not the paper by increased quantity from the gold.

Admitting such to be the fair inference, it becomes a curious matter of speculation to inquire how, with motives so strong to constant and progressive excess, and under the guidance of maxims and principles so unsound and of such apparently mischievous tendency, as those professed by the governors and some of the directors of the bank in 1810, such moderation and (with some exceptions which will be noticed hereafter), such regularity of issue should, under chances and changes in politics and trade, unprecedented in violence and extent, have been preserved, as that a spontaneous *readjustment between the value of the gold and the paper should have taken place, as it, did without any reduction of their circulation.*

The explanation of the difficulty seems to be this. The rule by which the bank directors professed to be, and were in the main, guided, viz. the demand for discount of good mercantile bills, not exceeding sixty-one days' date, at the rate of five per cent, per annum, did, with the necessary policy of government in periodically reducing the floating debt within certain limits by funding, operate as a principle of limitation upon the total issues of the Bank. And the reason of the rule having so operated, is to be found in the fact, that the market rate of interest *for bills of the description which were alone discountable at the bank*, did not materially, or for any length of time together, exceed the rate of five per cent per annum.

But the bank directors seem to have been unaware of the precise mode of operation by which their rule had the effect of a principle of limitation against great or permanent excess in their circulation; and the explanation by them in their evidence before the bullion committee of 1810 was so unguardedly given as to expose them to the *reductio ab absurdum.*

In the bullion report of 1810 it is stated, "that the bank directors, as well as some of the merchants who were examined, showed a great anxiety to state to the committee a doctrine, of the truth of which they professed themselves to be most thoroughly convinced, that there can be no possible excess in the issue of bank of England paper so long as the advances in which it is issued are made upon the principles which at present guide the conduct of the directors; that is, so long as the discount of mercantile bills is confined to paper of undoubted solidity, arising out of real commercial transactions, and payable at short periods." And the following are extracts of the evidence to that effect. Mr. Whitmore, governor of the Bank: —

Min. p. 91. "The Bank never forces a note in circulation: and there will not remain a note in circulation more than the immediate wants of the public require, for no banker, I presume, will keep a larger stock of bank notes by him than his immediate payments require, as he can at all times procure them."

Min. p. 127. "The bank notes would revert to us if there was a redundancy in circulation, as no one would pay interest for a bank note that lie did not want to make use of."

Mr. Pearse, the governor, stated distinctly his concurrence in the opinion upon this particular point, Min. p. 126. He referred to the manner in which bank notes are issued, resulting from the applications made for discounts to supply the necessary want of bank notes, by which their issue in amount is so controlled that it can never amount to an excess.

He considered "the amount of the bank notes in circulation as being controlled by the occasions of the public for internal purposes;" and, page 157., that "from the manner in which the issue of bank notes is controlled, the public will never call for more than is absolutely necessary for their wants."

The part, however, of the evidence which attracted most notice, and created no little surprise, was the following: —

"Is it your opinion that the same security would exist against any excess in the issues of the bank, if the late of the discount were reduced from 5 to 4 per cent?" Answer by Mr. Whitmore: "The security of an excess would be, I conceive, precisely the same" Mr. Pearse. "I concur in that answer." "If it were reduced to 3 per cent?" Mr. Whitmore: "I conceive there would be no difference, if our practice remained the same as now, of not forcing a note into circulation." Mr. Pearse: "I concur in that answer."

If the governor and deputy governor had added the proviso, that the market rate of interest should be, in the cases supposed, viz. of discounting at four or three per cent, as near to the bank rate *for bills of the prescribed description*, as it then was to 5 per cent, they would have escaped the severe criticisms to which their answers, so unguardedly given, were exposed.

The truth is, that if the market rate of interest for such bills as came within the prescribed rules of the Bank had fluctuated more than it did, and had likewise on an average very materially exceeded the fixed rate of discount, and more especially if it had risen progressively during the whole period of the restriction, not only would the fluctuations in the amount of bank notes have been greater, but there would also have been such a constant tendency to excess through this channel of issue, as would not have admitted of compensation by diminished issues through other channels, and the total increase of the circulation would have been greater than it has proved to be. But it so happened that the market rate of interest for *such bills as came within the bank rules* did not constantly nor materially exceed 5 per cent; nor did it rise progressively through the greater part of the interval of the restriction. The rate of interest for such bills was at its highest long before the termination of the war, as may be inferred from the circumstance, that in the three last years of it the applications for discount at the bank fell off, compared with what they had been for some years before.

The fact of a rate of interest in some degree steady at about 5 per cent, on this description of securities is perfectly compatible with a considerably higher rate for other securities. It is well known that, within these few years past, such bills have occasionally been eagerly sought by bankers and other capitalists at a rate as low as 2 per cent, per annum, while, on mortgages or other securities not immediately or readily convertible, advances were rarely to be had under 4, and frequently not under 5 per cent. On the other hand, during the war, while bills of undoubted solidity, and at short dates, were generally discountable at about 5 per cent, it was difficult to raise money on longer dated bills without a commission, or on mortgages or other securities imperfectly or distantly convertible, on any terms but such as, by annuities, premiums, or other evasions of the usury laws, were equivalent to from 6 to 10 per cent, per annum.

It was, therefore, the coincidence, through the greater part of the interval of the restriction, between the market rate and the bank rate of interest, that prevented the tendency through this medium to progressive increase and irremediable excess of issues, which might have been apprehended if the bank rate had been for any length of time much below the market rate.

The principal causes of the fluctuations in the amount of discounts at the bank down to 1816, besides those which are incidental to the growth and varying exigencies of trade, the greater or less inducement to speculation and occasional derangements of commercial credit, may be traced to the financial operations of Government.

When considerable public loans were negotiated, or when Exchequer Bills, to a larger amount than usual, were issued on the money market, the immediate effect was to create a temporary absorption of floating capital, and, consequently, to occasion a temporary rise in the rate of interest. This would naturally be followed by increased applications for discount at the bank. But in the intervals between loans, or when Exchequer Bills were in less amount than usual, either by Government not issuing so many, or by the bank taking a portion of them off the market, that is, making advances upon them, there would be diminished applications for discount.

SECTION 5 *On the regulation of the bank issues during the restriction*

With reference to the foregoing explanation it is to be observed, that the regulation of the bank issues, when the pressure on the exchanges for foreign payments was unusually great, became inevitably exposed to the alternative of very extensive and sudden variations of the exchanges *or* of the rate of interest.

If the circulation had been regulated, as it ought to have been, by a view to the exchanges, and had been contracted in proportion to the depressing causes acting upon them, the consequent diminution of bank notes would have been felt in a severe pressure on the money market, or, in other words, in a considerable rise in the rate of interest, attended with serious inconvenience, both commercial and financial, the former aggravated by the operation of the mischievous and absurd provisions of the usury law. During the intervals of such forced contraction of the circulation, sales of land and houses, and of fixed property generally, would have been difficult, and exposed to enormous sacrifices, in cases in which it was necessary to realise; and the prices of goods would, of course, have experienced considerable depression in all instances in which the supply at all exceeded the wants for immediate consumption. A fall of the late of interest would have followed upon the cessation of the causes for contraction, and upon the consequent necessary enlargement of the circulation.

On the other hand, a regulation on the principle, if such it can be called, by which the bank directors professed to be guided, disregarding the exchanges, and allowing the amount of the issues to be governed by, and in its turn to act upon, the rate of interest, was calculated, as long as the market rate did not materially exceed the bank rate of discount (for bills coming within the bank rules), to produce a considerable degree of uniformity in the circulation, and to prevent such violent changes in the state of the money market as would other wise have occurred; but it was calculated at the same time to leave the exchanges liable to extraordinary fluctuations, and such as did, in point of fact, occur — fluctuations which exposed all transactions connected with the foreign trade of the country to the greatest possible hazards and losses, in addition to those which were necessarily incidental to a state of war. The great depression of the exchanges added also enormously to the expenses of the war, and to the cost of production of all imported articles, and the depreciation, thence resulting, of the paper compared with its standard, was a flagrant breach of faith, and a national discredit.

In other words, the alternative in the regulation of the bank issues, presented by the extraordinary state of things which prevailed at particular periods of the war, but more especially during the closing years of it, was that of causing great and rapid changes in the quantity of money, with corresponding violent alterations in the rate of interest and in the state of credit, both commercial and financial, or, of preserving a greater degree of uniformity in the amount of the circulation and in the rate of interest, at the expense of very great fluctuations of the exchanges, and their enormous attendant and *preponderating* evils.

If the currency, during the war, had been purely metallic, then, must have been occasionally, and sometimes for a considerable interval, a very great diminution of the quantity of money, caused by the demand for gold for export, to defray the unusually large foreign payments beyond the amount that could, in the ordinary course of trade, be met by increased exports of commodities. But, independently of the interval which, in an uninterrupted state of foreign intercourse, would be required for the adaptation of an increased amount of exports of commodities to meet the demand for *extra* foreign payments, that interval was greatly extended in the latter years of the war, inasmuch as insurmountable impediments are well known to have been opposed to the export of commodities from this country to the Continent of Europe: so that the state of greatly diminished quantity of money, by export of coin, in order to meet the foreign expenditure, would, in a purely metallic currency, have been of considerable duration. And the same would have been the case if the regulation of the bank issues had been guided by the exchanges, and had consequently been such as to have preserved the value of the paper on a level with that of gold.

Thus, for example, in the latter years of the American war, and in the earlier part of the last war with France, prior to the suspension of cash payments, the alternations between contraction and enlargement of the bank issues (and, as far as can be judged, of the whole circulation) were very much greater than during the restriction.

The amount of Bank of England notes was, in February, 1773, 6,037,060*l.*, and in February, 1775, 9,135,930*l.*, being an increase of upwards of 50 per cent.①

---

① The extraordinary degree of contraction to which the Bank was obliged to resort m 1782, and again in 1796, in order to counteract the drain on its treasure, by the pressure on the foreign exchanges, is, independently of its importance in other points of view, deserving of remark, with reference to an opinion entertained by the partisans of the currency theory, namely, that the penalty on melting and exporting the coin, which existed prior to Peel's bill, operated, according to its extent, as a protection to the Bank, in maintaining a larger circulation than it otherwise could have done, or, in the language of that theory, that it operated to that extent, as a relaxation of the standard. (*Evidence before the Agricultural Committee of the House of Commons*, 1836. Third Report, p. 484.) But they overlook the consideration, that in proportion as the penalty on exportation admitted of a greater enlargement of the circulation, before the drain commenced, it rquired so much greater contraction to stop the drain, and still more to bring back the coin when the drain had been established.

As a specimen of the great fluctuation of the exchanges, and of the discrepancy between their indications and the *primafacie* inference presented by the amount of the bank issues, Mr. Van sittart moved the following resolution, among those that were passed in 1811:—

"That during the latter part of, and for some time after, the American war, during the years 1781, 1782, and 1783, the exchange with Hamburg fell from 34*s.* 1*d.* to 31*s.* 5*d.*, being about 8 per cent, and the price of foreign gold rose from 3*l.* 17*s.* 6*d.* to 4*l.* 2*s.* 5*d.* per ounce; and the price of dollars, from 5*s.* $4\frac{1}{2}$*d.* per ounce to 5*s.* $11\frac{1}{4}$*d.*; and that the bank notes in circulation were reduced between March, 1782, and December, 1782, from 9, 160, 000*l.* to 5, 995, 000*l.*, being a diminution

The variations, also, between 1793 and 1797 were very considerable; but these will be more particularly noticed in the subsequent historical sketch.

If, however, the greater exemption from violent changes in the amount of the circulation, during the restriction, than in the periods anterior and subsequent to it, had been still more striking than it is, it would not be a compensation for the manifold evils and dangers attending an inconvertible paper currency.

The observation of the comparative uniformity of the amount of the bank circulation, and of its not having exceeded, during the suspension of cash payments, the quantity which was found consistent eventually with the restoration of its standard value, is not here introduced for the purpose of vindicating the policy which imposed and continued the restriction, but it may fairly be adduced as an answer to the charge of *constant excess*① of

---

of above one third, and continued (with occasional variations) at such reduced rate until December, 1784. And that the exchange with Hamburg lose to 34*s*. 6*d*., and the price of gold fell to 3*l*. 17*s*. 6*d*. and dollars to 5*s*. 1 $\frac{1}{2}$*d*. per ounce, before the 25th of February, 1787, the amount of bank notes being then increased to 8, 688, 000*l*."

① But charges still wider of the truth have been urged against that measure. The most exaggerated statements have been made in general terms, of the violent changes occasioned by it in the quantity of the paper circulation. The following specimen of such charges is taken from a publication on "Corn and Currency", by Sir James Graham, which attracted considerable notice in its day: —

"Mr. Pitt, when be introduced his bold measure of the bank restriction, which rendered the paper of the Bank of England no longer convertible into cash on demand, and imposed no limit on its issues beyond the will of the Government, or the caprice of the Directors, declared, with prophetic warning, (*Hansard's Paihamentary Debates*, vol. xxxnt. p. 71) 'that, if the country be once surcharged with paper, it would have as ruinous effects as would be produced by lessening the quantity of the paper circulation, a sudden diminution of the paper currency would prove the most violent shock which the trade and credit of this country could receive.'"

issue, by which, in the arguments quoted, the whole period of the restriction is asserted to have been characterised, the term excess not being confined to mean an amount beyond what could, under the extraordinary circumstances, be maintained, consistently with the *par value*, but such an increase and excess as would, *under ordinary circumstances*, have entailed depreciation.

SECTION 6 *On the effect of the bank restriction in raising the prices of commodities*

It may be asked, whether, if it be admitted that there was no excess during the restriction of the amount of circulation beyond what might have been maintained, but for the pressure of foreign payments, the restriction can be charged with any part of the nominal rise of prices, which prevailed during the suspension of cash payments? The answer would necessarily be in the negative, as far as relates to depreciation attributable to an increase in the quantity of money. But the restriction admitted of a greater depression of the exchanges, than could have occurred in a convertible state of the paper. And as the depression of the exchanges constituted an element of increased cost of all imported commodities, and thus, directly or indirectly, affected the price of a considerable proportion of native

---

"Notwithstanding this sound prediction from the author of the measure, his successors, who profess to tread in his steps, and to venerate his name, have despised the warning, have rejected the admonition, and applied the power precisely in the two modes which Mr. Pitt thought most dangerous. 'The country *has been* surcharged with paper', —there *has been* a 'sudden diminution of the currency', not once, but repeatedly, and exactly as Mr. Pitt foretold, each violent change, in either direction, has shaken to then foundations 'the trade and credit of the country.'" p. 28.

productions, the restriction may be considered to have been the condition without which so much of the rise of prices as was attributable to increased cost by adverse exchanges could not have occurred. Besides that, it is the general tendency of a fall of the exchange to raise the prices of exportable commodities.

It is in this sense only, if, even in this sense, the word can be correctly so applied, that the bank restriction can be said to have been the *cause* of so much of the advance of prices may be measured by the depression of the exchanges below the point to which, previous to the restriction, they had, under the pressure of extra foreign payments in former wars, occasionally fallen. ① But the variations of the exchanges, taking them in the aggregate, and allowing for partial discrepancies of occasional quotations arising from impediments to exchange operations, and from hazards attending the transmission of bullion, allowing also for the difference arising from the varying proportions between silver and gold, will be found to correspond in the main with the variations in the price of gold. There would, therefore, be little difference in the result, whether the price of gold or the exchanges were taken as the measure of the utmost advance of prices during the restriction, beyond the rate at which, *ceteris paribus*, they could have been maintained in a convertible state of the currency. The same reasoning will apply as to the measure of the utmost fall of prices that can be ascribed to a return to the convertibility of the paper. But the price of gold is the simplest and clearest expression of the result of the quotations of all the different exchanges. On this ground, therefore, as well as

① During the American war, the exchange on Hamburg was occasionally, and for some length of time, at about 31*s*. 6*d*.. And it is only, therefore, for the fall below this late that the bank restriction is accountable.

because the price of gold is, by the definition of the standard, the measure of the depreciation specifically predicated of bank notes, the explanation about to be given of the causes of the great variations of prices, in the period which is to come under examination, is to be considered as subject always to an allowance (as a maximum, however) of the difference between paper and gold. But an admission to this extent, which is beyond what, in point of fact, is likely to be found necessary, is utterly insufficient, according to the currency theory, to account for the great rise of prices during the restriction, and for the great fall subsequently; the rise being, by that theory, ascribed to an excessive enlargement of the issues, which the bank was, by the restriction, enabled and induced to make and maintain; and the full being attributed to the contraction which, by the same theory, is considered to have been necessarily effected us a preparation and means for the restoration of cash payments.

SECTION 7 *On the alleged invariable connection of increase of price with the bank restriction, and on the effect of the near approach of the termination of the restriction producing a fall of prices greatly exceeding the difference between paper and gold*

Proceeding on the assumption of the constant excess of the issues of the Bank of England, and of the country banks, the concluding allegations, among the arguments which have been stated in support of the doctrine of ultra depreciation, are, "that the *constant and invariable* connection of increase of price with the bank restriction is a forcible proof of such a relation, as that of cause and effect subsisting between the two phænomena; and that the near approach of the termination of that restriction had produced a fall of prices, greatly exceeding the difference between paper and gold; thus still further corroborating that connection, and proving, almost demonstratively, that the prices from 1797 to 1814 were, to a certain degree, artificial, and that the comparison of paper with gold did not afford a test of the real amount of the fall in the value of our currency." Here it is evidently meant to imply. that the near approach of the termination of the restriction, and, still more, the actual passing of Peel's bill, had been the *originating and the chief, if not only, cause* of the fall of prices. And of course, if the mere removal of the restriction was the chief cause of the fall, the restriction must be supposed to have been the chief, if not the only, cause of the previous rise.

It appears to me that a total absence of knowledge of many facts bearing upon the question, a great misapprehension of others, and a general confusion of the order of time, in which the principal circumstances in connection with prices, and with the state of the circulation, are supposed to have taken place, can alone account for the prevalence of opinions so erroneous as those involved in the above propositions; opinions which, destitute as they are of any real foundation, are almost universally prevalent.

It is the purpose, therefore, of the following historical sketch to lay before the reader the most prominent of the facts, which are calculated to elucidate the causes of the great variations of prices from the close of 1792 to the present time; and as the result of the view, which it is thus proposed to take, I expect to be able to show —

1. That there were circumstances during the period under consideration, affecting the cost of production, and the casual supply relatively to the rate

of consumption of the principal articles, the fluctuations of which are in question, sufficient to account for the variations of prices, independently of any supposed influence of the currency, beyond the degree indicated by the difference between paper and gold.

2. That the theory which supposes the disengagement and reabsorption of gold by this country, arising from the restriction and the resumption of cash payments, to have sensibly affected bullion prices is independently of the inadequateness of the supposed cause as has already been shown not borne out by a reference to the periods in which, or to the circumstances under which, the great alterations of price took place.

3. That the alterations in the amount of the circulation did not occur in such order of time with reference to the variations of prices, as to justify the assignment of such a relation as that of cause and effect; for that in point of fact in the majority of instances the alleged effects preceded the supposed causes.

4. That the increase of the bank circulation during the restriction, although excessive, as being beyond what could, under the pressure of foreign payments, be maintained consistently with the preservation of the par of the exchanges, and of the price of gold, was not greater than it is probable would, in an undisturbed state of politics and trade, have been required to carry on the greatly extended pecuniary transactions of the country at bullion prices on then ordinary level with those of other countries. The proof, or at least the strongest possible presumption to this effect being, that upon every cessation of the pressure of foreign payments the exchanges tended to a recovery, and were, when those payments finally ceased, restored to par, not only without any reduction of bank paper, but coincidently with an increase of it.

5. That the growth and contraction of country bank notes greatly beyond, and within, the extent to which they served for ordinary local purposes, were governed during the restriction by the same general causes as operated before and since. They expanded under circumstances favouring speculation, and a rise of prices, and became contracted under the opposite circumstances.

6. That a contraction of the currency was not a necessary consequence of, or, in point of fact, produced by, Peel's bill, or by any anterior preparation on the part of the bank for cash payments; for that, according to the rules by which the bank regulated its issues, there is every reason to believe that, without any reference whatever to that bill, or to any anterior preparation, the circulation of Bank of England notes and coin together, constituting the basis of the currency, would have been neither more nor less than it actually proved to be.

PART IV

HISTORICAL SKETCH OF PRICES, AND OF THE STATE OF THE CIRCULATION, FROM 1792 TO 1837

CHAPTER Ⅰ
INTRODUCTION

The whole question of the degree in which the causes that have been severally assigned as accounting for the great variations of price in the period which is to come under consideration, viz. from the commencement of 1793 to the present time, mainly rests upon the sequence observable between prices, and the circumstances connected with them in the relation of cause and effect. It is absolutely essential in this view to trace the events in strict connection with prices. In a former work of mine on prices, a cursory glance only was taken of the state of things in relation to prices at particular periods, without, as I have since perceived, a sufficiently distinct arrangement of the whole series of them in chronological order. It is my present purpose, accordingly, to give them in that order. But with that view it is necessary to make a division into points, upon which the attention may rest, or, in other words, into epochs, through which the several sets of prices and circumstances may be traced distinctly. Shorter intervals, annual periods, for instance, would, properly speaking, be of the nature of annals, and would weary and distract the attention by the inevitable minuteness of the details, besides that an interval so short would not admit of continuous observation of the whole, or even of the greater part of the phases, within which the changes and alternations between periods of confidence and discredit, of the spirit of enterprise and despondency, have revolved. On the other hand, intervals of ten years would be too long for the purpose, as they would embrace too many particulars to admit easily of such arrangement and classification as are essential to the formation of any clear conclusions. Not only, therefore, as a medium between these extremes, but because, in point of fact, it so happens that intervals of about five years do afford resting-places, at each of which an examination may conveniently take place of the rise and progress, and in many instances of the termination, of a series of events, all tending to throw light on each other, and to bring out a legitimate conclusion, it is here proposed to adopt a division of the time which is to pass in review into intervals of about five years.

The first division will, however, most conveniently embrace six years, viz. from the commencement of 1793 to the close of 1798; and the period ending 1822 will comprise only four years, for reasons which will be obvious when those epochs come under consideration.

CHAPTER Ⅱ
ON THE STATE OF PRICES, AND OF THE CIRCULATION, FROM THE COMMENCEMENT OF 1793 TO THE CLOSE OF 1798

The commencement of 1793 is among the most memorable in the annals of this country, and of Europe, and indeed of the civilised world. It was in February of that year that the war with France, which, with the intermission of a few months, lasted for upwards of twenty years, was declared. ①

There had been immediately preceding that event a great revulsion and derangement of commercial credit, not only in this country, but in the principal trading cities of the Continent of Europe.

By some persons it was supposed, that the declaration of war had materially contributed to produce the derangement of credit. Thus Sir Francis Baring, in a pamphlet published in 1797, observed:—

"A circumstance which very materially contributed to produce the distress of 1793 was the sudden unexpected declaration of war. That dreadful calamity is usually preceded by some indication which enables the commercial community to make preparation. On this occasion the short notice rendered the least degree of general preparation impossible, and

① The preparations for war on both sides were made in January, but the actual declaration of war was made by France against this country on the 1st of February, 1793.

which may be ascertained by the prices of stocks in the preceding month of October and various collateral authorities."

Notwithstanding this deservedly high authority for the supposition, that the breaking out of the war had contributed in a considerable degree to the memorable derangement of commercial credit, which occurred about that time; I am disposed, both from my own recollection, and from all that I have been able to collect by research, to doubt whether the war had much influence in the origin of the discredit, although it can hardly have failed of operating in aggravation of the main causes. These seem to have been pre-existing in a great and undue extension of the system of credit and paper circulation, not only in the internal trade and banking of this country, but in the commercial transactions of the principal cities of the Continent of Europe, and in the United States of America.

The commercial failures both here and on the Continent of Europe, and in America, began in the autumn of 1792, while the price of the funds was still comparatively high, 3 per cent. Consols being at 90 in September, and at 88 in November of that year, and while, therefore, it could not be supposed, that the alarm of impending hostilities could have had much effect. Nor did it appear from the character of the mercantile failures which occurred, and which proved in most instances to have been insolvencies of some standing, how war, or the apprehension of war, could have produced their embarrassment. At the same time it must be admitted, that the breaking out or the war, although apparently not an originating cause, must necessarily have added to whatever were the pre-existing causes of derangement, not only by the increased rate of interest occasioned by the loan for the purposes of the war, but by the inevitable disturbance of some of the channels of demand.

There is a very prevalent impression, that the origin of speculations and high prices is to be dated from the commencement of the war in 1793. The fact, however, is, that there was a very general fall of prices, from the close of 1792 to the commencement of 1794. On looking over the Table of prices, it will be seen that there were very few commodities which were not lower at the close of 1792, and at different periods in 1793 and 1794, than they had been at the commencement of 1792. And the real fill was still greater than the apparent one; because the cost of production of all imported commodities was greater by the difference of freights and insurance, after the breaking out of the war.

This fall of prices does not seem to have been a direct or obvious consequence of the war: it was rather the effect of a recoil from extensive speculations, which had their origin two or three years before, connected with the extensive circulation of mercantile paper already alluded to. One of the chief causes of those speculations seems to have arisen on the ground of apprehended scarcity of colonial produce in consequence of the revolution in St. Domingo, which at that time constituted the largest source of supply of sugar and coffee to the Continent of Europe. Other grounds were afforded by the unsettled aspect of politics. As usual, in times of confidence and tendency to speculation, many articles, for the rise of which there was no sufficient ground of actual or apprehended scarcity, participated in the advance. But the rise proved to have been greater than the occasion justified, and prices fell. It may be observed, however, that as, during the previous rise, there had been no manifestation of extravagance of advance in any one article, so, in the fall, the number of articles to which it applied was extensive; but to none did it apply in a very marked degree. The lowest point of depression of the prices of such articles as had risen most between 1790 and 1792, seems to have been reached in 1794.

It was not till the latter part of 1794 and the commencement of 1795 that circumstances arose, which were calculated to create a great disturbance of prices, both of coin and of other leading articles of consumption. In proceeding to notice in some detail and consecutively the great variations in prices, which henceforth occurred, those of corn, as bearing most, according to general opinion, on the doctrine of depreciation, will be more particularly referred to and dwelt upon. Those of other commodities will be noticed only when under the influence of extraordinary circumstances, and more especially in connection with, and illustrative of, the influence of the circulating medium, the state of which will be the subject of consideration at the end of each interval.

The general character of the seasons, as to productiveness, will be noticed with more or less of detail, according as they may appeal to have been attended with less or more of influence on prices.

SECTION 1 *On the seasons in connection with the prices of provisions, from 1793 to the close of 1798*

"Summer was a very dry one, in which, though the wheat was moderate, the spring crops generally proved deficient."

The quotation of the Windsor market, which at Ladyday, 1793, had been 54*s*. 1*d*., fell at Michaelmas following to 45*s*.. And the ports, which had been open by proclamation in the spring, were shut again at the low duty in June of that year. ①

On the seasons of 1794 and 1795, the results of which form so prominent a feature in the history of the Cora Trade, it is necessary to dwell somewhat more in detail. Arthur Young, writing in 1795, says of the former,

"In the last summer, 1794, the wheat turned out, very *unexpectedly* to many growers, a fading produce; the drought in many parts of England parched the spring corn to that degree, that I believe the leguminous crops have scarcely returned even the seed committed to the ground for them."

"Here we find that there have been three seasons in succession unfavourable to the production of some kinds of grain, the dearness of all is a natural consequence."

The spring of 1794 was the most forward, and the summer was the most uninterruptedly hot and dry, of which I have been able to meet with any record: as, however, the degree of deficiency arising from the excessive drought and scanty crops of 1794, and the want of a surplus from 1793, had not, in consequence of the harvest being unusually forward (the cutting of wheat having been begun in the south and midland districts, by the middle of July, and the crops mostly secured by the end of that month), and the wheat having been brought in fine condition and very

① According to the Gazette return of the averages for England and Wales, there does not appear to have been so great a fall in the price of wheat immediately following the harvest of 1793, namely, from 51*s*. to 47*s*., but the discrepancy may be explained partly by the very incorrect manner in which the averages were taken and partly by the circumstance that the harvest weather of 1792 had been wet, while that of 1793 was dry, which would account for a greater difference than usual, between the better wheat and that of average quality in the spring of 1793. Notwithstanding, however, the objections which, as regards correctness, apply to the average returns, they will henceforth be referred to in preference to the Eton Tables for two reasons: the one is that the currency controversy has proceeded chiefly upon a reference to those returns; and the other is, that these admit of occasionally introducing into the same line of comparison the prices of spring corn.

early to the market, been sufficiently appreciated, the price did not rise soon enough to check the consumption; and it was not till the winter and spring following, that the insufficiency of the stock on hand, to meet the average rate of consumption, was discovered.

The winter of 1794-1795 had set in remarkably early, and proved to be of extraordinary severity and inclemency, so that independently of the increased consumption, thence arising, of the stock of dry food, apprehensions were justly entertained of injury to the growing crop. A very general alarm arose, and the average prices advanced as follows: —

Years	Wheat	Barley	Oats
1 Jan, 1795,	55*s*. 7*d*.	34*s*. 2*d*.	21*s*. 11*d*.
1 July, do.	77*s*. 2*d*.	41*s*. 10*d*.	27*s*. 8*d*.

Government had, early in 1795, and indeed, for some time before, taken the alarm at the indications of impending dearth, and adopted some extraordinary measures of precaution. All neutral ships bound with corn to France were seized and brought into this country, and their cargoes paid for, with an ample profit to the proprietors. This measure was adopted with a double view, of relief to ourselves and distress to the enemy, there being still greater scarcity in France than in this conntry. This was done because it was apprehended that our own merchants would be deterred from purchasing so freely as was desirable, by the great advance of prices, which had taken place in the North of Europe, in consequence of large purchases for account of the French government.

Of the policy of this measure, as interfering with the ordinary course and true principles of trade, Mr. Pitt spoke doubtingly; but rested the justification of it upon the extraordinary and alarming character of the emergency. Sir Francis Baring also offered a hesitating opinion in justification of the measure. Notwithstanding all these precautionary measures for obtaining a foreign supply, and the inducements held out by an unprecedentedly high price in this country, such was the scarcity in the north of Europe and in America①, and such the competition of the government of France with ours, that the importation in the whole of the year 1795, after deducting small casual exports, did not quite reach three hundred thousand quarters of wheat.

The spring of 1795 was very cold and backward, the summer was wet and stormy, and the harvest consequently unusually late. Under these threatening circumstances the prices experienced a continued advance, the average for England and Wales having reached 108*s.* 4*d.* in August of that year. The weather, however, having cleared up towards the latter part of August, and having proved fine throughout September, so as to admit of securing the whole of the crop in good order, the markets experienced a decline, the average price in October having got down to 76*s.* 9*d.*. But the original deficiency then manifested itself, and prices rose again considerably before the close of the year; on the meeting of parliament, 29th of October, 1795, the king in his speech alluded to the dearth in the following terms: —

"I have observed for some time past with the greatest anxiety, the very high price of grain; and that anxiety is increased by the apprehension that the produce of the wheat harvest, in the present year, may not have been such as effectually to relieve my people from the difficulties with which

① In the United States of America the crops of wheat, in 1795, were as deficient as they were in Europe. The deficiency was mainly ascribed to the ravages of an insect called the Hessian Fly.

they have had to contend."

And concluded with an assurance of his Majesty's hearty concurrence in whatever regulations the wisdom of Parliament might adopt.

Animated discussions took place on the nature and causes, and extent of the dearth, and on the remedies to be applied for the alleviation of its effects. On the 3rd of November, the Chancellor of the Exchequer moved, that a select committee be appointed, for inquiring into the circumstances of the present scarcity, and the best means of remedying it. As usual on such occasions, there was a disposition to account for the high price of provisions by the assignment of any but the simple, sufficient, and true cause, casual deficiency of supply from the visitation of two very unproductive crops. Monopoly[①], forestalling[②], and regrating were among the causes assigned. The war, however, was very generally considered as

---

① The following extract from among the speeches in the House of Commons may serve as a specimen to this effect: —

Debate 3rd of November, 1795, Mr Lechmere said, "We had, perhaps, had as plentiful a harvest as the great Author of all blessings ever gave us." "One of the great causes of the present distress he took to be the monopoly of farms."

② The charge of Lord Kenyon, at the Assizes for Salop, in 1795, will afford a specimen of the prejudices which extensively prevailed at that period as to the influence of unfair practices in raising the prices of provisions. —"For the sake of common humanity I trust it is untrue. Gentlemen, you ought to be the champions against this hydraheaded monster. T is your duty as justices to see justice done to the country. In your respective districts, as watchmen, be on your guard. I am convinced, from my knowledge of you, that I have no need to point out your duty in this case; and though the act of Edw. VI. be repealed (whether wisely or unwisely I take not upon me to say), yet it still exists an offence at common law, coeval with the constitution; and be assured, gentlemen, whoever is convicted before me (and I believe I may answer for the rest of my brethren), when the sword of justice is drawn, it shall not be sheathed until the full vengeance of the law is inflicted on them, neither purse nor person shall prevent it." — *Annals of Agriculture for* 1795, vol. xxv. p.111.

having had great influence in the rise of prices. ①

With regard to the extent of the deficiency, Lord Sheffield, in the House of Commons, December, 1795, stated it to be from $\frac{1}{7}$ to $\frac{1}{5}$ without any old stock, and without any prospect of adequate supply from abroad. Various remedies were proposed; that which was mainly relied upon and finally adopted, was an act, granting a bounty of from 16*s*. to 20*s*. the quarter, according to the quality, on wheat, and 6*s*. the cwt. on flour from the south of Europe, till the quantity should amount to four hundred thousand quarters; and from America, till it should amount to five hundred thousand quarters; and 12*s*. to 15*s*. from any other part of Europe, till it should amount to five hundred thousand quarters; and 8*s*. to 10*s*. after it exceeded that quantity, to continue till the 30th September, 1796.

Among the minor measures was a sort of self-denying ordinance②, by which the members of both houses of parliament bound themselves to reduce the consumption of bread in their households by one third, and to

---

① Mr. Fox said, "The war certainly has had a most decided effect, so far as it has tended to increase the consumption, to diminish the production, and to preclude the possibility of obtaining supplies, which might have been drawn from other quarters."—*Parliamentary Debates*, vol. xxxiii. p. 239.

It was with reference to this opinion that Mr. Burke observed, "As to the operation of the war in causing the scarcity of provisions, I understand that Mr. Pitt has given a particular answer to it; but I do not think it worth powder and shot." (*Thoughts and Details on Scarcity*, p. 33) As the seasons of 1794 and 1795 form so important a feature in the general impression of the high prices ascribed to the war and the restriction, and as those seasons were in every way remarkable, an extract, descriptive of them, from the publication by Mr. Burke here quoted will be found inserted in the Appendix.

② "Engagement by such members as may choose to sign the same: —"

"To reduce the consumption of wheat in the families subscribing such engagement by at least one third of the usual quantity consumed in ordinary times, and to recommend the same in their neighbourhoods. Agreement to be in force till fourteen days after the commencement of next session of Parliament, unless the average price of wheat should, in the mean time, be reduced to 8*s*. per bushel." — *Parliamentary History*, Dec. 11. 1795.

recommend, among those whom they could influence, a similar reduction.①

The prices of all other provisions having risen in a greater or less proportion to wheat, and there being a very general apprehension of a continuance of the scarcity, it had become manifestly impossible for the working classes to subsist on their ordinary wages. It was partly from a conviction to this effect, and partly in consequence of the tendency to disturbance and riots among the agricultural labourers, that the allowance system was at this time introduced. There was at the same time a general acquiescence on the part of employers in the necessity of some advance of wages, which, however, when conceded, bore still a very inadequate proportion to the increased price of the necessaries of life. The distress②, accordingly, of the working and poorer classes was very severe, and the privations of the classes immediately above them, and generally of all classes depending on limited money incomes, were great. The whole period, indeed, of this memorable dearth, was one of much suffering to the bulk of the community. But it was a time of great prosperity to the landed interests, that is, to the landlords who were raising, or had the prospect of soon raising, their rents; and to the farmers, who were realising enormous gains pending the currency of their leases. The following extract from an article by Arthur Young, in the Annals of Agriculture, for 1796, will serve as a practical illustration of the principle which I have had occasion to

① It was as one of the means of diminishing the consumption of wheat on the occasion or this scarcity, that the notable hair-powder tax was imposed a measure which hastened the discontinuance of that strange fashion.

② In a reference to this, period, in the Annual Register for 1796, it is observed that "the scarcity was woefully felt by the poorer sort, several of whom perished for want." p. 9.

notice; viz., of the effect of a deficiency in raising the price greatly beyond the ratio of the defect, and of the consequent larger sum distributed among the growers than could be derived from medium or abundant crops.

"The average price of wheat for the twelve months, from May 1795 to April 1796, has been, on an average, in England and Wales, 10*s*. 7*d*. per bushel, and that of barley 4*s*. 9*d*.. Now the price for twelve years, ending 1791, was for wheat 5*s*. 10*d*., and for barley 3*s*. 3*d*.. For the year above described, therefore, the price has exceeded that average 4*s*. 9*d*. per bushel for wheat, and 1*s*. 6*d*. for bailey. Let us suppose the annual consumption of wheat to be 8, 701, 875 quarters, and that of barley 10, 545, 000 quarters; and, further, that the deficiency of the crop on the average, of the two years, so far as they affect the period in question, has amounted, in wheat, to one fifth, and that the barley has, on an average of the two crops, been a medium: in this case there would have been consumed —

Of wheat 6, 961, 500qrs. the extra price on which at 4*s*. 9*d*. the bushel, or 38s the quarter, is 13, 226, 849*l*.

Of barley, 10, 545, 000qrs. at 1*s*. 6*d*. per bushel, or 12*s*. the quarter

– – – 6, 327, 000*l*.

– – – 19, 553, 819*l*.

If, therefore, these data are just, and they are ventured merely as calculation on uncertain foundations, the farmers have received in these two articles only near 20, 000, 000*l*. sterling beyond the deficiency of the crop, supposing the deficiency to be one fifth, which is a very great one, and without adding a word on the price of meat or any other article." — Vol. xxvi. p. 469.

The dearth of provisions, and the apprehensions of further scarcity, readied their height in the spring of 1796, the average price of wheat having advanced to 100*s*.. When, however, the influence of the Bounty, in addition to the encouragement of the markets in this country, was ascertained to be effectual in preparations for a large importation, the prices of corn began to give way, and the fall was hastened by the mildness of the season, the winter of 1795-1796 having been one of the warmest, as that of 1794-1795 had been one of the coldest upon record.

The harvest of 1796 was abundant, and tolerably well secured. This, with the addition of an importation of upwards of 800, 000 quarters, reduced the average price of wheat before the close of the year, to 57*s*. 3*d*.; and the fall continued, progressively, till the summer of 1797, when the average ranged between 49*s*. and 50*s*..

In 1797, the spring was backward, the summer variable, and rather cold, and the harvest wet and stormy, and the general reports of the crops unfavourable, both as to quality and quantity. In consequence of the apprehensions entertained of injury from the weather, the prices of wheat advanced from an average of 50*s*. in June, to 60*s*. in October. But, notwithstanding that all that could be ascertained of the crops proved the existence of some deficiency of quantity, as well as inferiority of quality, the price declined again by the close of the year to an average of 52*s*. 9*d*., and in February, 1798, to 49*s*. 10*d*.. This decline was apparently occasioned by the surplus of the former year, combined with a further importation of 407, 242 quarters of wheat, in 1797. It is consequently clear, that if this year's crops had been abundant, the fall of price would have been more considerable.

The season of 1798 proved to be moderately productive. The summer was dry and warm, the harvest forward, and the crops secured in good order. The spring crops had suffered from the heat and drought. The wheat crop was the best, although not considered to be large; but coming early to market, the average price which in August had been 51*s*. 3*d*. , fell in November of that year to a fraction below 48*s*. .

The following statement of the average prices will show the subsidence of the prices of corn at the close of 1798, to nearly the level of what they had been at the close of 1792—

Years.	Wheat.	Barley.	Oats.
1792. Dec.	47*s*. 2*d*.	29*s*. 10*d*.	18*s*. 6*d*.
1798. Nov.	47*s*. 10*d*.	29*s*. 0*d*.	19*s*. 10*d*.

So that after six years of war, involving a greatly increasing expenditure, defrayed by loans, much larger towards the later than at the earlier period, we see the prices of corn, after having been elevated by scarcity, obviously arising from the seasons, falling, upon the return of only moderate abundance, to the level whence they had risen.

SECTION 2 *On the prices of commodities from 1793 to 1798*

While the prices of provisions had been undergoing such great variations from the vicissitudes of the seasons, the prices of other articles experienced were also an extraordinary fluctuation.

There had been, as has been noticed, a general fall of prices at the commencement of the war, and they continued at a comparatively low range through the greater part of 1794. In 1795, several circumstances combined to occasion a range of high prices, besides those of provisions. Two successive bad seasons on the Continent of Europe as well as in this country had rendered all European agricultural produce scarce and dear, such as linseed and rapeseed, olive oil, and tallow. Silk in Italy and the vintages in France had suffered from the inclemency of the season. There was an extraordinary competition between our government and that of France in the purchase of naval stores in the north of Europe, thus greatly raising the prices of hemp, flax, iron, and timber. The prospect of a war with Spain, which broke out in the year following, affected several descriptions of Spanish produce. Colonial produce, of which a scarcity consequent on the failure of the supplies from St. Domingo was now generally felt throughout Europe, experienced a fresh rise. All these classes of commodities continued to rise through 1795 and part of 1796, Those which were affected by the seasons in Europe, fell in the latter part of 1796, and in 1797, although from the increased cost of production, and in the case of naval and military stores from the increasing demand, not to their former level.

The following are specimens of the fluctuation of this class of articles: —

	1793-1794	1795-1796	1796-1797
Ashes, per cwt. –	24*s*. to 31*s*.	60*s*. to 70*s*.	39*s*. to 55*s*.
Flax, per ton –	28*l*. – 32*l*.	54*l*. – 57*l*.	44*l*. – 45*l*.
Hemp, do. –	22*l*. – 23*l*.	58*l*. – 59*l*.	32*l*. – 34*l*.
Foreign non, do.	12*l*. – —	22*l*. – 5*s*.	19*l*. – 15*s*.
Linseed, per qr. –	35*s*. – 40*s*.	60*s*. – 63*s*.	30*s*. – 35*s*.
Oil, Gallipoli, per ton –	42*l*. – 46*l*.	70*l*. – 71*l*.	60*l*. – 63*l*.
Rice, per cwt. –	15*s*. – 16*s*.	41*s*. – 43*s*.	15*s*. *to* 16*s*.
Tallow, do. –	38*s*. – 39*s*.	78*s*. – 80*s*.	46*s*. – 47*s*.
Timber, per load	48*s*. – —	80*s*. – —	50*s*. – 55*s*.

But a very important class of articles, viz., coffee, sugar, indigo, pepper, cotton, cochineal, and other articles of colonial produce, which had begun to rise in 1795, continued to advance till the close of 1798, insomuch that, at the end of the latter year (and in the first two or three months of 1799) they attained a greater height than at any subsequent period between that and 1814, when the great speculative exports to the Continent took place. The following are some of the instances of the rise of prices which the leading articles of colonial produce experienced from different periods in 1793 and 1794 to the close of 1798, and the three months following: —

	1793 – 1794		1798 – 1799	
Coffee, Jamaica, per cwt.	77*s*.	to 95*s*.	185*s*.	to 196*s*.
Sugar, Muscovado, do –	32*s*.	– 58*s*.	62*s*.	– 87*s*.
—, East India, white	60*s*.	– 70*s*.	96*s*.	– 115*s*.
Cotton, bowed Georgia. per lb. –	1*s*. 1*d*.	– 1*s*. 4*d*.	3*s*. 6*d*.	– 4*s*. 6*d*.
Cochineal – – –	12*s*.	– 12*s*.	3*d*.	– 51*s*.
Indigo, E. I. superior –	7*s*. 6*d*.	– 9*s*. 6*d*.	11*s*.	– 13*s* 9*d*.
Pepper, black, per 1b. –	13*d*.		22*d*.	
Logwood, per ton –	6*l*.	– 8*l*.	48*l*.	– 50*l*.
Tobacco, per 1b. –	3*d*.	– 5*d*.	$11\frac{1}{2}d$.	– 16*d*.

This enormous advance of prices of a class of articles involving a vast amount of capital, had its origin, or at least received its main impulse, in 1796. And the rise continued almost uninterrupted through 1797 and 1798, notwithstanding a progressive coincident rise of the exchanges which in the latter year attained an unprecedented height, that on Hamburg having reached 38*s*.. The demand was chiefly for export to the Continent of Europe, and the principal channel was Hamburg. It is further to be observed, that this large class of articles was rising while corn was falling;

and that they attained at the close of 1798, some a little less, and some a great deal more than 100 per cent, above their previous rate, while corn had fallen 50 per cent below the rate which it had attained in 1796.

I have been the more disposed to dwell upon this remarkable feature of the state of prices in the interval under consideration; because I am quite satisfied that, among those who recollect or have heard of those enormous prices of colonial produce, there is a vague impression that, as they occurred two years after the bank restriction, and in the height of the war, they were the consequence of one or the other.

That these high prices were not the consequence of any enlargement, but were in spite of a great contraction of the basis of the currency, will be seen presently; and it is quite clear that they were not caused by a demand arising out of the expenditure of our government, seeing that the demand was chiefly from abroad, and they were not connected with war on the Continent, seeing that the powers of the Continent were at peace from the spring of 1797 till 1799. The negative of the influence of war applies, however, only to the supposition of any extra consumption or demand thence arising to account for the high prices. That the effect of the war was to obstruct supplies and to increase the cost of production, if it were only by the difference of freight and insurance, has been already stated, and is in this, and all other instances, to be considered as being implied. But this is not the sense to which the supposed influence of war on prices divested of taxation is commonly confined.

Thus, we have seen that at the close of 1798 (and this is the reason for having extended the epoch to six instead of five years), while corn and provisions generally, and some other articles of European produce, had, as a consequence of two remarkably unproductive seasons, risen upwards of

100 per cent in 1795 and 1796, and had subsided at the termination of the interval to the level from whence they had risen, another and a most important class of commodities reached, by the end of 1798, to an enormous and unprecedented height, and were then much higher than during any subsequent period of the war.

SECTION 3 *Bank circulation, 1793 to 1798*

In the preceding sketch of prices they have been considered without reference to the state of the circulation.

To what extent, if at all, the great fluctuations were influenced by the currency, will appear in a clearer point of view by taking a survey of the state of the circulation during the whole of the interval which has been under consideration, than if detached references had been made to it in the progress of the examination of the circumstances which immediately affected the prices through the medium of supply and demand; and this mode of examining, at the close of each interval or epoch, the regulation of the bank issues, and the general state of the circulation, during such interval, will be adopted in the succeeding epochs.

There has before been occasion to observe, that at the commencement of 1798, the general circulation was greatly deranged by the failures of many of the country banks, and of many considerable mercantile establishments. The commercial discredit and distress thence arising, surpassed in degree and extent of suffering any of which there had been any previous example. The causes of the mercantile failures and consequent commercial discredit, have been before noticed. They were not confined to this country but were connected with a very general excess of the circulation of mercantile paper, and a great prevalence of the spirit of speculation in the principal trading towns of the continent of Europe, and in America. But the peculiar feature, as related to this country, was in the failure of an extraordinary number of country banks①: the more extraordinary, as the previous existence of such numbers of them, and such an extent of circulation, seems hardly to have attracted notice, or to have come in any way within the knowledge of the public. In this, as in subsequent instances, the growth of the country circulation followed the extension of agriculture, and trade, and manufactures. It is observed by Mr. Henry Thornton, in his work, published in 1802, on Paper Credit, that "a great increase of country banks took place during the time which intervened between the American war and that of the French revolution, and chiefly in the latter part of it; a period during which the population, the agriculture, and the trade of the country had advanced very considerably."

The circumstances of the period following the termination of the American war were, doubtless, very favourable to the extension of that description of circulation.

After the forcible and extraordinary contraction which the Bank of England had resorted to in 1783 and 1784, with a view, in which it succeeded, to stop the drain of its treasure, which had been reduced to the lowest ebb, there was a steady and uninterrupted influx of gold into its

① The following is an extract from the list of Bankruptcies: —

		Total number of commissions.	Against country bankers.
1791	-	769	1
1792	-	934	1
1793	-	1956	26

Appendix to the Report of the Lords' Committee on the Resumption of cash payments, 1819.

coffers during the five following years; and the basis of the currency was necessarily increased by the issue of bank notes in payment for the gold. The circulation, accordingly, of the bank, which had ranged at a little more than 6,000,000*l*. between 1783 and 1785, had in 1789 reached 11,121,800*l*., and its bullion amounted to 8,645,860*l*.[①] This influx of bullion, and the consequent increase of the bank issues, had the natural effect, as it was in a period of confidence, of reducing the rate of interest; and the fall of the market rate of interest, while the bank did not lower its rate of discount, enabled the country banks to extend their issues in advances and discounts, which, if the current market rate of interest had been higher, would have been, in part at least, applied for at the Bank. The discounts at the Bank, which in 1785 had been 4,973,926*l*., were reduced in 1789 to 2,035,901*l*.

There was another circumstance which had, probably, more than any other single cause, contributed to the growth of the country circulation. It is well known that rising prices of corn and farming stock, and the consequently improved state and credit of the farmers, have been among the principal occasions of an increased issue and circulation by the country banks: and this was a state of things which prevailed between 1787 and 1791. During that interval, after a low range of prices preceding the harvest of 1787. There was, without any extraordinary scarcity, such a degree of comparative deficiency of produce as raised and maintained a relatively high range of prices till the harvest of 1791, the abundance of which occasioned a temporary considerable fall of prices. It might be thought by those who consider every increase of the circulation as a cause,

① Being one half of its liabilities, which were 17,521,250*l*..

of a rise of prices, that those of agricultural produce from 1787 to 1792 had been raised by that increased circulation. But as a proof, that the rise was not the effect of any increase of currency, peculiar to this country, it is requisite to advert to the fact, that the advance of prices had been greater on the continent of Europe, and especially in France, than here; and that in order to prevent the effect of that higher state of prices abroad from drawing supplies from this country, our own crops of 1788 and 1789 having been considered rather deficient, the exportation from this country was prohibited by proclamation; and if the prices of corn had been raised by the amount of the circulation between 1788 and 1790, the still increased amount ought to have prevented the fall which occurred at the close of 1791 and the beginning of 1792.

It is not improbable, indeed, that the fall of prices of agricultural produce, which occurred in the early part of 1792, as a consequence of the abundant harvest of 1791, had the effect of impairing the securities of the country banks, through that medium of issue, and may thus, concurrently with the recoil from over trading in other branches, have occasioned the extensive failures and discredit that marked the close of 1792 and 1793. Of that calamitous time, some contemporary accounts will be found in the Appendix.

This somewhat detailed explanation of the circumstances connected with the country circulation, which experienced so great a derangement, has appeared to me to be desirable, as affording means for the better judging of the position of the Bank of England in 1793, and of the influence of the regulation of its issues in the eventful period now under consideration.

There had been a decline of the foreign exchanges in 1792, which may account, in some degree, for the drain; the greater part however of the drain seems to have been occasioned by a demand from the country bankers, for the purpose of enabling them to meet the run which they experienced. But although the bank fully kept up the amount of its issues, while it had supplied a large amount of gold to the country, the total of the circulating medium at the beginning of 1793 was in a very contracted state, or, in other words, the pressure on the money market was very severe; and this, notwithstanding that the bank was liberal in its discounts①, which had increased from 1, 898, 640*l*. , in August, 1791, to 6, 450, 041*l*. , in February, 1793.

It has been already observed, that prices of almost all commodities, with the exception of corn, were lower in 1793 than they had been in the two years preceding; and the price of wheat was below the average of the three years previous to the harvest of 1791. The price of 3 per cent consols had fallen from 96, in 1792, to 72, in 1793, at which price the first loan in preparation for the war, amounting to 4, 500, 000*l*. , was contracted. ②

This general depression of credit and of prices was the main cause of the contraction of the circulation, and not the contraction of the circulation a cause of the depression. A grant had been made by parliament of exchequer

① It may here be observed, that a demand for increased discounts at the Bank of England is rarely, if ever, felt in the early stages of a speculative tendency, or as a means of making purchases, with a view to a further advance. It is chiefly when a pause takes place in the expected advance, and still more after the commencement of a fall, that the applications for discount become urgent, for the purpose of enabling the parties to meet engagements entered into some time before, and for which they may be supposed to have reckoned on funds to have been realised by advantageous sales.

② "It was originally intended to have raised this loan on a 4 or 5 per cent, stock; but the embarrassed state of commercial credit having caused a scarcity of money, the minster only received offers from one set of subscribers, and as they preferred 3 per cent, it was judged expedient to conclude the bargain in that stock at the above pine, which was between 4 and 5 per cent, under the current price. Mr. Pitt admitted that the terms were much more disadvantageous to the public than might have been expected; but having done every thing in his power to excite a competition without effect, they were the best he could procure. "—*Terms of Loans*, by J. J. Grellier, 1802.

bills to be advanced on loan in aid of commercial credit. But this measure appears to have had no influence on the circulation, or on the state of prices. And in point of fact the pressure and discredit and stagnation had ceased before the proposed advance of exchequer bills came into operation.

The bullion in the Bank in August①, 1791, amounted to considerably more than one third of its liabilities, and the exchanges till the autumn of that year maintained a high range; but they afterwards gave way, that on Hamburg having fallen from 36-37, in May, to 34-35, in November, in consequence of the large foreign payments which were then to be made. This decline of the exchanges, with the knowledge or intimation of the foreign expenditure in progress, should, according to a correct system of management, have operated as a warning and inducement to contract the circulation. But as under circumstances, in some respects, analogous, in 1782, and again in more recent instances, when the critical moment arrived, upon the turn of which depended the preservation of the value of the paper, the regulation of the issues proved to be the reverse of what it ought to have been. Instead of a contraction there was an enlargement. And although the increased issue was of very short duration, it could hardly fail, while it lasted, of giving additional force to the causes operating to a depression of the exchanges, and to a consequent increased tendency to an efflux of the metals, and greatly increasing the difficulty of counteracting a further pressure on the exchanges. If the difference of the issues on

①

	£		£
Circulation –	10, 286, 780	Securities –	12, 446, 460
Deposits –	5, 935, 710	Bullion –	6, 770, 110
Liabilities –	16, 222, 490		19, 216, 573

In 1794 the bank, first issued notes under 10*l*..

particular days be taken, the increase will be very striking:—Thus, on the

30th August, 1794, the amount was, 10, 286, 780*l*.

28th February, 1795 – 14, 017, 510*l*.

a difference accounted for by the well known circumstance of the bills drawn for account of the Austrian government on the treasury of this country, and accepted by the treasury, payable at the bank. But this comparison of particular days, although they are those on which the usual returns are made, gives an exaggerated view of the case, and it is more fair to take the average issues for the quarter, thus: — Quarter ending

30th September, 1794 – 10, 422, 900*l*.

31st December – – 10, 964, 980*l*.

31st March, 1795 – – 12, 421, 260*l*.

Here in the last quarter of 1794, there was an increase of 500, 000*l*. , and in the first quarter of 1795 an increase of 2, 000, 000*l*. . But it is not a little singular, and the fact may serve as a proof of the anomalies which perplex the question of the regulation of the bank issues, that, coincidently with this increased issue, the exchanges actually experienced some improvement. The quetations were,

On Hamburgh,	Dec.	1794	–	34 · 9 to 34 · 6.
, ,	Jan.	1795	–	34 · 6 to 35 · 6.
, ,	Feb.	, ,	–	35 · 6 to 36 · 6.
, ,	March	, ,	–	35 · 8 to 36 · 5.

And in order to prove that this rise of the exchanges was not partial or artificial, it may be observed that the price of standard silver fell from 5*s*. $2\frac{1}{4}$*d*. per oz. in December, 1794, to 5*s*. 1*d*. in the first three months of 1795, the price of gold continuing at 3*l*. 17*s*. 6*d*. per oz. ; the

Lisbon exchange improved in the same proportion; and the whole of the reduction of the treasure of the bank, between August, 1794, and February, 1795, had been only 650,000*l*., leaving still a stock of 6,127,720*l*., against liabilities amounting to 19,990,530*l*.

It must be added, in justice to the bank directors of that time, that they thenceforth retraced their steps, and resolutely contracted their issues, which in the quarter ending June 30th of 1795, were lower by one million and a half than they had been in the preceding quarter, and lower than they had been on the average of the preceding three years. And if a specimen of the degree of reduction be taken on particular days, as the previous increase has been, it would stand thus in juxtaposition with the exchange: —

				Exchange.
28th February, 1795	–	14,017,510*l*.	–	36 · 0
31st August, ,,	–	10,862,200*l*.	–	32 · 6

the bank treasure having been reduced in the interval from 6,127,720*l*. to 5,136,350*l*.. But, notwithstanding this reduction of issue, and a diminution of a million of the stock of bullion, such was the overpowering pressure of foreign payment, now increased by the necessity for an import of foreign grain, and by the enormous prices to which the competition of the French government had raised the prices of naval stores in the Baltic, that the exchanges gave way rapidly, as is seen by the above quotation, and the drain on the treasure of the Bank, chiefly, if not exclusively, for export, continued through the remainder of 1795, and the greater part of 1796.

At the close of 1795, a notice was exhibited at the doors of the Bank, announcing that, in future, only a certain proportion of the applications for discount would be complied with, however high might be the credit of the parties.① This announcement, combined with the actual contraction of the issues, occasioned a very severe pressure on the money market; and in the spring of 1790 there were great complaints of an insufficiency of circulating medium for the trade in the metropolis. As a specimen of the feeling of the time, it may be worth while to notice the heads of some resolutions passed at a meeting of merchants and bankers, held at the London Tavern, on the 2nd of April, 1790.

"At a select meeting of gentlemen interested in and acquainted with the principles of internal circulation, held at the London Tavern, on Saturday, the 2nd of April, 1790, Sir Stephen Lushington, Bart., in the chair: — Resolved,

1. That it is the opinion of this meeting that there has existed, for a considerable time past, and does exist at present, an alarming scarcity of money in the city of London.

2. That this scarcity proceeds chiefly, if not entirely, from an increase of the commerce of the country, and from the great diminution of mercantile discounts which the Bank of England has thought proper to introduce in the conduct of that establishment during the last three months."

After some other resolutions to the same effect, a committee was appointed, consisting of the Chairman, Walter Boyd, Esq., Sir James Sanderson, Bart., Mr. Alderman Anderson, Mr. Alderman Lushington,

---

① The notice was to the following effect: —

31. Dec. 1795.

"That in future, whenever hills sent in for discount shall in any day amount to a larger sum than it shall be resolved to discount on that day, a pro rata proportion of such bills in each parcel as are not other wise objectionable, will be returned to the person sending in the same, without regard to the respectability of the party sending in the bills, or the solidity of the bills themselves."

John Inglis, Esq., J. J. Angerstein, Esq., for the purpose of digesting the outlines of a plan for augmenting the circulating medium of the country.

A plan was afterwards drawn up by Mr. Boyd, for a board to be constituted by act of Parliament, for the support of credit. They were to issue promissory notes, payable six months after date, bearing interest at the late of $1\frac{1}{4}d.$ per 100*l.*, or 1*l.* 18*s.* per cent, per annum, upon receiving the value in gold and silver, Bank of England notes, or in bills of Exchange not having more than three months to run.

The details of the plan were given in a report drawn up by Mr. Boyd. These were laid before the chancellor of the exchequer, with whom the committee had an interview. They there learned that it had been proposed by the bank directors, as the best remedy for the scarcity of money, that the floating debt should be funded. The minister said, that he would first try what this would do towards removing the scarcity of money, and if it should answer the purpose, the establishment of aboard for the support of credit would be unnecessary.

Mr. Boyd, in his pamphlet from which these extracts are made, adds: —

"The floating debt was funded by means of the loan of 7,500,000*l.*, which was contracted on very liberal terms, upon the prospect held out to the contractors of a total change of system on the part of the Bank. How this prospect was realised, the distresses of the city in the end of May, 1796, can testify."

The pressure on the money market here recorded, is particularly deserving of notice, as showing that the high price of provisions, in the spring of 1796, was not in any degree owing to an enlarged circulation. And Mr. Henry Thornton appears to have been struck by the same circumstance, as he observes, —

"The following facts furnish a convincing proof that the late high prices of corn have not been owing to the enlargement, of Bank of England paper. By the account which the bank rendered to Parliament, it appears that the amount of Bank of England notes, was, on the 25th February, 1795 ①, 13, 539, 160*l*.. In the three months immediately following, the average price of wheat in the London market was about 57*s* per quarter.

By the same account it appears that the amount of Bank of England notes was, on the 25th of February, 1796, 11, 030, 116*l*.. In the three months immediately following, the average price of wheat in the London coin market was about 94*s*. per quarter." p. 314.

In point of fact, with the single exception of the increase which took place in the first months of 1795, and which was withdrawn before the expiration of the quarter, the bank circulation was lower, on the average, during the prevalence of the highest prices in the interval under consideration, than it had been, on the average, in 1791 and 1792. This contraction of the Bank of England circulation, coincidently with so great an advance of the prices of provisions, and of a large proportion of commodities, as had taken place in the spring of 1796, seems to have been countervailed in some degree by an expansion of country bank and private credit circulation; that expansion being usually, if not inevitably, the consequence of a *tendency*, from causes real or imagined, to an advance of prices.

The very circumstance of the derangement of the country bank circulation at the close of 1796, supposes a previous enlargement of it. It

① The difference between this amount and that, which has just before been quoted as the amount on the 28th of February, 1795, arises from the amount of bank post bills being included in the latter and not in the former.

is probable that the great fall of the prices of corn and cattle, after the spring of 1796, was among the causes tending to produce the derangement of the country circulation.

But low as the amount of the circulation had been, on the average of the last nine months of 1795, and the early part of 1796, it was still further reduced in the last six months of 1796, as will be seen by the following return of the quarterly averages: —

January to March	–	10, 824, 150*l*.
April to June	–	10, 770, 200*l*.
July to September	–	9, 720, 440*l*.
October to December	–	9, 645, 710*l*.

It might have been imagined that the contraction had thus been pushed far enough, inasmuch as the exchanges had improved, and were evidently improving, so as almost to ensure a return of the bullion that had been exported. But a fresh cause of drain supervened. This cause is thus explained in the report of the Lords' Committee of Secrecy in 1797: —

"The alarm of invasion which, when an immediate attack was first apprehended in Ireland, had occasioned some extraordinary demand for cash on the Bank of England, in the months of December and January last year, began in February to produce similar effects in the North of England. Your Committee find, that, in consequence of this aspprehension, the farmers suddenly brought the produce of their lands to sale, and carried the notes of the country banks, which they had collected by these and other means, into those banks for payment; that this unusual and sudden demand for cash reduced the several banks at Newcastle to the necessity of suspending their payments in specie, and of availing themselves of all the means in their power of procuring a speedy supply of cash from the metropolis, that the effects of this demand on the Newcastle Banks, and of their suspension of payments in cash, soon spread over various parts of the country, from whence similar applications were consequently made to the metropolis for cash, that the alarm thus diffused, not only occasioned an increased demand for cash in the country, but probably a disposition in many to hoard what was thus obtained: that this call on the metropolis, through whatever channels, directly affected the Bank of England as the great repository of cash, and was in the course of still further operation upon it when stopped by the minute of council of the 26th of February."

The landing of some troops from a French frigate which had accidentally got into the port of Fishgard, in Wales, tended to increase the prevailing alarm.

The contraction of the circulation, immediately previous to the issuing of the order in council, had been carried to an extreme degree, the issues on the 25th of February having been reduced to 8, 640, 250*l*.. ①

---

① The policy, on the part of the Bank, of this extreme contraction was questioned by Mr. Henry Thornton, in his evidence before the committees in 1797, as also in his publication on paper credit in 1802. The rationale of the objections that have been urged against that degree of reduction of the circulation is, that having earned it to a degree that was effectual in restoring the exchanges, and thus securing the return from abroad of the gold that had been exported, the expedient course, on the part of the Bank, when the demand for gold became confined to the interior, and evidently arose from the discredit of the country circulation, was to enlarge its issues, instead of further contracting them, as the bank did; for, by such further contraction, the difficulties and discredit of the country banks were aggravated, and the demands upon them, and by them upon the Bank, for gold became more urgent. And the success of an opposite course in a memorable instance of more recent date has given considerable force to the reasoning upon which that objection proceeds. But the doctrine is to be received with great caution, as it may easily be perverted into a justification of a very lax and improvident management.

The directors, in 1797, pursued a clear and steady course in the reduction of the amount of their paper, in order to counteract the drain on their treasure; and there is reason to believe, that if, instead of applying to the government with a statement of their apprehensions, which led to an interference by the order of council on the 26th of February, they had, as the directors in 1783 did, gone on with the

The effect of this extreme contraction was felt chiefly, as may be supposed, in the money market. Exchequer bills, bearing 3 $\frac{1}{2}$*d*. per day, were sold at 3*l*. and 3*l*. 10*s*. per cent, discount, and it was said, that in some instances sales were made at 5*l*. per cent discount. Navy and victualling bills were also at an enormous discount, and the 3 per cent consols fell below 50. Mercantile bills, excepting such as came within bank time and regulations, were hardly negotiable at all, or were subject to heavy commissions, by way of evading the operation of the usury law.

But while in the rate of interest, and in the price of public securities, the effect was naturally very great, it was hardly perceptible in the markets for goods. The price of corn ① had previously been falling from restored abundance, while from the opposite cause, scarcity, actual or apprehended, colonial produce continued to rise, notwithstanding not only the pressure on the money market, but notwithstanding also the great

---

intention of paying to their last guinea (when at worst they could but have stopped), they would have surmounted the run. The reason for this opinion is, that the circulation was already so contracted that the reduced number of notes then outstanding were become so much wanted for immediate payments, as to be less and less likely to be returned to the bank for gold; while, on the other hand, the tide of the metals was setting in so strongly from abroad as almost to insure a sufficient supply to meet the internal demand. A strong corroborative ground for such a supposition is, that before the order in council for the restriction had reached Dublin, the run on the bank of Ireland had altogether ceased, and the directors of that establishment expressed great reluctance at being prevented from continuing to pay in specie, which they considered themselves well able to do. And it is a fair presumption that as a demand for gold, under the alarm of invasion in Ireland, had been one of the predisposing causes of the run in this country, the same general circumstances which restored confidence in the circulation there would quickly operate in arresting the progress of discredit here.

① So the corn markets were buoyant, notwithstanding the contracted state of the currency, that, in consequence of bad weather at the harvest of 1797, the price rose in September of that year 10*s*. the quarter, and afterwards fell again slowly when the sufficiency of the supply was ascertained.

advance of the exchanges. ①

On the day following the order in council, the bank increased its issues, and on the 28th of February② the amount stood at one million higher than it had done on the 25th. The average for the whole year was somewhat higher than it had been in 1796, although lower than in 1795. But in the amount of the bank circulation in 1797 are included notes under 5*l.*, amounting to somewhat under a million, which must be considered as wholly in the place of so much gold, which would otherwise have circulated. Indeed the increase of bank notes was in a small proportion only to the increase of bullion, which was between three and four millions.

The exchanges, which had given way a little on the post day following the older in council, under an impression that there was likely to be an excessive issue of paper, rallied immediately after, upon its being found that there was no tendency to such excess. And as a great part of our

---

① It is not possible to adduce an instance more striking than that which is here adverted to, of the inefficacy of a contraction of the circulation in counteracting the tendency to an advance of prices under the influence of actual scarcity, or of the force of opinion of prospective scarcity, relatively to the estimated rate of consumption. For in the present instance, instead of a use of prices of exportable commodities having been *caused* by an exchange adverse to this country, and therefore holding out a compensation to the foreign buyer for a higher price, the prices of such commodities advanced 50 to 100 per cent, while the exchanges likewise advanced 10 to 20 per cent.

② The position of the bank on the 28th of February, 1797, being the day following the restriction, was: —

		£			£
Circulation	–	9, 674, 780	Securities, public	–	11, 714, 431
Deposits	–	4, 891, 530	private	–	5, 123, 319
Liabilities	–	14, 566, 310			16, 837, 750
Bullion	–	1, 086, 170			17, 923, 920

The above amount of liabilities is lower than it bad been since 1787.

government expenditure abroad had ceased, in consequence of the peace between Austria and France, by the treaty of Leoben, they continued to rise till they got considerably above par.

The Hamburgh exchange attained, before the close of that year, a quotation which it had never before reached, viz. 38; and it ranged at about that high rate through the whole of 1798. This extraordinarily high state of the exchange was attended with a great influx of bullion, the stock of which in the bank, by the end of August, amounted to six million five hundred thousand pounds①; and at the end of that year, was above seven millions, being in the proportion of more than one third of its liabilities. The bank was, in consequence, in a condition to resume its payments in specie, and an announcement was made by the directors to government to that effect. The government, however, from a consideration of the political state of the country, deemed it expedient to continue the restriction.

But the great rise of the exchanges, and the rapid influx of bullion, and a great fall in the prices of provisions, were coincident with an increased issue of bank paper; thus proving that the intermediate depression of the exchanges, and the consequent great efflux of bullion, were not caused by an increased amount, and consequent diminished value of the currency of

① The position of the bank in August 1798 was: —

	£		£
Circulation, bank notes of 5*l*. and upwards, and post bills under 5*l*.	10, 649, 550	Securities, public	10, 930, 038
Deposits	1, 531, 060	private	6, 419, 602
	12, 180, 610		17, 349, 640
Liabilities	8, 300, 720	Bullion – –	6, 546, 100
	20, 481, 330		23, 895, 740

this country, but by a great and sudden emergency, which occasioned an extraordinary demand for, and consequent temporarily increased value of foreign currencies, as measured in our currency; for immediately upon the cessation of that demand, the value of those currencies fell even below their usual level as compared with ours.

Of the magnitude of the extra demand for means of making immediate payments abroad, some idea may be formed from the following statement of the foreign expenditure of government, extracted from an account inserted in the Appendix to the Report of the Lords' Committee of Secrecy in 1797[①]:—

			£	*s.*	*d.*
1794	–	–	8, 335, 592	5	5
1795	–	–	11, 040, 236	13	0
1796	–	–	10, 649, 916	0	8

To the above sums is to be added 4, 702, 818*l.* 18*s.* 8*d.*[②], as *excess* of payments abroad for naval stores imported in those years. And the value of grain imported was in[③]—

1794	–	–	–	1, 983, 856*l.*
1795	–	–	–	1, 535, 672*l.*
1796	–	–	–	3, 926, 484*l.*

making an aggregate of extra foreign expenditure of no less than 42, 174, 675*l.*, in those three years of which the largest proportion fell

① Appendix to Lords' Report, No. 23. In these sums are included the loan and advances to the Emperor of Austria, 5,570,000*l.*

② Appendix to Lords' Reports, No. 27.

③ Appendix to Lords' Reports, 1797, No. 31.

upon the two last.

It is quite clear that, practically, no conceivable increase of exports in the way of trade could be immediately brought into operation, so as to obviate the pressure on the exchanges of so enormous and so sudden an increase of the balance of payments to be made abroad. And it was only, as has been seen, by an extraordinary contraction of the circulating medium, and by the transmission of all the bullion that could be collected, whether from the coffers of the Bank, or from the channels of circulation, that the pressure could be at all met, consistently with the maintenance of the convertibility of the paper. But the contraction of the issues of the Bank, combined with the export of bullion, *did* prove efficacious in restoring the value of the currency of this country, as compared with the currencies of other countries; and it was only an accidentally supervening cause of drain for internal circulation, that endangered the convertibility which was *prematurely* suspended by an interference of government. *Prematurely*, inasmuch as the stock of bullion had not, on the 26th of February, 1797, been reduced below a million, while the circulation had been contracted to the very low amount of 8, 640, 250*l*. ; this proportion of the circulation to the treasure of the bank being lower than it had been in 1783, or again in 1825, in each of which instances the run had been surmounted. Whatever, therefore, might be the motives of *policy* which dictated the suspension, it was clearly not justified at that precise time as a measure of *necessity*.

SECTION 4 *Summary of the preceding survey*

From the preceding view of the slate of the circulation and of prices, from 1798 to 1798, it appears,

1. That it was the extraordinary adverse balance of foreign payments, and not an increased circulation or quantity of money, that caused the depression of the exchanges, and the efflux of bullion in 1795 and 1796, inasmuch as the exchanges rose and bullion flowed rapidly back comcidently with an increase of the bank circulation, when the foreign payments ceased.

2. That the bank directors of that time acted upon the principle, and found it efficacious, of controlling the exchanges by a contraction of their issues.

3. That in consequence of the two very deficient harvests of 1794 and 1795, a great rise of the prices of provisions took place in 1795 and 1796, coincidently with a remarkable contraction of the bank circulation; and that there was, comcidently with an enlargement of the circulation, a rapid fall of the prices of provisions, and a complete subsidence of them at the close of 1798, to the level of what they had been at the commencement of 1793.

4. That while, from 1796 to the close of 1798, the prices of provisions and of European produce generally were falling, the prices of all transatlantic produce were rapidly rising, coincidently with a great rise of the exchanges, and reached a greater height than they ever afterwards attained, until the commencement of 1814.

5. That the great fall of the prices of corn, and of European produce generally, from 1796 to the close of 1798, took place coincidently with a progressively increasing government expenditure, defrayed chiefly by loans.

6. That there is as little ground, therefore, for the hypothesis of the influence of war demand (except in the case of articles constituting naval

and military stores), as there is for that of the circulation, in accounting for the very extraordinary, and thus far unprecedented, fluctuations of prices which characterised the interval that has passed under review.

CHAPTER Ⅲ
ON THE STATE OF PRICES, AND OF THE CIRCULATION, FROM 1799 TO 1803

At the commencement of the period now coming under consideration, while the prices of coffee, sugar, cotton, and generally of all transatlantic produce were, in consequence of a continued speculative demand for export, immediately high; and while various of other articles were in consequence of increased cost of production, arising out of the circumstances of the war, at a greater or less advance upon what had been their ordinary level before the war, the prices of provisions were moderate; or rather if the increased cost of production of a foreign supply, of which it was supposed that we then stood habitually in need, be taken into account, might be considered extremely low.

Of corn, the Gazette averages for England and Wales were, in January, 1799, —

For Wheat	–	49*s*.	6*d*.
Barley	–	29*s*.	4*d*.
Oats	–	19*s*.	10*d*.

And the following were the prices of meat: —

Beef, in Smithfield,		–	3*s*. to 3*s*. 4*d*. per st.
Mutton	–	–	3*s*. to 4*s*. 2*d*.
Pork	– –	–	2*s*. 8*d*. to 3*s*. 8*d*.
Hay, aver. St. James's mar.			45*s*. 6*d*. per *ld*.
Straw,	– ditto,	–	31*s*.

Prices, as low as they had been on an average of several years before 1793. And the exchanges were at such a high rate as indicated a greater value of the currency relatively to the currencies of other countries, than had existed with a trifling exception during the preceding part of the century. But a great change was about to take place; the prices of provisions, and of other European produce, rising to an enormous height, while transatlantic produce experienced a very great fall, at the same tune that the exchanges underwent extraordinary fluctuations.

SECTION 1 *Rise of the prices of provisions and other articles of European produce from the spring of 1799 to the spring of 1801*

The winter of 1798-1799 was extremely rigorous, and had set in very early. The autumn of 1798 had been very unfavourable for wheat sowing (which, partly perhaps from this cause, was said to be to a smaller extent than usual), and the subsequent weather was throughout adverse to vegetation. ① Severe frosts setting in early, and alternating with rapid thaws, and heavy falls of snow occurring into an advanced period of the spring, gave a general character of untowardness to the season of 1799, which the subsequent progress of it more than realised.

Under this unpromising aspect of the season, the prices of grain advanced, slowly however at first, the averages for March having risen in a very trifling degree. But the spring proving to be excessively cold and ungenial, and the appearance of the growing crops very unpromising, a rapid rise took place in May, when the averages for grain were,

Wheat	–	–	61*s*. 8*d*.
Barley	–	–	35*s*.
Oats	–	–	27*s*. 4*d*.
Beef, in Smithfield		–	3*s*. 8*d*. to 5*s*. per st.
Mutton	–	–	4*s*. 4*d*. to 5*s*. 4*d*.
Hay –	–	–	70*s*.
Straw –	–	–	52*s*.

To this dry, harsh, and ungenial spring succeeded a cold and almost uninterruptedly wet summer and autumn. The consequence was, great injury to all, and destruction to some, of the crops; and henceforth the prices of grain rose without intermission. At the close of the year the averages of corn were,

① The severity of the frosts and the suddenness of the thaws during this month have, in many respects, been unfavourable to the young wheats, especially those which were sown early. These causes have likewise prevented the operations of the plough in preparing turnip and other grounds for wheat, rye, &c., as well as for the making of summer fallows. In the more western parts of the island our reporters also observe that less wheat than usual has been sown on account of the frosts, and some other impediments. — *Monthly Agricultural Report for* January, 1799.

Wheat	–	–	94*s*. 2*d*.
Barley	–	–	45*s*. 5*d*.
Oats	–	–	33*s*. 3*d*.

Although parliament had met in September 1799, there do not appear to have been any discussions in it on the high price of provisions till the 18th of February, 1800, when the House of Commons resolved itself into a committee on the report respecting the assize of bread, and the deficiency of the last crop of grain. Lord Hawkesbury then took occasion to make some statements which it may be worthwhile to record.

"As to the quantity of wheat consumed," he said, "a quarter of wheat in the year for each man was the general calculation. This, allowance would require between eight and nine millions of quarters to supply this country for a year. The produce of the country varied in different years, but the average computation between very high and very low seasons might come nearest the truth. This average did not feed the country; for the average importation for several years back might be estimated at one twentieth of the consumption. The deficiency of the late crop might be estimated at one third of the usual crop, which must be added to the one twentieth usually imported, in order to estimate what importation would be necessary this season. It must, however, be considered that there was in the country a stock in hand from the preceding harvest sufficient to supply one month. But if we also take the foreign supply in the country at the same period, there was certainly much more than would be consumed in a month. Considering all these circumstances, the probable amount of importation necessary this season would be about 600, 000 quarters of wheat, whereas, in 1796, the importation was more than 800, 000 quarters. The millers and others skilled in the subject had recommended some regulations as to the use of new bread, and had computed that by such regulations there might be a saving of one fortnight of the whole consumption. It had also been stated that millers, when the price of grain was high, and, consequently, when bread was dear, extracted from the grain a greater quantity of flour than they did at other times. This would afford a second saving. A third would arise from the use of substitutes for bread. As the price of grain, even in those countries from which we could receive a supply, was high, it was to be feared that the high price of grain in this country was inevitable, but from a review of all the circumstances, it might be collected that there was no real danger of scarcity." ①

If this very statement was not descriptive of real scarcity, it is difficult to say to what degree of deficiency the term could with propriety be applied. So formidable were the appearances at that time of increasing dearth, that, in pursuance of the recommendation of the committee, recourse was again had to a bounty, and an act was accordingly passed, guaranteeing to the importer the difference between the average price of English wheat in the second week after importation and 90*s*. on wheat from the south of Europe, Africa, and America; 85*s*. from the Baltic and Germany; and 90*s*. from Archangel, if imported before the 1st of October, 1800.

Notwithstanding the reasonable probability from the encouragement thus held out of a large forthcoming importation, such was the scantiness of the supply in the markets, and such the apprehension excited by the

---

① Lord Hawkesbury concluded by moving "That leave be given to bring in a bill to prohibit any person or persons from selling or offering for sale any bread which has not been baked for a certain number of hours." Leave was given. The blank for specifying the number of hours was filled up with "twentyfour." The bill went through all its stages on the following day. Various other regulations were afterwards proposed and some of them adopted.

unfavourable appearance of the growing crops in the spring of 1800[1], that the prices of provisions continued to advance until June, 1800, when they had reached the following quotations: —

Wheat, Gazette average,	134*s*. 5*d*.
Barley – –	69*s*. 1*d*.
Oats – –	51*s*. 1*d*.

In Smithfield market,

Beef sold for 4*s*. 6*d*. to 6*s*. 4*d*. per stone.

Mutton and Pork 5*s*. 4*d*. to 6*s*. 8*d*.

In Newgate and Leadenhall markets,

Beef –	–	9*d*. to 1*s*. 2*d*. per *ld*.
Mutton –	–	8*d*. to 10*d*.
Veal – –	–	9*d*. to 1*s*.
Pork in St. James's market,		9*d*. to 10*d*.
Hay, – –	–	64*s*. to 122*s*. per *ld*.
Straw –	–	54*s*. to 63*s*.

The summer of 1800 was hot and dry, and as the harvest approached, the crops assumed a more promising appearance. The weather, till the third week of August, was favourable for securing the corn in the more forward districts, and some quantity was well got in.

At the same time a considerable importation was in progress. There was, in consequence a sudden and great fall in all the principal markets, and the averages in August, 1800, declined to

① The autumn of 1799 had again been unfavourable for sowing wheat; the winter had been somewhat like the preceding, marked by early severity of frost, with alternations of rapid thaws and the spring of 1800 was exceedingly wet .

96*s*. 2*d*	for	Wheat.
54*s*. 3*d*.	–	Barley.
35*s*. 9*d*.	–	Oats.

The promising appearances of restored abundance were, however, soon changed into the sad reality of renewed and aggravated dearth.

A portion, not exceeding, according to the reports, one half of the crops, was secured in good order before the 19th of August, when heavy and almost incessant rains set in, accompanied by a high temperature and a close atmosphere, in consequence of which a great deal of the wheat was sprouted, and otherwise injured. The portion that had been secured in the southern division of the kingdom, before the rains set in, and therefore good as to mere condition, and greatly superior to that of 1799, proved to be coarse and shrivelled and light, and consequently greatly deficient in yield. This description applied to the quality of the grain generally. But the rains, which came on in August, caught a considerable proportion of the wheat still in the fields, even in the home and some of the southern districts, and injured the whole of the crops in the northern parts of the island. Accordingly, bad as the crops were in England, they were still worse in Scotland, and considerable purchases were in consequence made in Mark Lane for shipment thither. Under these circumstances, notwithstanding an importation of foreign corn to a very large amount, that of wheat alone being 1, 242, 507 quarters, prices rose as rapidly as they had just before fallen.

The rise, in the present instance, had been accelerated by the circumstance of the Russian government having, in the autumn of 1800, laid an embargo on British shipping. This act was considered, as it proved to be, equivalent to a declaration of war; and as the Danish government was known to be unfriendly to ours, apprehensions were naturally entertained, as they were eventually realised, that in the ensuing season the Baltic might be closed against us. The Prussian government, moreover, had a few months before, viz. in July, imposed a duty of 10*s*. per quarter on the exportation of wheat. It can hardly therefore be a matter of wonder that a renewed range of high prices should be the consequence, and accordingly the averages in December 1800 were,

For Wheat	–	133*s*.
Barley	–	76*s*. 7*d*.
Oats	–	41*s*. 8*d*.

The sufferings of the bulk of the community, under this severe visitation of dearth, were very great. The expression of them broke out in tumultuous meetings and riotous proceedings in different parts of the kingdom, in the autumn of 1800, and the peace of the metropolis was with difficulty preserved.

Parliament met on the 11th of November, 1800; and the speech from the throne slated, that the meeting of it was called at an earlier period than had otherwise been intended, for the purpose of taking into consideration the measures proper to be adopted with a view to alleviate the severe pressure of distress, which was felt in consequence of the high price of provisions. The speech also alluded to the supposition of combination and fraudulent practices, for the purpose of raising the price of grain, and expressed concern with reference to the disturbances which had broken out in some parts of the kingdom.

In the discussions in both Houses, to which the speech and the motions for the address gave rise, several members denied the existence of scarcity, or admitted it only in a qualified degree, and ascribed the high prices, some to war and taxation, and excess of paper circulation; while others laid most stress on monopoly and improper practices on the part of farmers and dealers.

Mr. Pitt, with reference to the allegation of improper practices, deprecated, only in general terms, any such regulations as might interfere with the freedom of trade, and of the application of industry and capital. But he more particularly applied himself to answer the arguments of those who ascribed the high price of provisions chiefly, if not exclusively, to war and taxation.

"Since this question has been started," he said, "I beg leave to hint a few general observations, which seem completely to overthrow the argument of those who impute the dearness of provisions to the war. In a more detailed discussion, I shall be ready to examine separately the effect of every tax which has been imposed since the year 1793, to state the utmost effect which it could be supposed to have produced directly or indirectly on the price of grain; and to prove that these taxes could form, even on the most exaggerated computation, a very inconsiderable part of the increased price of provisions. To show that the war has not any general effect to raise the price of grain, consider only the price of grain at different periods of the present war, though the argument would be strengthened by a review of former wars. Three or four years have been years of comparatively high price. In 1794 and 1795, the price was high, but in the interval of nearly three years that succeeded, that is, from about Michaelmas 1796 to Midsummer 1799, the price sunk perhaps too low for the fair profit of the farmer. The general price then in England was from 48*s*. to 49*s*. a quarter. From Michaelmas 1798 to Ladyday 1799, it was not above 48*s*.. How then, if the war was the cause of the dearness, did it happen that the effect, which on the hypothesis should have been increasing, was suspended during an interval of nearly three years; and when likewise some of the taxes to which the effect is chiefly ascribed bad been imposed? Previous to the last-mentioned period (one of great cheapness) the triple assessment had existed a twelvemonth, and must have produced its full effect. This plain fact is alone worth a thousand instances deduced by circuitous reasonings. I shall not enter into a comparative statement of the prices in former wars, nor insist on the ingenious arguments that have been adduced to show, that war is favourable to lowness of puce. It is deserving of remark, however, that this country, which, from the period of the revolution, for a great part of the present century, had been used to export great quantities of grain, ceased to export and began to import in the middle of that peace which succeeded the most successful war in which this country was ever engaged. Thus it is clear, from a deduction of facts, that war of itself has no evident and necessary connection with the dearness of provisions."

He added,

"As to the extent of the deficiency of the late harvest (1800), it would be no less rash than unnecessary to give any opinion. For the practical remedies proposed, a knowledge of the precise deficit is not required. This, however, we know, that notwithstanding the clamour about monopoly, previous to the harvest, it is now universally admitted, that the old slock was very nearly exhausted. An early harvest, therefore, found us with less stock than usual; of course, that stock, unless aided by importation from abroad and economy of our own resources, must be applicable to the consumption of a shorter period than usual."

Of the assignment of the bank circulation as a cause of the high price, Mr. Pitt seems to have taken no notice in that day's debate; but in a debate a few days after, on a motion of Mr. Tierney's, on the state of the nation, he observed shortly, —

"As to the stoppage of the Bank, that stoppage has taken place for some time, and the difference between the paper circulating medium of that time and the present, is very inconsiderable."—*Parliamentary History*, vol. xxxv.

On the 24th of November, Mr. Ryder presented the first report from the Commons' committee on the high price of provisions, from which the following are extracts: —

"There appears upon the whole of this information, reason to believe, that the general deficiency of the crop of wheat in England and Wales does not amount to quite so much as one fourth."

"The accounts of the stock on hand, furnished by these returns, are necessarily more uncertain; they are in some degree various, but they do not on the whole furnish any ground for doubting the prevailing opinion, confirmed by the general information of the members who have attended your committee, that the stock of British corn at the harvest was reduced far below its usual amount, and was in most places nearly, in many absolutely, exhausted."

"In addition to what has been stated respecting the produce of the crop and the stock in hand, it is to be observed, with a view to the state of the markets, in the time which has elapsed since the harvest, that the farmers, during that period, have had a double demand for the new crop for consumption and for seed."

"It appears to your committee, that these circumstances might be expected to have produced a very high price at this season, even if the late harvest had been abundant; that the degree in which it has been deficient must naturally have added to such prices, whether with or without the concurrence of any other causes, the existence and effects of which your committee propose to investigate."

The committee then state their expectation, that the deficiency will be remedied by the double operation of importation and economy. With respect to importation the committee state that,

"Within twelve months from the 26th of September, 1799, to the 27th of September, 1800, there have been imported into Great Britain no less than 1, 261, 932 quarters of wheat and flour, 67, 988 of barley, 479, 320 of oats and 300, 693 *lbs.* of rice. This happened under the unlavourable circumstances of a harvest abroad uncommonly deficient in quality, and not abundant in quantity, and of the late period of the season, when the bounty was granted by parliament. "①

The committee proceed to offer various suggestions; the encouragement of the fisheries, the stoppage of the distilleries, a bounty on importation, a recommendation from the highest authority, pointing out the advantages which would be derived from the general practice of economy and frugality in articles of food. And with reference to this last suggestion, the

---

① In a sixth report, presented in December, 1800, are the following computations of the estimated consumption, and of the resources to meet the supposed deficiency: —

The usual consumption of wheat cannot be supposed to exceed 7, 000, 000 quarters per annum.

Amount of resources to meet the deficiency:— Importation of wheat since the beginning of

October above	– – – –	170, 000 qrs.
Importation of flour from the United States equal to	– – – –	580, 000
Importation of wheat from Canada	– – – –	30, 000
Rice, equivalent to	– – – –	630, 000
Stoppage of starch manufactory	– – – –	40, 000
Stoppage of distilleries	– – – –	360, 000
Use of coarse meal	– – – –	400, 000
Retrenchment	– – – –	300, 000
		2, 510, 000

committee observes: —

" In order to give the greatest weight and solemnity to such a recommendation, your committee submit to the House, whether it may not be proper to desire the concurrence of the other House of parliament, in a humble address to his Majesty, requesting that his Majesty would be graciously pleased to issue a proclamation for this purpose. "

A royal proclamation was issued accordingly, and circulated by the magistrates and the clergy throughout the kingdom. An act was passed, granting a bounty which guaranteed the difference between the average price of foreign wheat in the third week after importation, and 100*s*. to the importer of *all* wheat weighing 53 *lb*. per bushel, if imported within the time limited by the Act. ①

These proceedings, while on the one hand they had the effect of giving the assurance, that measures were in progress calculated to diminish the consumption and to increase the supply, and thus eventually to reduce prices; yet, on the other hand, they naturally conveyed a strong impression of alarm. An official letter from the Duke of Portland, then Secretary of State for the Home Department, to the Lord Lieutenant of the county of Oxford, strongly dwelling on the deficiency of grain, and recommending

---

① On the policy of this measure it is, perhaps, scarcely necessary to remark, as it is not probable (although our subsequent policy in legislation about corn, in the opposite direction, is hardly less absurd, and certainly more injurious, as it is more permanent), that any such gross error in legislation will be repeated. It ought, indeed, to have been quite evident, that the enormously high prices then prevailing, and the further rise anticipated, would have the effect of inducing preparations, on the part of the merchants, to bring forward all the corn that could be collected, and to hasten the importation as much as possible. The very extravagance of the measure, however, proves the magnitude of the apprehensions, which were then entertained of the further progress of the dearth.

economy in the use of it, was animadverted upon at the time, as being calculated to increase the general feeling of alarm.

There was, doubtless, sufficient cause for apprehension; because although there were reasonable grounds for supposing, that the measures in progress would be effectual in ultimately reducing prices, yet various contingencies of the season, and of obstructions arising out of the war, might frustrate the expectations of relief; and although the occurrence in immediate succession of a third year of deficient produce was not within moderate probability, it was not to be considered as out of calculation, there having been instances of such a succession of unproductive seasons.

Under these circumstances of actual and apprehended deficiency, the prices of provisions continued to advance. The averages of grain in December, 1800, have already been given. They advanced progressively till March, 1801, when they were —

For Wheat	–	156*s*. 2*d*.
Barley	–	90*s*. 7*d*.
Oats	–	47*s*. 2*d*.

And the following were the prices of meat: —

Beef, in Smithfield,			5*s*.	to	6*s*. 6*d*.
Mutton,	–	–	6*s*. 6*d*.	to	8*s*.
Veal,	–	–	6*s*.	to	8*s*. 6*d*.
Pork,	–	–	6*s*. 6*d*.	to	7*s*.
In retail,					
Beef,	–	–	10*d*.	to	$10\frac{1}{2}d$.
Mutton,	–	–	11*d*.	to	12*d*.
Veal,	–	–	12*d*.	to	14*d*.

A rise in the price of dairy produce would naturally follow from the same general causes.

And not only had there been this enormous rise in the prices of provisions, between the close of 1798 and the spring of 1801, but many other articles of European raw produce had experienced a simultaneous advance, partly as the consequence of the same inclemency of the seasons as had prevailed in this country, and partly from the extraordinary obstructions to importation from political causes. Thus wool and tallow rose from the twofold cause of the seasons in diminishing both the home and foreign produce, and flax, hemp, timber, foreign iron, linseed, in short, all articles for our supply of which we depended wholly, or in part, on importation from the Baltic, experienced a very considerable rise, not only in consequence of the embargo in Russia, in the autumn of 1800, but also in consequence of the threatened hostility of Denmark, which was likely to close against us the passage of the Sound. In addition to this extensive dearth of raw produce was the dearness of many articles of general consumption, occasioned by the progress of taxation, such as the heavy duties of excise on salt, soap, candles, and leather, which may be considered as necessaries, and on malt and beer, sugar, tea, and tobacco and spirits, which are secondary necessaries, or, perhaps, more correctly speaking, necessaries to all the classes above the very poorest. Fuel of every description had risen considerably from the same general causes.

SECTION 2 *Rise of wages from 1799 to 1801*

Such and so great being the rise of prices of provisions, and of nearly all consumable commodities, it was quite impossible that the lowest of the working classes could, upon their wages, at the rate of what they were before 1795, obtain a subsistence for themselves and their families, on the lowest scale requisite to sustain human existence; and the classes above the lowest, including some portion of skilled labourers, could do little, if at all, more than provide themselves with food, clothing, and shelter, without any of the indulgences which habit had rendered necessaries. If under these circumstances there had been no rise of wages, no contributions by parishes and by individuals, in aid of wages, great numbers of the people must have actually perished, and the classes immediately above the lowest would with difficulty have preserved themselves from the same fate. In such case the suffering from dearth would have been correctly designated as a famine, a term which has been somewhat loosely applied to the period under consideration. For, severe and intense as were the sufferings and privations of the people of this country, in the dearths of 1795 and 1796, and of 1800 and 1801, there were few recorded instances of death from actual destitution.

A rise of wages was imperatively called for by the urgency of the case, and was complied with to some extent in most of the branches of industry, the claims for increase being aided by the resource which workmen and labourers had of enlisting in the army and navy. There had already been an advance of wages in 1795 and 1796, and the allowance system had been begun and carried to some extent in those years. A further advance of wages took place in 1800 and 1801[①]; but still so inadequate, compared with the prices of provisions, as even with parish allowances and private

① Arthur Young (Annals of Agriculture, vol. 37 p. 265, 1801,) says, "a person is now living in the vicinity of Bury (Suffolk) who, when he laboured for 5*s*. a week, could purchase with that 5*s*..

				While in 1801 the same articles cost		
				£	*s*.	*d*.
A bushel of wheat		–	–	– 0	16	0
A ditto of Malt		–	–	– 0	9	0
A pound of Butter	5*s*.	–	–	– 0	1	0
A pound of Cheese		–	–	– 0	0	4
One pennyworth of Tobacco		–	–	– 0	0	1
				1	6	5
Suppose in 1801 his wages produced him – 9*s*.				–0	15	0
Suppose as a pauper from the parish rates – 6*s*.				0	11	5

"So that to enable him to purchase the same quantities he procured when his week's wages were 5*s*., would now require 11*s*. 5*d*. more than his wages and the parish allowance together. The comparison is," says Mr. Young, "fair as far as it goes, because the extreme in both cases, the very lowest in the first, and the very highest in the last."

There was a rise also in artisan and manufacturing labour, between 1792 and 1801; but in a small proportion only to the use in the prices of necessaries. Various statements were put forth by different classes of artisans, setting forth the inadequateness of the rise of wages, including the most recent advance in 1801. Among other statements was one from the journeymen tailors, by which it *appeared* that their wages, from 1777 to 1795, had been 1*l*. 1*s*. 9*d*. per week, which, at the price of $7\frac{1}{4}$*d*. for the quartern loaf, would purchase thirty-six loaves; while the utmost advance of wages, which, in 1795, was to 25*s*., and, in 1801, to 27*s*. per week, would purchase only eighteen loaves and a half in the latter year. A statement from printers' compositors, whose weekly wages were advanced from 24*s*. to 27*s*. in 1795, and to 30*s*. in 1801, gives a similar result in the disproportion of the advance of wages to the rise of necessaries.

By the Greenwich Hospital table, the wages of carpenters, bricklayers, masons, and plumbers appear to have experienced very little advance, according to the quotations of 1800, as compared with the twenty years preceding, viz. —

contributions, to leave a vast mass of privation and misery. Mr. Whitbread had, in 1795, and again in 1800, proposed bills in the House of Commons for regulating the wages of labour by the price of provisions, and prescribing a minimum of wages. There was enough of good sense to cause the rejection of such a measure.

If it had been adopted, high as the prices of provisions were, they would have been still higher; as on the other hand, if wages had not risen, and if there had not been the supplementary aids to wages, the prices would not have risen so much as they did; for it must be evident that there could not in that case have been so large a sum devoted to the purchase of necessaries. The rise in the wages of labour, therefore, with the parish allowances, may be considered as having been, in the first instance, a consequence of the high prices of provisions, and subsequently a cause of the prices reaching a higher level than they could otherwise have attained.

SECTION 3 *Statement of the general causes of the rise of the prices of commodities and labour from 1799 to 1801*

If the circumstances, such as they have been here imperfectly described, leading to the great elevation of the prices of provisions, and of raw materials, and of articles subject to the duties of excise, and the consequent necessary rise of the wages of labour from 1799 to 1801 be

---

		s. d.	*s. d.*		*s. d.*	
Carpenters –	–	– from 2 6 and	2 8	to	3 2	per day.
Bricklayers –	–	– – 2 4		to	3 0	
Masons –	–	– – 2 8		to	2 10	
Plumbers –		– – 3 0		to	3 3	

carefully examined, they will he found to resolve themselves into the agency of the following causes, namely, two seasons in succession of extraordinary dearth, — taxation, —and impediments arising out of the war to importation of articles which, whether as food or as raw materials, for our manufactures were of indispensable necessity.① But simple and obvious as were the causes of the great advance of prices, there were persons who then denied, or professed to doubt the existence of scarcity to account for the high prices, as there have been persons who, in more recent times, have denied the existence of abundance as accounting for a

---

① The great lise of the price of provisions and other necessaries, combined with the progress of taxation consequent on the war, occasioned an enormous increase of the late of living, as is instanced in the following: —

"Estimate of the Expenses of House-keeping, between 1773 and 1800, by an inhabitant of Bury St. Edmunds, extracted from the Appendix to the Report of a Committee of the House of Commons in the year 1800.

	1773			1793			1799			1800		
	£	*s.*	*d.*	£	*s.*	*d.*	£	*s.*	*d.*	£	*s.*	*d.*
Coomb of Malt	0	12	0	1	3	0	1	3	0	2	0	0
Chaldron of Coals	1	11	6	2	0	6	2	6	0	2	11	0
Coomb of Oats	0	5	0	0	13	0	0	16	0	1	1	0
Load of Hay	2	2	0	4	10	0	5	5	0	7	0	0
Meat	0	0	4	0	0	5	0	0	7	0	0	9
Butter	0	0	6	0	0	11	0	0	11	0	1	4
Sugar (Loaf)	0	0	8	0	1	0	0	1	3	0	1	4
Soap	0	0	6	0	0	8	0	0	$9\frac{1}{2}$	0	0	$10\frac{1}{2}$
Window Lights (30 winds.)	3	10	0	7	10	0	12	12	0	12	12	0
Candles	0	0	6	0	0	8	0	0	$9\frac{1}{2}$	0	0	$10\frac{1}{2}$
Poor Rates per Qr.	0	1	0	0	2	6	0	3	0	0	5	0
	8	4	0	16	2	8	22	9	4	25	14	$1\frac{1}{2}$

As far as the items included in this estimate are concerned, and they appear to be correctly stated, they exhibit an increase of about 200 per cent, in 1800, compared with 1773, and this was before any material difference between paper and gold bad become observable."

fall of prices. And a complete parallel may be found, *mutatis mutandis*, in the arguments against the belief in scarcity at that time, to those which more recently have been urged against the belief in abundance.

The following extracts from a pamphlet, published by Mr. Boyd, in the form of a letter to Mr. Pitt, in the autumn of 1800, which attracted considerable attention at the time, may serve as specimens of ingenious arguments, brought forward to disprove the most palpable facts, and to substitute for them a perfectly unfounded hypothesis.

Nearly at the outset (page 3.) the writer states his suspicion "that the increase of prices of almost all articles of necessity, convenience, and luxury, and, indeed, of almost every species of exchangeable value, which had been gradually① taking place during the last two years, and which had recently arrived at so great a height, proceeded chiefly from the addition to the circulating medium, which he conceived to have been made by the issue of bank notes, uncontrolled by the obligation of paying them on demand." He then proceeds, in terms which have been almost verbally repeated, in recent times, by persons who apply the doctrine of depreciation to the state of prices throughout the whole period of the suspension of cash payments: —

"Can you, sir, or any man, assign any cause sufficiently general in its effects and powerful in its operation, to account for a change so general in the prices of all, or very nearly all, articles of necessity, convenience, and luxury, as well as of every species of property or exchangeable value, within so short a space of time, except the one to which I attribute it? I by no means pretend that the high price of grain (which the general voice

① A rise of 100 to 200 per cent, in two years, can hardly be called gradual.

seems to attribute to the effect of an unfavourable season) is solely occasioned by the general cause of excess of paper circulation, not founded as all paper circulation ought to be, in the precious metals. I only contend, that if there be (as is alleged) a *real scarcity* of grain, the effects of this scarcity must be very much increased by the *general cause* which I conceive to have produced the *general rise* of the price of every thing. Your mind must look down with scorn upon the stale and inadequate causes of the high price of provisions which have been assigned for it by some men, more distinguished by their station than their acquirements. You well know that *partial causes* never can produce *general effects*. You cannot fail to have sought for a great and general cause for the solution of the phenomenon which excites the general wonder. That phenomenon, I again assert, in all probability, arises from an increase of the representative signs of money totally disproportioned to the time in which it has been effected, and to any progress which the industry of the country can possibly have made within that time; and such an increase never could have existed but for the rash attempt to extend the empire of credit beyond those limits which the eternal laws of nature had marked out for it.

A great use has taken place in every species of exchangeable value during the short period of two years. The public mind is on the rack to discover the cause of this rise, of which the most alarming effects are manifested in the article of bread. One says that there is a *real scarcity of grain*, owing to an uncommonly bad season last year, and a scanty crop this year. *How* this knowledge was acquired, I am utterly ignorant; but as it comes from a noble duke, (alluding to a letter addressed by the Duke of Portland to the lord lieutenant of the county of Oxford,) high in the administration of the internal affairs of this country, it is to be presumed that it was not promulgated on slight or doubtful grounds. This, however, I must be permitted to say, that if there did exist sufficient reason to believe the scarcity to be *real*, the influence of that cause cannot have lost any of its force by the extraordinary publicity given to it.

Another says, there is no scarcity; but a set of forestallers and regraters have monopolised the grain of the country, and sell it out at such prices as they think proper to fix from time to time."

The writer very justly ridicules and reprobates this absurd and unjust clamour, but at greater length than the topic is worth, and then continues: —

"The opinion of a third person is, that the scarcity and high price of bread corn proceed from a great addition made to the population of the country. How such a cause should so suddenly produce an effect of such magnitude does, I own, exceed my comprehension. At what period the seeds of this extraordinary increase were sown I cannot even guess, but it is necessary to suppose that there must have been some one or two years of uncommon fecundity, in order to account for the extraordinary addition to our population which, in this particular year, has so greatly enhanced the price of corn. The progress of population, like the growth of an individual, is so gradual and imperceptible as to escape the notice of the most vigilant observer, otherwise than in its effects, and, as in the growth of an individual it can never happen to any parent to be surprised with a child of two years old starting into the dimensions of one of twelve, so, in my bumble opinion, it is not probable that it should happen to any country to find its population, in one or two years, made such an extraordinary shoot as only could have been expected in half a century; and yet such a shoot it must have made, if an increased population be admitted as the cause of the very high price of provisions in this particular year.

By a fourth, the high price of provisions is placed to the account of the war. This is a good general head for carrying all doubtful points to, —all unappropriated disasters, all stray calamities and incidental disappointments of every description. I shall not touch upon this extensive subject further than to say, that I see nothing in the mode of *conducting this war*, during the last two or three years, which ought to occasion any result affecting provisions, different from what all other wars, and this very war during the first four years of its duration, have generally produced. Whether the mode by which the means of earning on the war have been raised, have or have not contributed to the high price of corn, as well as of every other necessary of life, is quite another consideration, and belongs to the general object of this inquiry, which is, to consider the influence of the present paper currency on the prices of commodities in general. It is sufficient for the present purpose of estimating the credit due to the assertion, that the high price of grain is occasioned *by the war*, to say, that no such conclusion is warranted by what has happened in other wars.

It has been reserved for me to assign, as the cause of the general use which almost all things have experienced within the last two or three years (and which grain, as the article that comes most frequently in contact with money, feels the soonest and the most) the existence of a great bank, invested with the power of issuing paper, professing to be payable on demand, but which, in fact, the bank which issues it is not obliged to pay."

These are the very arguments conveyed in the language almost *verbatim et literatim*, of the more modern partisans of the doctrine of indefinite depreciation of the currency during the bank restriction. There is the same disposition to profess to doubt, or utterly to deny, the existence *of the fact of scarcity arising from political and physical causes*, in spite of evidence the most conclusive in the case of every description of produce, that exhibited so great an advance of price, in the period under consideration.

The writer of the letter, here quoted, is a striking instance of the degree in which the desire to maintain a tenet hastily adopted is apt to render a person, otherwise well informed, blind or averse to see the most palpable facts passing around him, which, if seen or known at all, must be conclusive against him. Else how could it be possible, that, whether as an extensive merchant, and much in society, and still more as a member of the very parliament which was then sitting, and engaged in collecting the most extensive information from all parts of the kingdom, on the state of the crops, and the stock of provisions, he could seriously entertain a doubt of the existence of great scarcity, arising from two consecutive remarkably deficient harvests, is wholly inconceivable. But what would be still more marvellous, if it had not also its parallel among otherwise well-informed persons at a later period is, that neither in Mr. Boyd's letter, nor in the publications in answer to him, is the slightest notice taken of the important fact, that, coincidently with the rising prices of provisions, and of other European produce, all Colonial and American produce (rice excepted), which during the three preceding years had been rising, while corn was falling, declined rapidly in 1799 and 1800, while corn was rapidly rising, and all transatlantic produce was, at the date of that letter, in a state of great depression.

SECTION 4 *Great fall of the prices of transatlantic produce from the spring of 1799 to the spring of 1801*

In the examination of prices, in the interval ending in 1798, we have seen that colonial produce had begun to rise in 1796, in consequence of a demand from Germany, and that the demand which had become extremely speculative, continuing on an increasing scale, the prices had reached an unprecedented height at the close of 1798. In a few instances, the rise was continued through the first three months of 1799. As usual, in such cases, the consumption of the commodities, which had been the objects of speculation, was reduced by the advanced cost, and consequently proved to be much less than had been anticipated, while the supplies were much larger.

The prices thenceforward began to fall; and, as the circulation by bills of exchange and other forms of credit had expanded with and promoted the rise of prices, so it was contracted by, and in its turn accelerated the fall of prices until the final adjustment to the metallic standard. This process was attended with very disastrous results in the great commercial towns of Germany and Holland. The number of houses that failed at Hamburg, between August and November, 1799, was eighty-two, and the amount of their engagements upwards of twentynine million five hundred thousand banco marks, or about two million five hundred thousand pounds. The rate of discount at Hamburg rose during that interval to 15 per cent per annum.

The fall of prices and the commercial failures in Germany entailed a corresponding fall of prices in this country, and discredit and failures to a considerable extent, not only among the houses immediately embarked in the trade with that part of the Continent, but also of some eminent houses in the West India trade. The following extracts, from printed commercial reports of that period, convey a description of the circumstances attending the fall of prices of colonial produce: —

"1st of October, 1799. —The trade of this country with the principal part of Europe having of late been confined almost wholly to one channel, the unusual flow of business it produced to those places through which it was carried on, led many persons to extend their concerns in a degree to which their capital was inadequate, and encouraged a spirit of adventure and speculation, particularly in the chief articles of sugar and other West India produce, which at length has been earned too far; the consequence of which has been the failure of some considerable houses at Hamburgh and other places, which has affected their connections in this country, so far as to cause the stoppage of several houses winch had hitherto maintained no small degree of commercial reputation."

"1st of November, 1799. —The embarrassments of the merchants at Hamburgh have increased to an alarming degree; and during the whole month of October every mail that has arrived has added several names to the unfortunate list of houses which have stopped payment in that city, where there are scarcely any persons in the mercantile line, whatever may be their wealth and connexions, who have not experienced considerable difficulties, while the effects there of have extended to Bremen, Frankfort, Amsterdam, and many other of the principal trading towns on the Continent. The general and extensive connexion which has of late subsisted between the greater part of our merchants and those of Hamburgh, naturally excited apprehensions of the most serious consequences in this country, which have been in part too justly verified by the failure of several commercial houses, in addition to those alluded to in our last report. The loss of the Lutine frigate, winch had on board 600, 000 dollars, destined for Hamburgh, has been a very unfortunate circumstance, both in itself, and, with respect to the object in view, as it must occasion a great disappointment, and delay the intended relief considerably."

The losses connected with the Hamburg failures, and the great fall of prices of West India produce, seem to have been felt with peculiar severity in Liverpool. Mention is made in the Annual Register of

"An act passed in the parliament which met in the autumn of 1799, granting a loan of 500,000*l.* in exchequer bills to the West India merchants in Liverpool, in order to avert the evils which hung over their heads from very heavy failures in Hamburgh. Security was given for this loan, in property in their warehouses amounting to upwards of two millions."

The subjoined statement will show the extent of the depression of transatlantic produce, which took place between the spring of 1799 and the spring of 1801, being the interval during which all European produce had been rising, and had leached an unprecedented height: —

		1798-1799			1800-1801	
Coffee, Jam. Sup., per cwt.	185*s.*	to	196*s.*	116*s.*	to	130*s.*
Sugar, Mascov. Jam., do.	62*s.*	–	87*s.*	28*s.*	–	50*s.*
—, East India, white, do.	96*s.*	–	115*s.*	50*s.*	–	70*s.*
Saltpetre, do –	140*s.*	–	145*s.*	60*s.*	–	61*s.*
Cochineal per *lb.* –	52*s.*	–	54*s.*	14*s.*	–	19*s.*
Cotton, Bowed Georgia –	3*s.* 6*d.*	–	4*s.* 6*d.*	1*s.* 5*d.*	–	2*s.* 8*d.*
Indigo, East India, superior	11*s.*	–	13*s.* 9*d.*	8*s.*	–	9*s.* 6*d.*
Spices, Cinnamon –	8*s.*	–	10*s.*	4*s.*	–	5*s.*
—, Pepper –	–	–	22*d.*	–	–	13*d.*
Tobacco, Virginia –	$11\frac{1}{2}d.$	–	16*d.*	4*d.*	–	5*d.*
Logwood, per ton –	48*l.*	–	50*l.*	12*l.*	–	15*l.*
Rum, per gallon –	7*s.* 2*d.*	–	8*s.*	3*s.*	–	5*s.* 6*d.*

The prices of most of our manufactured articles likewise experienced a considerable fall in the interval from 1799 to 1801. The following is from a Monthly Commercial Report, dated 1st of April, 1801: —

"The trade of Birmingham is in a very distressed situation. A large proportion of the workmen are entirely out of employ, and those who still have work have the utmost difficulty to gain a subsistence, from the exorbitant price of all kinds of provisions. The ribbon trade of Coventry is in a most deplorable state, and the woollen trade of Yorkshire, if possible, still worse"①

But it is not this great fall only of prices of so many, and so important, articles of consumption, that affords a negative of the presumption of the agency of so general a cause, as that of the currency or war demand, — in the rise which took place from the spring of 1799 to the spring of 1801, in the prices of provisions, and of other articles of European produce; for it will now be seen, that, upon the cessation or abatement of the operation of the seasons, and of obstructions to importation, the prices of provisions, and of other objects of exchange (labour alone excepted) which had so

---

① So much for the assertion so confidently made in Mr. Boyd's letter, that, "a great rise had taken place in the price of every species of exchangeable value, during the short period of two years." I am at the same time inclined to believe, that the writer expressed what was really the impression on his mind for, I find that even among men of business there is a very great vagueness of recollection within even moderately short periods, of the order of time, within which large classes of produce have fluctuated relatively, each to the other, and a preponderating impression, produced by the attention having been at the tune drawn more to one than the other, is applied to the whole mass, although it maybe, as it was in the case here alluded to, and again in more recent periods, that while the prices of one great class of commodities has been using, another has been falling in nearly the same ratio. The simple fact of the opposite tendencies, more especially where in each case the tendency may be explained, by distinct circumstances producing it, destroys the conclusion derived exclusively from one only of those tendencies, as to the universality of the operation of a given cause."

risen, fell, and continued to fall till they subsided to the level from which they had been raised.

SECTION 5 *Fall of the prices of provisions from the spring of 1801 to the close of 1803*

As the several steps of the rise in the prices of provisions to, so, an extraordinary elevation have been noticed, it may not be uninteresting to trace the circumstances leading to the fall.

After the great elevation of prices had been reached in March, 1801, the aspect of things, both as to the influence of the seasons and the state of politics, experienced a marked change for the better.

The winter had been less rigorous than the two preceding. The seed time, both for wheat and spring corn, had been favourable, and an increased breadth of cultivation was in progress. The spring of 1801 was genial, and the crops were forward and promising. The death of the emperor Paul of Russia, and the peace with Denmark, which followed the battle of Copenhagen, had reopened the navigation of the Baltic to British shipping, thus removing the obstruction which had been apprehended to supplies from thence; and the bounty, therefore, with the high prices, insured a large importation of corn.

Under these improved prospects of future supply, the markets gave way rapidly. The averages of corn in England and Wales, on the 30th of June, 1801, were, —

For Wheat	–	–	129*s*. 8*d*.
Barley	–	–	69*s*. 7*d*.
Oats	–	–	37*s*. 2*d*.

The harvest proving to be of moderate abundance had, with the large importation①, the effect of reducing the averages by the end of 1801②, to

75*s*. 6*d*. for wheat;

44*s*. for bailey; and

23*s*. 4*d*. for oats;

being a fall of upwards of 50 per cent since the month of March preceding. Beans and peas fell in the like proportion; but meat continued to be dear, because the stock of cattle and sheep, which had been reduced by the previous scarcities, had no time to be restored.

It may here be observed, as an instance of the imperfect information, and the fallacy as to any correct conclusion, to be derived from a mere reference to *annual* averages, that, although the year 1801 saw the termination of the great dearth, that it was in fact a comparatively abundant season, and that it was signalised by a fall of upwards of 50 per cent in prices, it yet passes, according to the yearly averages of the price of wheat, for the dearest of the whole series; while 1799, which was the most disastrously sterile, might from such reference be inferred to have been but slightly deficient. Thus,

---

① The importations in 1801 were, of

Wheat	–	1, 424, 766 quarters
Barley	–	113, 966
Oats	–	583, 043

② The preliminaries of peace with France, which were signed in October, 1801, do not appear to have had any material influence in accelerating the fall, the greater part of which had, indeed, taken place before that event, which, however, was calculated to extend the sources of supply, and to diminish the cost of importation.

1799, yearly average	–	–	67*s*. 6*d*.
1800, – –	–	–	113*s*. 7*d*.
1801, – –	–	–	118*s*. 3*d*.

The seasons of 1802 and 1803 were considered to be of ordinary, and certainly not of superabundant, produce; but they had the effect of progressively depressing the prices of grain. The averages at the close of 1802 were, —

For Wheat	–	–	57*s*. 1*d*.
Barley	–	–	25*s*. 7*d*.
Oats	–	–	20*s*.

And notwithstanding the renewal of the war with France early in 1803, the fall of prices continued, with only trifling oscillations, to the close of that year, when the averages were, —

For Wheat	–	–	–	52*s*. 3*d*.
Barley	–	–	–	23*s*. 11*d*.
Oats	–	–	–	21*s*. 1*d*.

In the course of the first three months of 1804, the price of wheat experienced a further decline to 49*s*. 6*d*. But the foregoing quotations sufficiently establish the fact, that by the end of 1803 a complete subsidence had taken place in the prices of grain, to the level from which they had been disturbed; and if the very low prices at which barley and oats ranged in 1803 be taken into the account, it is manifest that grain generally was then as cheap as, with the exception of a few months, it has been in the whole period following the peace, and since the resumption of cash payments. ①

SECTION 6 *On the state of the circulation from 1799 to 1803*

We have now to see how far the state of the circulation, during this interval, differed from what it might be supposed to have been, if the paper had been convertible under the usual system pursued by the Bank; and how far there exist any grounds for thinking that the rise of prices was caused by an increase and the subsequent fall by a diminution of the quantity of money.

The currency, at the outset of 1799, may be considered as having been at its strict bullion level with the rest of the commercial world, or, if anything, at a somewhat higher value, inasmuch as the exchange on Hamburg, from January to March of that year was 37*s.* 7*d.*, being higher than it had been for any length of time before the restriction. And it may be instanced, as a proof that the directors considered the position of the bank to be such as, but for the restriction, which from political considerations the government were induced to continue, would admit of their paying in specie, that on the 3rd of January, 1799, the following notice was given: —

"That on and after the 14th instant the bank will pay in cash all fractional sums under five pounds, and that on and after the 1st of

① The prices of meat declined slowly. The extreme dryness of the summer of 1803 had made turnips and cattle food generally scarce and dear. The quotations at the close of that year were,

Beef, in Smithfield,	–	–	–	4*s.* to 5*s.* 4*d.*
Mutton,	–	–	–	4*s.* to 4*s.* 6*d.*

But it will be seen, that the prices continued to fall in the interval, which is to come next under consideration.

The pirces of commodities, exclusive of provisions, were not marked in 1803 by any such variations as to require particular notice.

February next, the bank will pay cash for all notes of one and two pounds value, that are dated prior to 1st of July, 1798, or exchange them for new notes, at the option of the holder."

The position of the bank on the 28th of February, 1799, being two full years after the restriction, was as follows: —

		Securities	
Circulation of bank notes of 5*l*. and upwards, and Bank post bills – –	11, 494, 150	Public –	11, 510, 677
Under 5*l*. – –	1, 465, 650	Private –	5, 528, 353
	12, 959, 800		17, 039, 030
Deposits – –	8, 131, 820	Bullion –	7, 563, 900
Liabilities – –	21, 091, 620	Assets –	24, 602, 930

The stock of bullion was thus in the proportion of more than one third of the liabilities, and was, in fact, larger than the bank had ever before (with the exception of two years, from August, 1789, to August, 1791) possessed.

After this period there arose a combination of circumstances, which entailed the necessity for the payment of *unusually* large sums abroad. The violent commercial revulsion, which took place at Hamburg in the autumn of 1799, required, on the part of the merchants here, an immediate transmission of funds to a very large amount. Good bills to a sufficient extent (many of the German houses here being in a state of discredit) could not be procured, and would not, if obtained, have been negotiable at Hamburgh, at the moment of such a suspension of credit, the rate of discount there having risen to 15 per cent per annum, at which only the best bills, and to a limited amount, could be made available. The only alternative was to send bullion, which was accordingly exported (chiefly silver) in large quantities.

The harvest in this country had, as has been seen, failed to such an extent, as to require an unusually large importation of corn, which, as it was scarce on the Continent of Europe and in America, could only be, obtained at very high prices. The war on the Continent, by the second coalition against France, had been resumed on such a large scale, in the summer of 1799, as of itself to create a great absorption of gold and silver for the military chests; and it was, moreover, accompanied by subsidies to Russia and Austria. The celebrated expedition, too, under the Duke of York, to the Helder, in the autumn of 1799, contributed to swell the amount of foreign payments.

Under this combination of extraordinary circumstances requiring an immediate transmission of such enormous sums abroad, while the currencies of the principal commercial cities of the Continent of Europe *were greatly contracted* by the state of mercantile discredit, and by the demand for specie for the purposes of the war, the exchanges fell, without any previous enlargement of the bank issues worth mentioning, and with an actual amount of circulation below what, with reference to the state of its treasure, the bank would have been justified in issuing, previous to these occurrences.

The following are the quarterly average amounts of the Bank of England notes of five pounds and upwards, for 1799, with the exchanges, and the prices of gold and wheat at the close of each quarter: —

			Ex. on Hamb	Gold	Wheat
March	25.	11, 585, 210	37*s*. 5*d*.	3*l*. 17*s*. 9*d*.	52*s*. 6*d*.
June	25.	12, 118, 690	36*s*. —	3*l*. 17*s*. 9*d*.	64*s*. 4*d*.
Sept.	25.	12, 155, 360	32*s*. 9*d*.	No price.	80*s*. 8*d*.
Dec.	25.	12, 335, 920	32*s*. 6*d*. to 31*s*. 6*d*.	–	92*s*. 7*d*.

It will here be observed, that a great fall of the exchange (and a great rise in the price of wheat) took place by the end of September, although the increase of bank notes, as compared with the preceding quarter, is not worth notice, and that the circulation in the last quarter exceeded that of the two preceding quarters, by only the insignificant amount of 180, 000*l*. , while the exchange was 10 per cent, lower, and the price of wheat nearly 50 per cent, higher in December than in June. But considering the state of commercial discredit, and the high rate of interest which prevailed at the close of 1799, the presumption is, that the circulating medium was virtually contracted, and that the value of money was increased.

It is true, that supposing the regulation of the issues to have been under a very vigilant and correct system of management, with a view to preserve the value of the paper on a level with its standard, the Directors would, in consequence of the great fall in the exchanges, and the consequent drain of their treasure, have reduced their circulation at the close of 1799, and at any rate they would not have extended it as they did then, and further under a still increasing pressure of foreign payments in 1800. But in the first place, the exchanges would not have fallen so much if the bank had then been paying in specie, inasmuch as the gold drawn from it for exportation, would in so far have diminished the demand for bills. And, in the next place, judging by the conduct of the bank in 1782, and again in 1795, when in the face of a similar fall of the exchange, the issues were extended instead of being contracted, the probability is, that the amount of the circulation would equally have been extended in 1800. As in point of fact they were extended by about a million of notes of 5*l*. and upwards, as compared with 1799, or by a million and a half, as compared with the three years ending in 1795, the average amount, in 1800, having been 13,421,920. ①

---

① It was upon the extension of the issues of the Bank, in 1800, that the first important controversy respecting their influence on prices arose. The letter of Mr. Boyd on the subject has already been noticed, as far as relates to the rise of prices. In a postcript dated 31st of December, 1800, he adds: —

"By the return to an older of the House of Commons, it appears that the amount of bank notes in calculation was 15,450,970*l.*, which exceeds the sum in circulation on the the 26th of February, 1797 (viz., 8,640,250, by nearly four fifths of that circulation). Compared with the average circulation of three years, ending December, 1795; viz., 11,975,573, the circulation on the 6th of December, 1800, exceeds that average cnculation by nearly three tenths of its amount." "The exchange with Hamburgh, which, when this letter was written, was 31*s.* 10*d.*, is now 29*s.* 10*d.*, by which means the difference which then existed of nearly 9 per cent, against out currency is now increased to upwards of 14 per cent. If, therefore, a person residing on the Continent remit funds to this country to be invested in the 3 per cent, at the price of 62 it is evident that by purchasing the money so remitted at 14 per cent, discount the real price of his 3 per cent, will be $53\frac{8}{25}$, or nearly $53\frac{1}{3}$. The price of gold has fortunately not advanced in the same proportion within the same period. The price which, on the 11th Nov. was 4*l.* 5*s.* per ounce, is now 4*l.* 6*s.*, which is little more than $1\frac{1}{6}$ per cent, thus making the whole premium upon gold 10*l.* 8*s.* 8*d.*, for every 100*l.* or something more than $10\frac{5}{12}$ per cent."

This letter of Mr. Boyd's elicited, among other answers, one from Sir Francis Baring, in which, after observing upon the inconsistency of Mr. Boyd, who had been at the head of those persons that had remonstrated on the insufficiency of the circulation in 1796, in now attributing such vast effects to the increased amount of the bank issues, has the following apt remark:

"Perhaps Mr. Boyd is not aware in what manner his own quotations and his own arguments may return against him, by the delay of a few days. In the postcript, dated the 31st, December, 1800, he observes, that since his letter was written, the exchange on Hamburgh had fallen from 31*s.* 10*d.* to 29*s.* 10*d.*, which he considers as an additional proof of what he has advanced. In that case, he must admit that when the exchange rises, it must produce a comparatively favourable effect. On the 2nd of January, 1801, the course of Hamburgh is printed 29*s.* 8*d.*, and on the 30th of January it is printed 31*s.* 8*d.* — a difference of very near 7 per cent, and yet we do not perceive the slightest effect it has produced in lowering the price of provisions or other commodities grown and consumed in Great Britain, and affords a most unequivocal corieet answer to the whole of his argument with regard to the foreign exchanges."

But admitting that there had been the increase of issues, by the Bank of England, to the utmost* extent of Mr. Boyd's exaggerated view of it, and allowing also for an increase of the country circulation, it can hardly be considered as compensating for the chasm which must have been caused in the metallic circulation by the clandestine export of guineas, which the low exchange must have forced abroad.

The amount of gold in circulation, before the restriction, was by a

---

Mr. Henry Thornton, in his work on Paper Credit, makes the following remarks, suggested by Mr. Boyds publication:—

After observing that the two millions of notes under 5*l.* issued by the Bank of England should be considered as mere substitutes for the guineas which they displaced, and should therefore be deducted from the total amount of the bank issues, in any reasoning upon the effect produced by these on the cnculating medium, he proceeds to say, "I have to consider how far, allowing for that difference of two millions of which mention has been made, the circulating quantity of Bank of England paper has lately corresponded with that of antecedent periods. The average amount of Bank of England notes in circulation during three years ending in 1795, appears to have been 11, 975, 578. The amount in circulation on the 20th of February, 1797, the day antecedent to the suspension of the cash payments of the Bank, has been already stated to have been about 8, 600, 000, this being that very low sum to which they were then reduced. By a statement of their amount on the 6th of December, 1800, laid before the House of Commons, they appeal to have been then 15, 450, 970. This last mentioned sum includes* the two millions of one and two-pound notes. If these two millions are deducted, the amount, on the 6th of December, 1800, will exceed the average amount in three years antecedent to the suspension of the cash payments of the Bank, by 1, 475, 397*l.*. It remains, however, to be observed, that the notes of the Bank of England were stated to the House of Commons by the governor of that company in the spring of 1801, to have been then reduced to a sum less by about a million and a half than their amount on the 6th of December, 1800. The total quantity, therefore, of the Bank of England notes in cnculation in one part of the spring of 1801, if the two millions be deducted, almost exactly agrees with their average amount timing the three years ending December, 1795."

* By a return to Parliament from the Bank, dated 6th, February, 1801, the amount of notes under 5*l.* in circulation.

From 25th of November to 25th of December 1800, was 2,148.700

And from 25th of December to 25th of January 1801, - 2,519.100

moderate computation, twenty-two millions five hundred thousand pounds (by some it was estimated at forty millions). Supposing, therefore, eight millions to have remained in circulation in 1800 (an outside supposition), there would be fourteen millions and a half, at least, to be replaced by Bank of England and country bank notes. Now the increase of the Bank of England issues, including the small notes in 1800, as compared with the three years ending in 1795, was somewhat under three millions five hundred thousand pounds, and it would be a most extravagant estimate, which would assume an increase in that interval of country bank notes to the extent of eleven millions, which would be requisite to make up the difference. Indeed, the increase to that extent, if it took place at all, must have been effected in a wonderfully short space of time, because, as has been seen, there had been a great reduction of the country circulation in 1796, and from that time till after the commencement of 1799 there was not much facility or inducement for its increase. The subsequent rise of prices, no doubt, favoured the extension of the country bank issues ①, but it is

① With reference to the country bank calculation at this period, the following further extract from Sir Francis Baring's answer to Mr. Boyd may not be without interest. "An alarm has been raised against country banks, which have been accused of enabling the farmers to hoard then corn by making them advances of money: but the inhabitants of this metropolis arc not aware of the total change in the situation of the country banks, in consequence of the war. Those who are established in seaports and great manufacturing towns may still he considered as having commercial deposits with which they must, in prcfcrence, accommodate their commercial friends; but the general mass of banks through the country look to the farmers for deposits and support, as the only persons who have money to employ. It is very rare that a farmer wants to borrow; but the instances are not rare when he is able to accommodate even his landlord with a loan."

In truth, such were the enormous gains of the farmers at this time, that, while their credit must have been so high as would have enabled them to borrow to any amount they might desire, it is not conceivable that they could have had sufficient motive for borrowing on an extensive scale It is mush more probable, and Sir F Baring mention it as a fact that they were rather lenders than borrowers.

utterly improbable, or rather absolutely absurd, to suppose that it can have been to anything like the above amount. The fair conclusion, therefore is, that the quantity of money, during the range of high prices in 1799 and 1800, although greater than could he maintained, under the pressure of demand for foreign payments, was not only not increased, but was probably less than it had been in the three years ending in 1795, without taking into account the great increase of transactions, and consequently of the functions of money that must have taken place since that time. But, whether less or greater, it was the duty of the Directors of the bank to preserve the value of their paper on a level with gold, and this they could not have done without contracting their issues, or, at least, without limiting the amount in 1800 to what it had been in 1799. It is very possible, that the simple limitation to that amount might have effected a restoration of the exchanges and the price of gold, because, notwithstanding the enlargement of between a million and a million and a half of notes of 5*l*. and upwards in 1800, the exchanges were not materially lower than they had been at the close of 1799; whence it should seem that an increase of our commercial exports was in progress to accommodate itself to the increased and increasing foreign payments, which were going forward under the two important heads of government expenditure abroad, and of imports① of grain.

The question here occurs, what would have been the effects on commercial credit and prices, and on the rate of interest, if the issues of the bank had been so limited at the close of 1799, and through 1800, as to have preserved the value of the paper on a level with gold?

① The computed value of grain imported, in 1800, was 8,755,995*l*., in 1801, 10,149.098*l*..

All hypothetical reasoning, as to what *might have been*, instead of what *was*, admits of wide difference of conclusion, and is at best unsatisfactory. According to the best of my conception of the state of things, under the supposed forcible contraction by the bank of its issues, it would have been this. There would have been a greatly increased pressure on the money market, severe as it already was. The public funds would have been lower, and the financial operations of government would have been on terms more disadvantageous to the public. The commercial discredit and failures which occurred at the close of 1799, and the commencement of 1800, in consequence of the revulsion of credit at Hamburgh and other continental towns, would probably have been aggravated, and the fall of prices of colonial produce, and of all other commodities that were in full supply, or were held on credit, or depended for purchase on the usual credit, would, great as it was, have been more rapid. But the prices of corn, and of other provisions, and of articles generally, the supply of which was below the ordinary rate of consumption, would in all probability have been full as high. The prices of provisions were determined by the highest sum which the wages of the lowest classes, aided by contributions from parishes and individuals, would afford for food, and the rate of wages would not be affected, or in the most trifling degree only, by the casual expansion or contraction of the bank issues, and certainly not within a short period as a twelvemonth. There appears, moreover, in the rise of prices of provisions following the harvest of 1799 to have been little of either buying or holding on credit, for there is, as we have seen, according to the best evidence of which the subject is susceptible, the strongest proof or reason for supposing that the stock of corn was exhausted, and that the dearth, great as it was, would have been more severely felt, had it not been for the earliness of the harvest of 1800.

The renewed rise of the prices of provisions after the harvest of 1800, took place without any increase of the amount of bank notes of 5*l.* and upwards, which for the last six months of that year was rather less than in the first six months. And the average amount for the whole of the year 1801 was 13,454,370, being, as nearly as might be, the same as in 1800. Now this amount upon the grounds already stated, with the addition of about 2, 700, 000*l.* of notes under 5*l.*, and with the utmost probable extension of the country paper, and with the progressively diminishing number of guineas, did not probably make up an aggregate nearly equal to that which constituted the currency in the three years ending in 1795. There is accordingly the strongest possible reason to believe, that the quantity of money was not increased, and could not, therefore, be the *cause* of the rise in the price of provisions between the summer of 1799 and that of 1801, independently of the incongruity which attaches to the supposition of its having caused the rise of one class of commodities, at the same time that another great class of commodities was falling in nearly an equal proportion to the rise of the former, while it has been in evidence, that there was a great scarcity of the commodities which did rise. The argument, therefore, is sufficiently made out, that it was a case of *dearth* and not of depreciation.

If any doubt, however, should still remain on that score, a fact decisive against the supposition, that an increase of the quantity of money, or of the circulating medium, as indicated by the bank issues, had been the cause of the rise is, that coincidently with an increase of the circulation of the Bank of England notes, prices subsided upon the cessation of the scarcity to the level from which they had advanced. For if it was the amount of bank notes that raised prices in 1800 and 1801, how happened it that an increased amount in 1802 did not sustain the prices, and much more prevent a fall of above 50 per cent? And if the exchanges had been depressed, and the price of bullion raised by the amount of the circulation, how happened it that they tended upon the abatement of foreign payments to their par level coincidently with an increased issue, as will appear by the following statement. The average circulation of—

		Ex Dec. 31.		Foreign Gold.			Silver Dllrs.		Wheat.	
	£	*s.*	*d.*	*l.*	*s.*	*d.*	*s.*	*d.*	*s.*	*d.*
1800 was	13,421,920	30	0	4	6	0	5	9	133	0
1801 –	13,454,370	31	11	4	3	6	5	$10\frac{1}{2}$	75	6
1802 –	13,917,980	31	0	4	0	0	5	$4\frac{1}{4}$	57	1

In as far, therefore, as a negative admits of being established, it is clearly so, in favour of the conclusion, that the bank restriction had *no* effect of depreciating the currency beyond the degree indicated by the difference between paper and gold, in the period now under consideration, and the presumption is the strongest possible that the prices of provisions, and of other produce, which attained their greatest elevation in the spring of 1801, would have reached the same height under a convertible state of the currency; and that, therefore, as regards these, it is doubtful whether *any* allowance for the difference between paper and gold ought to be made.

But although in a convertible state of the currency, the articles which were of *first necessity*, and which existed in an extraordinary degree of scarcity, would, in all probability, have been as high as they were, all articles not so circumstanced would have been lower in consequence of the forcible contraction of the circulation, which would have been necessary to counteract the pressure on the exchanges, of the unusually large foreign expenditure. And it is probable, that after the spring of 1801, when scarcity, and the apprehension of it, had ceased, the fall of the prices of necessaries would have been more rapid than it was. At the same time, there is no reason to believe that the subsidence would have been to a lower level than that to which prices did eventually fall under the actual system. If prices had fallen more rapidly, the importations of 1801 and 1802 would have been less and the exportations greater, and the prices of 1803 would have been probably higher, instead of continuing to fall as they did. Among the grounds of presumption in favour of this view is the fact, that the prices of corn and of meat were, in 1802, higher in France, and some of the other countries of the Continent of Europe, than in this country. ①

The circulation of the bank in 1803 was —

Of 5*l*. notes and upwards, including

---

① In truth, the use and high range of prices, with short intervals only of subsidence, which have been noticed in the review of this and of the preceding epochs, have their parallel in the state of prices on the Continent of Europe during the corresponding period. Thus, Mr. Jacob, in his report of March, 1826, states the manner in which the competition of France for foreign corn tended to raise the price in the markets of the rest of Europe.

"During the ten years from 1791 to 1801, there was a constant demand in France for foreign corn; several deficient harvests had been experienced at the beginning of the Revolution. The agents of France were employed both in Europe and America in purchasing corn, and hiring neutral vessels to convey it to France, paying little regard to the price they paid for it, or the rate of freight at which it could be transported. Holland, which scarcely has ever grown corn sufficient for its own consumption, felt a great want, owing to its internal sources of supply from Germany and Flanders being diverted from the usual channels by the circumstances of the war." (P. 51)

At the same time, it is to be observed, that France either was not visited by such great dearths in 1799 and 1800 as prevailed in this country and in the north of Europe, or that the government, by operating on the averages, endeavoured to conceal the fact.

bank post bills	–	–	12, 983, 477*l*.
And of notes under 5*l*.	–	–	3, 864, 045*l*.
Together,	–	–	16, 847, 522*l*.

being nearly one million of the former, but only two hundred thousand of the total less than in 1802.

The comparative diminution, however, was in the first six months of 1803. In the last six months of that year there was an increase, as compared with the last six months of 1802, and the prices of corn were lower at the close of 1803 than they had been at the close of 1802: —

			Dec. 1802.			Dec. 1803.	
Wheat	–	–	57*s*.	1*d*.	–	52*s*.	3*d*.
Barley	–	–	25*s*.	7*d*.	–	23*s*.	11*d*.
Oats	–	–	20*s*.	0*d*.	–	21*s*.	1*d*.

The great fall of prices between 1801 and 1803 was followed, as might be supposed, by extensive failures. A comparison of the number of bankruptcies stands thus: —

1798	–	911	1801	–	1199
1799	–	717	1802	–	1090
1800	–	951	1803	–	1214
	–	2579		–	3503

being an increase of more than one third.

It is probable that the excess of failures in the latter period would have been still greater, if, in consequence of the peculiar nature of the bounty on importation of corn, which ensured a minimum price till the 1st of October, 1801, the importers had not been preserved from the full effect of the decline of the markets between the spring and autumn of that year. There does not, at the same time, appear to have been so great an extension and abuse of credit during the rise of prices, between 1799 and 1801, as on some former and subsequent occasions, nor, consequently, so great a derangement of the circulation in consequence of the fall; nor in point of fact were there any failures of consequence among the country bankers.

SECTION 7 *Summary of the preceding survey*

On a review, then, of the whole period from the commencement of 1799 to the close of 1803, it appears —

1. That the prices of provisions, which, at the beginning of 1799 were as low as they had been on an average of some years anterior to 1793, advanced, in common with other articles of European produce, to an unprecedented height, as a necessary consequence of the two very deficient harvests of 1799 and 1800, combined with actual and apprehended obstructions to importation.

2. That upon the recurrence of moderately productive harvests in 1801, 1802, and 1803, combined with a removal of some of the impediments to a foreign supply, the prices of corn and other European produce at the close of 1803, subsided to the level from which they had been raised by the before-mentioned scarcities from seasons and political obstructions.

3. That coincidently with the great rise in the prices of provisions and of European produce in 1799 and 1800, a very great fall took place in all transatlantic produce; thus negativing the inference of the operation of a common cause, such as that of mere increase of money.

4. That the rise in the prices of provisions, and of European produce generally, in 1799 and 1800, was attended with an increase of the bank circulation, and with a rise in the price of gold, and a fall of the exchanges.

5. That the fall in the prices of grain, and of all European produce, subsequent to the spring of 1801, and a fall in the price of gold and a rise of the exchanges, were attended with a further increase of the circulation of bank notes; thus affording a negative of any inference that the increase of bank notes had been the cause of the previous alteration of prices and exchanges, because if it had been so, the further increase of bank notes should have prevented the subsidence of prices, and the restoration of the exchanges.

6. That the prices of provisions, and of many other leading articles of consumption, were lower in 1803, a period of war on a most extensive scale, and of very large loans raised by government towards defraying the expenses of it, than they had been in 1802, a year of peace.

And, finally, that with the exception of the prices of naval and military stores, not a trace can be found in the state of prices, in the interval that has passed under review, of *war demand*, and as little of *depreciation* of the value of the currency, understanding by that term, a rise of prices *caused* by an increase of money, and not by a relative scarcity of commodities.

CHAPTER Ⅳ
STATE OF PRICES AND OF THE CIRCULATION FROM THE COMMENCEMENT OF 1804 TO THE CLOSE OF 1808

The state of stagnation and declining markets which has been noticed as prevailing from the time of the renewal in the spring of 1803, of the war with France, in agriculture and trade, but more especially in the former, continued through the early part of 1804.

The prices of coin by the gazette averages for England and Wales, were, —

March, 1804,	Wheat	- -	49*s*. 6*d*.
	Barley	- -	22*s*. 9*d*.
	Oats	- -	19*s*. 9*d*.

No instance in the whole period under discussion from 1793 to the present time, nor indeed any in the whole course of last century exhibits so great a fall of the price of wheat within the same space of time, as that which occurred between March, 1801 and March, 1804, namely from an average of 155*s*. to 49*s*. 6*d*.. ①

① Thus, after twelve years of war, and eight years of suspension of cash payments, we find that the prices of corn subsided a second time to the level from which they had been, in two memorable instances, so violently disturbed by the causes which have been described. And as this renewed subsidence forms a most important feature in the discussion, it may here be desirable to exemplify it by the following comparative statement: —

This fall and low range of prices is the more observable, because the cost of production had been considerably increased. The wages of labour had as has been seen, risen considerably in consequence of a recurrence of periods of great dearth; and all the implements of husbandry had experienced a very great advance in price. The rate of interest too was much higher in consequence of the absorption by the government expenditure of a large part of the savings of individuals. Moreover some, although, perhaps, an inconsiderable proportion, of the progressive taxation attached to agricultural production; and while the cost in labour, in capital, and taxation, applicable to native production was thus raised, the cost of a foreign supply of which we were then supposed to stand habitually in need, was also raised by the increased charges of freight and insurance incidental to the state of war. ①

These considerations render the real fall of the price still greater than the apparent one, and this, notwithstanding the continuance of the war on an enlarged scale of expenditure, and notwithstanding an amount of inconvertible Bank of England notes greater in the first six months of 1804 than it had been in the first six mouths of 1801, when the price was 200 per cent, higher.

		Wheat.		Barley.		Oats.	
		s.	*d.*	*s.*	*d.*	*s.*	*d.*
1792, December	– –	47	2	29	10	18	6
1798, November	– –	47	10	29	0	19	8
1804, March	– –	49	6	22	9	19	9

The higher price of wheat in 1804 is compensated by the lower price of bailey, and with this allowance the subsidence is complete.

① The extra charge of freight and insurance cannot be taken at less than from 5*s.* to 10*s.* per quarter on wheat from abroad, in the interval from the breaking out of the war till 1806, when, in consequence of the introduction of the continental system, the risks, and consequent charges attending commercial intercourse with the continent, were greatly increased.

It might naturally be expected that a fall so tremendous of the markets for grain and for agricultural produce in general, by the transition from scarcity to abundance, would he severely felt by the agricultural interests, always excepting the labourer. Accordingly there were meetings held in Essex and other counties for the purpose of petitioning parliament for additional protection as a remedy for the prevailing agricultural distress. The committee of the House of Commons, to whom the petitions were referred, not having any theory of "preparations for cash payments," or of "transition from war to peace," by which to account for the recent fall of prices, or for their former elevation, give the following very rational explanation of the causes of the rise and fall between 1791 and 1804:—

"It appears to your Committee, that the price of corn, from 1791 to the harvest of 1803, has been very irregular; but, upon an average, increased in a great degree by the years of scarcity, has, in general, yielded a fair profit to the grower. The casual high prices, however, have had the effect of stimulating industry, and bringing into cultivation large tracts of waste land①, which, combined with the two last productive seasons, and other causes, have occasioned such a depression in the value of grain, as, it is

① The number of inclosure bills had been: —

1795	–	–	–	39
1796	–	–	–	75
1797	–	–	–	86
1798	–	–	–	52
1799	–	–	–	65
1800	–	–	–	63
1801	–	–	–	80
1802	–	–	–	122
1803	–	–	–	96
1804	–	–	–	104

feared, will greatly tend to the discouragement of agriculture, unless maintained by the support of parliament.

A bill was in consequence brought in by Mr. Western, and an act passed by which a duty was imposed of 24*s*. 3*d*. per quarter, when the price should be under 63*s*.; and 2*s*. 6*d*. per quarter, when at or above that rate and under 66*s*.; and 6*d*., when above 66*s*. It would be foreign to the purpose of this work to enter into a consideration of the justice or policy of this measure, which proved to be inoperative. It is only here mentioned for the purpose of showing that, neither the state of the currency under the bank restriction, nor the continued and increasing consumption arising out of the war, were at that time relied upon for the recovery, or even for the maintenance, of prices by those persons who, having since lost sight both of the facts and of their own contemporaneous explanation of them, now adopt a purely fanciful theory on the subject. If the bank restriction, or war demand, had been the cause of the rise, how happened it that they did not prevent the fall, or, to repeat the words of Mr. Pitt, applied to a similar state of things three years before, "How happens it that the effect which, on the hypothesis, should have been increasing, was suspended during an interval of nearly three years?"

There were then no preparations for cash payments, and the loans to defray the expenses of the war were on a larger scale than ever. So hopeless, indeed, would be the task of endeavouring to reconcile the state of prices at the close of 1803, and in the first half year of 1804, with either of the two theories of modern times, that I have met with no instance of any reference to, or attempt at an explanation of, this period of cheapness consistently with those theories.

It could not, however, have been so slurred over had it not been for the shortness of its duration. An early recurrence of scarcities occasioned a fresh disturbance of prices, and buried the instance of cheapness here referred to in a heap of high averages.

SECTION 1 *Deficiency of the harvest of 1804*

If the harvest of 1804 had proved only moderately productive, and still more if it had been abundant, a continuance of low averages would very materially have modified the character of all the reasonings on the effects of the bank restriction on the price of corn. But the crops, more especially that of wheat, contrary to the expectations entertained in the earlier part of the season, turned out to be *very deficient*.

The occurrence of this year of deficiency, between two periods of only three seasons each, of moderate produce, immediately preceding and succeeding, is an essential consideration in accounting for the high average price of corn during the war and the restriction; for it hence appears that *there were not four seasons in succession without the occurrence of one harvest or more of decided and acknowledged deficiency*. So that no sooner had the influence of the preceding deficiency ceased to operate, and the price consequently subsided to the level from which it had been greatly raised by the accidents of the season, combined with political obstructions to importation, than a fresh disturbing cause came immediately into operation. In proportion to the importance in this point of view of the result of the harvest of 1804, is the anxiety on the part of those who refer all the phenomena of high prices to the bank restriction, to represent the produce as having been sufficient, if not abundant. In several publications, having that object in view, the produce of that harvest is represented as having been abundant.

Sir. James Graham, in a tract entitled "Corn and Currency," which when it appeared (1826) attracted considerable notice, after giving a table containing the amount of Bank of England notes, in juxtaposition with the average prices of wheat for each year, adds, —

"From the comparison of the issues of the bank with the correspondent average of the price of wheat throughout this long series, it will appear that an increase of issues has, with *wonderful precision*, *created a rise of price*, not always in the same year, but more generally in the one immediately succeeding; and a decrease of the issue has produced in a like manner a correlative decline. The effect of increase[①] is illustrated by the years

① Even if the harvest of 1804 had been as abundant as it was indisputably deficient, according to the very authority quoted for the strange assertion of the reverse, the state of the bank circulation would most assuredly not account for the rise of price. The following is a comparison of the annual average circulation of bank notes with the average prices of wheat at the end of each year, 1803, 1804, and 1805: —

	Bank Notes of 5*l.* and upwards. *	Prices of Wheat in December.
1803,	£ 12, 983, 477	51*s.*
1804,	12, 621, 348	86*s.*
1805,	12, 697, 352	76*s.*

And the discrepancy between the state of the circulation and the price of wheat will be still more striking, if we compare them in the first and last half years of 1804 respectively, there having been an actual diminution in the last six months of that year coincidently with a great advance in the price of wheat. But what, if there were no other ground, is decisive against the hypothesis of an excess of bank notes having *produced* this rise of prices is, that coincidently with such rise, the bullion in the coffers of the bank was experiencing a progressive increase; for instance,

		Bullion.
February, 1804	–	£ 3, 372, 140
August	–	5, 879, 190
February, 1805	–	5, 883, 800
August	–	7, 624, 50

* In this and all the other references to the position of the Bank the amount of the circulation of notes of 5*l.* and upwards includes bank post bills.

1803, 1804, and 1805, in which the harvests were good and the produce abundant; vide *Joplin on Currency*, Appendix, No. 14., and in which the rise of price cannot therefore be attributed to a deficiency of supply."

Curiously enough, the authority quoted in the above extract gives a directly opposite and a true statement of the fact, the following being the description in Joplin, on the currency, Appendix, No. 14. (extracted from the Farmer's Magazine), "1804. In scotland, wheat an average crop, but of inferior quality; in England, *a very short crop*, and the quality very inferior." It happens, whimsically too, that Mr. Joplin (in order to prove his theory, that the variations in the price of coin are owing more to variations of demand than of supply), in the text of the pamphlet, from the appendix to which the above quotation is made, has the following passage: — "In the years 1804 and 1805, wheat rose from 50*s*. to 100*s*. without any scarcity at all." The assertion of abundance is repeated in a publication entitled, "A Letter to Lord Archibald Hamilton, 1823", in which the writer, in contradiction of a statement of mine, expressly says, "1804 was not a year in which the harvest was deficient, it was rather a year of plenty."

It has been requisite to notice these unfounded assertions, although made so long ago, because the state of the corn trade, at this most important period, has not, as far as I am aware, been since distinctly adverted to, or attempted to be explained consistently with either of the two theories. And such assertions, so confidently made as those here referred to, have served to confirm the impression, so universally prevalent, that there was nothing in the seasons, excepting the notorious scarcities of 1795-1796 and 1800-1801, to justify the high prices during the remainder of the war and the restriction.

The fact of the deficiency of the harvest of 1804 is attested by evidence which leaves no room for doubt.

The forty-third volume of the Annals of Agriculture, edited by Arthur Young, is nearly filled with answers from persons in different parts of the country, to whom circulars had been addressed by order of the Board of Agriculture, containing inquiries as to the nature and causes of the failure of the wheat crop of 1804, and as to the extent of the deficiency. The cause of failure seems to have been an extensive prevalence of blight and mildew; and nearly all the answers concur in stating a deficiency of from one fourth to one third in England and Wales; while in Scotland, to which the cause of injury had extended only partially, there was an average produce. The Farmer's Magazine, vols. v. and vi., contains statements in great detail relative to that harvest, and the effect of it on prices. The following is an extract from that work of a cornfactor's circular: —

London, Oct. 30. 1804.

"From the general bad quality of the new wheat presented at Mark Lane, I am sorry to say that the injury from blight appears to have been more extensive than was supposed when I wrote you last year. The best samples are inferior to last year's; and the great bulk of what has been yet produced will not yield more than two thirds of the fine flour which the average of last year produced. In consequence of this, the price of wheat has very considerably advanced, notwithstanding the considerable supply of foreign wheat which has been quickly brought to market."

The average prices accordingly which had been,

	Wheat.	Barley	Oats.
March, 1804,	49*s*. 6*d*.	22*s*. 8*d*.	19s. 9*d*.
were, Dec., 1804,	86*s*. 2*d*.①	43*s*. 10*d*.	26*s*. 11*d*.

This sudden and great rise of prices having immediately followed the passing of the Corn Bill in 1804, considerable dissatisfaction prevailed, and petitions were presented to parliament, in the spring of 1805, against the bill, alleging, among other things, that it had been the cause of the rise of the price of corn. In the opinion of some of the witnesses examined, the first tendency to an advance of prices, in the summer of 1804, was in

① The quality of the wheat being very inferior, the average price gives an inadequate idea of the extent of the rise, which will be best shown by the quotations of wheat in Mark Lane.

April 23. 1804.		30*s*. 45*s*. 52*s*. per quarter.
	Essex and Kent,	56*s*. 57*s*
	Foreign Red,	35*s*. 48*s*
	White Dantzic,	50*s*. 54*s*. 58*s*.
Oct. 29. 1804.	New	48*s*. 63*s*. 72*s*. 78*s*. 84*s*.
	Old	52*s*. 76*s*. 88*s*.
	Fine White,	90*s*. to 92*s*.
	Foreign Red,	52*s*. 78*s*. 82*s*
	White Dantzic,	75*s*. 85*s*.
	Fine	90*s*.
Jan. 28. 1805.	New	65*s*. to 100*s*.
	Old	79*s*. 105*s*. 116*s*.
	Foreign Red,	80*s*. 95*s*. 105*s*.
	White Dantzic.	100*s*. 120*s*. 126*s*.

consequence of the new corn bill; but they all agree that the subsequent rise was in consequence of the great failure of the wheat crop. ①

The acknowledged failure of the crop was quite a sufficient cause of the rise of price, without the aid of the corn bill, which, in point of fact,

---

① The following are extracts from some of the evidence, May, 1805: —

Mr. John Dixon, cornfacter (who had stated his opinion that the first rise had been caused by the corn bill), was asked, "Do you know of no other causes of the rise?"—Answer, "I know of no other causes, except in allusion to the general blight, which was not known till a few weeks before harvest." And when further asked, "Would not the price have risen, although the act had not passed?"—answered, "I do not ascribe the high prices which we have witnessed since harvest to the effect of the bill, but *to the general failure of the last year's crop.*"

Mr. Joseph Stonard, cornfactor, said, "I do apprehend that the advances from the 2nd of July to the 6th of August were in consequence of the bill then before the house; that the subsequent advances arose from the unfavourable weather, and the apprehensions of a defective harvest." "Did you hear of any blight in June to the wheat? —No. —Did you hear in the first week of July of the wheat harvest being likely to be defective? —I recollect on the second Tuesday in July, from the excessive cold rain, and from what I heard afterwards of its being pretty general through England, I believed that to be the cause of the great defect in the crop of wheat." *

Mr. Peter Giles, cornfacter, said, "I think wheat and oats advanced in July from 8*s*. to 10*s*. per quarter; but not wholly occasioned by the agitation of the bill." "What other causes? — The appearance of the crops on the ground not being very favourable. When did you apprehend that the last crop might be defective? — The report of the blight and mildew commenced the first week in August. When did that apprehension affect the price of grain? — It began the first week in August, and continued to advance till the last week. Do you attribute the second rise entirely to the apprehension of a defective crop? Entirely?

Mr. Samuel Scott (now Sir Samuel Scott, Bart.), a member of the house, being examined, chiefly upon some of the details of the bill, was asked, "Do you consider any material rise in price to have taken place in the market previous to the knowledge of the blight?"— Answered, "No material advance had taken place previous to the first rumour of an injury to the crop."

* The following is an extract from a Meteorological Journal for July, 1804:—"A considerable quantity of rain fell on the 7th; on the 8th, some heavy showers, with thunder and lightning. The mercury in the barometer rose rapidly till the next morning, when it fell, preparatory to that heavy rain, which, on account of its long continuance, was remarked by every body."

became wholly inoperative. ① But, if the corn bill had been operative, so much of the rise as might be clearly attributable to that cause would obviously be distinct from the supposed agency of war demand, or of the currency.

There has been the more reason for dwelling upon the fact of the great rise of the price of corn following the harvest of 1804, and upon the causes of that rise, not only because it negatives the theories of the currency and war demand, as applicable to this period, but because this renewed dearth, so quickly following that from which there had been just before a transition to plenty, is important in other points of view. It was calculated to maintain an elevation of the average price thrown over a series of years, and it was the specific occasion of renewed demands by the working classes for advanced wages; claims which were rendered the more effectual by the resource which the increasing employment in the army and navy held out to the workmen who

---

① On the continent of Europe the prices of corn rose considerably between 1802 and 1805. It appears that the seasons of 1802 and 1803, which were of fair average produce in this country, had been unfavourable in the south of Europe. So great was the scarcity in Spain during those two years, that the price of wheat rose in the spring of 1804 to nearly six times what it had been in 1800.

"The medium price of the load of four funegas of wheat at the market of Medina di Rio Seco in Leon, which was in May, 1800, at 115 reals vellon, rose as follows:—

May, 1801,	172 reals vellon.	
1802,	263	—
1803,	$247\frac{1}{2}$	—
1804.	620	—

(*Appendix to Bullion Report*, 1810, p. 185.)

The Monthly Magazine, in its commercial report for July, 1805, has the following passage. —

"In the late general rise of the price of grain in Germany, the bushel of wheat, that had been usually sold in Saxony for a dollar and a half, rose to ten dollars. In Lausitz, the price rose as high as fifteen dollars a bushel. In Brunswick, rye had advanced to between two and three dollars a bushel. Owing to the scarcity and dearness of provisions, the last great fair at Vienna was ill attended. Goods either went at very low prices, or remained unsold"

engaged in the numerous strikes of that time. It was on this occasion that the price of artisan labour especially experienced a considerable advance.

It will be seen that the following harvests, combined with the state of politics, were not of a character calculated to restore abundance, nor consequently to allow of a subsidence of the prices of corn to the level from which they had been disturbed by the failure of the crops of 1804. ①

SECTION 2 *Seasons of 1805 to 1808, both included*

The winter of 1804-1805 was mild; but the spring was ungenial; the summer was cold and unsettled; the harvest backward; and the appearance of the crops at the approach of harvest unfavourable; the consequence was, that the average price of wheat, after an intermediate fall, reached 98*s*. 4*d*. in August. But the weather then taking up, and continuing propitious for securing the crops, and these turning out better than had been expected, although far from being considered generally abundant, the price of wheat fell more than 20*s*. per quarter before the close of the year, and continued to decline till the spring following, when the Gazette average was 74*s*. 5*d*., or a fall of about 24*s*., since the preceding harvest.

The winter of 1805-1806 was attended with more frost, and snow than the preceding season, but was not a very rigorous one. The spring, like the preceding one, was backward; and the appearance of the crops was

① The harvest to which, as far as I can judge, it bears the nearest resemblance, is that of 1828, the effect of which was to raise the average price of wheat from 50*s*. in January, to 76*s*. in November, and this, be it observed, when we found in the south of Europe, and in Spain especially, a source of very considerable supply, instead of competition, as in 1804-1805, for sharing with us in supplies form the north of Europe.

unpromising. This circumstance, combined with political events, namely, the hostile proceedings of Prussia① against this country, under the dictation of France, which threatened in their consequences to cut off our supplies of corn from the Baltic, and which had the immediate effect of raising greatly the rates of freight and insurance, occasioned a rally in the average price of wheat to 84*s*. in June; but, thenceforward, notwithstanding, that the weather was variable, and rather wet during the harvest, and notwithstanding the apprehension of increased political obstructions, in consequence of the overthrow and final subjugation of Prussia by the battle of Jena, followed by the Berlin decree, in the autumn of 1806, prices declined slowly, but progressively, to 73*s*. 5*d*. before the next harvest. The quality of the wheat was considered to be inferior to that of the preceding year, and the quantity a bare average, which was not then computed to be sufficient for the consumption.

The winter of 1806-1807 presented nothing remarkable of mildness or severity, The spring of 1807 was rather forward, and the summer was fine and dry, to nearly the completion of the harvest in the southern division of the kingdom. In England and Wales, the wheat crop, although thin on the ground, was considered as an average in point of yield. But in Scotland, where the weather was extremely unfavourable for the operations of the harvest, the wheat crop proved to be very deficient. Thus, in the Farmer's Magazine, —

"1807. The crops generally of little bulk. Wheat, in some districts, equal to an average, but in others suffered from bad weather."

The spring crops were throughout scanty, and the potato crops in Ireland had failed to a considerable extent. Still, as the wheat in England had been

---

① The Prussian government issued a proclamation, dated in March, 1806, prohibiting the entrance of British ships into any of its ports or rivers.

got in mostly in good order before the bad weather set in, and was brought early to market, prices declined to 66*s*. in November, being a fall of upwards of 30*s*. per quarter since August 1805. This fall, be it observed, took place notwithstanding the increasing gloom of the political horizon, which led to the apprehension, well founded as the events proved, of great, and at one time nearly insurmountable, impediments to importation.

The orders in council issued by our government, in retaliation of the French decrees, formed the grounds for the non-intercourse act of America, the year following. And the bombardment of Copenhagen in the autumn of 1807, was followed on the part of Denmark by a closing of the passage of the Sound, and on the part of Russia by an embargo on British shipping. While the Prussian ports of the Baltic had, under the dictation of France, been for sometime before shut against the commerce of this country. Under these circumstances, the farmers were naturally induced, as by their increased capital from their great gains of late years they were enabled, to hold larger stocks. There is, therefore, every reason to suppose that if political appearances had been less threatening, and the crops less scanty, the subsidence in 1807, to the level from whence the rise in 1804 took place, would have been complete.

But in 1808, and at the very commencement of it, the grain markets began to recover. The scantiness of the preceding crop was beginning to be felt, and at the same time the apprehensions which had been entertained of the exclusion of the British flag from trade in the Baltic were realised. Thus we were threatened with an almost total cutting off of a foreign supply, if we should have occasion for it, as it was thought inevitable that we should; it being considered as a settled point that this country did not produce corn enough for its own consumption.

The winter of 1807-1808 set in very early, which of course increased the consumption of all kinds of grain, more especially as hay was scarce and dear. The appearances that a serious scarcity of food was likely to be felt before the coming harvest, induced parliament, on a report of a committee of the House of Commons, to prohibit the distillation from grain.① The same prospect had a natural effect on the corn market, and prices advanced accordingly in the spring of 1808.

The crops of 1808 proved more deficient than those of the preceding year. The memorably hot days in the early part of July② were considered to

---

① One of the motives which induced the legislature to prohibit the distillation from grain was, doubtless, to afford some relief to the West India planters, by the substitution of sugar in the distilleries, but the immediate occasion and the professed object of the measure were distinctly stated to be the actual and apprended deficiency of grain and of potatoes.

② A temperature in this climate. Of the season of 1808, the following extracts from the Farmer's Magazine convey the general character: —

"The first four months of the year were singularly stormy and cold, displaying all the horrors of winter, even till the last day of April. The month of May was ushered in with the most promising appearances; and vegetation, from that time, proceeded with a rapidity rarely witnessed in this country. The last two weeks of June, and the first three weeks of July, furnished warmer weather than had been remembered by the oldest man living*; and this unprecedented warmness was followed by dreadful thunder storms in every quarter of the island, accompanied with heavy rains, more resembling those of the torrid zone than what are usually experienced in the temperate climate of Great Britain. The loss and damage sustained by such heavy rains, can only be correctly ascertained at an after period. It is enough, in this place, to say, that, in consequence of them, the wheats have been mildewed considerably; a great part of the hay crop absolutely rotted; whilst field labour have been thrown out of shape, and placed in a condition not to be remedied at this advanced period of the season." — September 1808. vol. ix. p. 375.

"The failure of the wheat crop, noticed in our last, proves greater than at first imagined, and appeals to have taken place in almost every district, though in different degrees, according to the nature of the soil, the stage of growth at which plants had arrived when adverse weather set in, and the situation of fields occupied with that grain."—December, 1808.

* *Extract from a Meteorological Journal, two miles north-west of London*: —

"*July* 1. 1808. — The leading feature of this month has been the extreme heat of the 12th, 13th, and 14th days. We have paid much attention to the state of the atmosphere, as the reports in this work will show, since January, 1802, and remember nothing approaching to the heat of the days referred to.

"We have used the same thermometer through the whole period, nor has the plan been changed, it hangs on the outside of a window frame looking N. E.. In this situation on the 12th, it was as high as $88\frac{1}{2}°$;

have done great injury to the wheat, and they were followed by a great deal of wet and stormy weather, from that time till the getting in of the harvest. Some of the other crops suffered, although not in the same degree with wheat, and the aggregate produce was estimated to be below an average.

This was the period, too, when our communication with the Continent had become very much obstructed, so as to preclude the expectation of any considerable relief from foreign supply. In point of fact, there was an excess of export of about 15, 000 quarters of wheat, occasioned by the wants of Spain and Portugal. The high price, therefore, (wheat having advanced by July to an average of 81*s.* 1*d.* per quarter, and by January following to 90*s.* 4*d.*.) was a necessary condition for eking out a reduced supply of our own growth, when the obstructions to importation had become great, and were thought in that year to be insurmountable. Nothing, indeed, can better prove the magnitude of those obstructions, than the circumstance that an average price of upwards of 80*s.* when the exchange and the price of gold were nearly at par, was insufficient to bring forward any foreign supply worth mentioning. But such was the spirit of caution then prevailing in the

---

on the 13th, 91°; and, on the 14th, it was at the astonishing height of 93°, at which it continued nearly an hour. At the timber yard near Westminster Budge, we were informed, it was at the same height. In a shop in Holborn, on the 13th, we saw the thermometer at 89°, at a time that the shop appeared to the feelings very cool in comparison of the external air.

"Mr. Capel Lofft of Troston, writes, that on the 12th and 13th, his thermometer stood both days at 91°, and his observations were confirmed by those of a neighbour; and at Bury St. Edmunds, the thermometer was 93° on the 12th, and at 95° on the 13th. Mr. Lofft observes, that 'twenty-seven years' observation, very little interrupted, has never given me an equal result in two days, or even in a single day.'"

corn trade which had been suffering from a slow but long continued fall of prices, that the advance, although under circumstances so favourable to it, was very gradual. Thus it was not till May, 1808, that the average got up to 73*s*. 6*d*. for wheat. But thenceforward a backwardness of the crops, and unfavourable appearances of them, and very stormy weather during a great part of the harvest, which was considered to be deficient, occasioned a more decided rise, viz., to 92*s*., at the close of the year.

Under these circumstances, instead of having recourse to the bank restriction and to war consumption, for the purpose of accounting for the rise in price, it should be rather a matter of wonder that it did not go much higher; and it is a tribute to the prudence of the trade at that time, that there was so much less speculation in it than, as will be seen, prevailed contemporaneously in other branches of trade, in consequence of an actual or apprehended cessation of all foreign supply. It is at the same time worthy of remark, that while in the interval under consideration, viz. from the commencement of 1804 to the end of 1808, so great a rise had taken place in the prices of corn there was a considerable fall in the prices of meat to the close of 1808, and first quarter of 1809.

In Smithficld Market

	Beef.	Mutton.
1804,	4*s*. 6*d*. to 5*s*. 8*d*.	5*s*. to 6*s*.
1808,	3*s*. to 5*s*.	3*s*. 4*d*. to 5*s*. 4*d*.

The contract by the Victualling Board for the supply of fresh beef, was[①] Dec. 1803, at 55*s*. 6*d*. per cwt..

Dec. 1808, 50*s*.

And Irish provisions, which might be considered to be directly acted upon by government demand, were,

Dec. 1803,	Mess Beef,	152*s*.	to	160*s*.
	Mess Pork,	105*s*.	to	115*s*.
1808,	Mess Beef,	120*s*.	to	125*s*.
	Mess Pork,	65*s*.	to	92*s*.

It is not easy to find a more striking instance than this of the little influence of government demand on the general prices of provisions, seeing that in that interval the demands for victualling the navy and army, were on an enormous scale, and progressively increasing, more especially at the close of 1808, when fleets and armies were despatched for the war in the Peninsula, which had just then commenced. If the rise in the prices of corn is to be explained by the supposed operation of the bank restriction, or government demand, how is the fall in the price of meat to be accounted for? Leaving the supporters of either, or of both of the two theories, to offer a consistent explanation of the opposite tendencies of those two great classes of human food, I have now to call the attention of the reader to some most extraordinary variations, in this interval, of the prices of other descriptions of produce.

---

① In November, 1801, after preliminaries of peace with France, the contract was at 69*s*. 7*d*. per cwt.. This is the first date quoted at Deptford, but there is a quotation for Plymouth yard in March, 1801, as high as 80*s*..

SECTION 3 *Instances of some of the most prominent of the variations of the prices of commodities besides those of corn*

It would be irksome to the general reader to trace with much minuteness the changes and the causes of those changes in the great number of articles which underwent those fluctuations (which any person wishing to follow them more in detail may do by reference to the list of prices in the Appendix), I shall therefore confine myself to a view of some of the most prominent of them, for the purpose of seeing how far they are calculated to countenance the theories in question.

Sugar and coffee, and some other articles of Colonial produce, which had reached an extreme point of depression at the close of 1801, advanced from that time till 1805. The Berlin and Milan decrees, by narrowing the channels for export, depressed these articles in 1806 and 1807, and subsequently after experiencing a short-lived speculative improvement between 1807 and 1810, they were, till the opening of the ports on the Continent, some years later, viz. in 1811 and 1813, at a ruinously low range of prices.

Copper, in consequence of a greatly increased demand, not only for the sheathing of ships, but for an extensive coinage which was then in progress, attained, in 1805, to 200*l.* per ton, a price which it never afterwards exceeded, and below which it has constantly ranged, subsequently to 1808, when, for a short time, it was, after intermediate fluctuations, again at that price. Lead, which had ranged at about 20*l.* per fodder, previous to 1800, rose to 41*l.* in 1805, and after declining again to 28*l.*, rose in the autumn of 1808 to 43*l.*, a price which it never after wards reached. British iron attained, in 1803, as high a price as it ever subsequently reached till 1818 and 1819. Foreign iron had been at its maximum in 1800 and 1801.

The close of the year 1807[1] found us, by the events of the war, excluded from direct commercial intercourse with every country in Europe, Sweden excepted; and there was consequently, besides in many instances a short actual supply, a prospect of scarcity of every article of European produce, required as raw materials for our manufactures, or as naval stores. About the same time, too, began our disputes with the United States of America, which produced first a nonintercourse act, and eventually a war. The prospect of scarcity thus held out, naturally excited a spirit of speculation; and in proportion as that prospect became realised, was the speculative demand extended through different periods in 1808, and the early part of 1809, when the obstructions to importation, from political causes, nearly reached their height. After the attack on Copenhagen, and the final withdrawing of our naval and military forces from thence, Russia and Denmark joined in the war against this country.[2] The Baltic being thus shut against any direct commercial intercourse with this country, it was not clear that any part of our usual supplies of necessary articles from thence could be obtained by any channel, however circuitous, or at any expense, however great. It was naturally supposed that Russia might, whether compelled by France, or of her own accord, make a point of depriving this country of some of the materials essential to the maintenance of our navy, and of these the foremost was hemp. This

① The celebrated Milan decree was issued about this time,

② A Revolution in Sweden in March, 1809, placed that country also in hostility against us.

article, in consequence of such apprehensions, in aggravation of actual deficiency of supply, advanced from 58*l*. in the summer of 1807 to 118*l*. per ton in the course of 1808. Flax, on nearly the same grounds, rose from 68*l*. to 142*l*. per ton. Memel timber reached 17*l*. per load, having varied dining 1806 and 1807 from 3*l*. 13*s*. to 8*l*. 10*s*.. Deals and other descriptions of wood rose in proportion. Baltic linseed rose from 43*s*. to 150*s*. per quarter; Russia tallow, from 53*s*. to 112*s*. per cwt..

In consequence of the occupation of Spain by the French, it was imagined that the exportation of wool from thence would be rendered impracticable, or that, at any rate, the unsettled state of that kingdom would materially diminish the produce. Under this impression, a very great speculation was entered into, and the price rose from 6*s*. 7*d*. and 6*s*. 9*d*. to 22*s*. and 26*s*. per lb. for the Leonessa, and from 2*s*. 6*d*. and 5*s*. to 13*s*. and 18*s*. for Seville wools.

Our principal dependence for a supply of silk was, at that time, on Italy; and there was a double ground on which the French, who then exercised dominion over that country, might be expected to do their utmost to prevent our obtaining any from thence. One motive would be, that of distressing us, and another would be, that of giving a more decided superiority to their own manufactures. It is not to be wondered at, therefore, that this article advanced considerably, —viz. Piedmont thrown silk from 30*s*. and 47*s*. in 1807, to 96*s*. and 112*s*. in 1808; China raw silk, from 19*s*. and 22*s*. to 33*s*. and 45*s*.; and Bengal, from 25*s*. and 33*s*. to 52*s*. and 85*s*..

The orders in council, on our part, and the nonintercourse act and various embargoes, on the part of the United States of America, were calculated to favour speculation in the produce of that country; and, accordingly, Georgia cotton advanced from 9*d.* and 1*s.* to 2*s.* and 2*s.* 6*d.* per lb.; and Virginia tobacco from 4*d.* and 8*d.* to 1*s.* 4*d.* and 2*s.* per lb.. ①

Under an impression of the permanence of the causes of dearth of provisions and of other necessaries, increased as these were by the effects of progressive taxation, the rate of wages, particularly of artizan labour, experienced in the interval between 1803 and 1808, a further advance, and in 1808 and 1809 attained, in many branches of industry, its greatest height.

SECTION 4 *New fields of enterprise opened for exports*

There was, coincidently with the great advance in imported commodities, a new and very extensive field opened for our exports.

The transfer of the seat of government from Portugal to the Brazils, and the virtual emancipation of the colonies of Spain from the control of the mother country, opened the trade of a great part of South America in 1808②; and as by the course of the war we possessed the entire dominion of the seas, it was, in fact, to this country, exclusively of the rest of

① Of the falling off of supply, which gave occasion to this great advance of prices, take the following instances. Many others might be brought forward, which it would be tedious to enumerate.

Imports into Great Britain.

	Sheep and Lambs' Wool.	Raw and Thrown Silk.	Cotton.	Tallow.	Hemp.
	lbs.	lbs.	lbs.	cwts.	cwts.
1806	7,333,993	1,317,841	58,176,283	536,652	729,786
1807	11,768,926	1,123,943	74,925,306	367,398	756,824
1808	2,353,725	776,414	43,605,982	148,282	259,687

② There had been in 1806, a considerable excitement in the export trade, in consequence of the expedition of Sir. Home Popham to Buenos Ayres. But both the expedition and the commercial speculations founded upon it ended disastrously.

Europe, that this opening was presented. So vast and comparatively untried a field was not held out in vain to the merchants and manufacturers of this country; and, accordingly, the spirit of speculation was on the alert to export every article, not only that might probably, but that could possibly, come into demand.

Mr. M'Culloch, in illustrating the effects of ignorance and miscalculation in the overstocking of such new markets as are occasionally opened, and in filling them with articles totally unsuited to the wants and habits of the people, gives the following graphic description of the shipments to South America in 1808: —

"The exportations consequent on the first opening of the trade to Buenos Ayres, Brazil, and the Caraccas were most extraordinary. Speculation was then carried beyond the boundaries within which even gambling is usually confined, and was pushed to an extent and into channels that could hardly have been deemed practicable. We are informed by Mr. Mawe, an intelligent traveller, resident at Rio Janeiro, at the period in question, that more Manchester goods were sent out in the course of a few weeks, than had been consumed in the twenty years preceding, and the quantity of English goods of all sorts poured into the city was so very great, that warehouses could not be provided sufficient to contain them, and that the most valuable merchandise was actually exposed for weeks on the beach to the weather, and to every sort of depredation. Elegant services of cut glass and china were offered to persons whose most splendid drinking-vessels consisted of a horn, or the shell of a cocoa nut, tools were sent out, having a hammer on the one side and a hatchet on the other, as if the inhabitants had nothing more to do than to break the first stone that they met with, and then cut the gold and diamonds from it, and some speculators actually went so far as to send out skates to Rio Janeiro."—*Principles of Political Economy*, *2rd ed* p. 329.

This description of the exports in 1808 is the more especially to be borne in mind, as, in conjunction with the speculations in imports, and with the general excitement which is about to be noticed, it affords reasonable grounds for anticipation of the great reaction, and the ruinous results which are to be recorded, as having occurred in the following two years.

SECTION 5 *General excitement and speculations in shares in 1807 and 1808*

The encouragement thus offered for speculative exports coinciding with the inducements held out by actual, and still more by prospective scarcity, to speculation in so many articles of general consumption, combined, in 1807 and 1808, to produce an almost universal excitement, leading, as usual on such occasions, to hazardous adventure, and extending itself to new projects of various kinds, such as canals, bridges, fire offices, breweries, distilleries, and many other descriptions of joint stock companies.

The speculations in shares had already proceeded to a considerable extent in 1807.① In many of the instances these speculations as well as

① This will appear by the following extract from one of the contemporary periodical publications. — "To the Editor of the Monthly Magazine."

"Several of your correspondents have noticed the prevailing disposition for the establishment of joint stock companies for almost every branch of trade, but none of them have attempted to show the progress we had made towards reviving the infatuation of the celebrated year 1720. These stock jobbing speculations have received a check, which will probably prevent their increase for the present, but in older to convey to future readers of your Magazine some idea of our commercial ingenuity and enterprising

those in goods reached the utmost height in the beginning of 1808, and the

---

spirit, you probably will find room for the enclosed list. All the projects it comprehends have been laid before the public in the course of the last year, and the greater part of them will cease to be publicly known before the end of the present year. Yours, &c.."

January 12. 1808.

List of Public Companies proposed to be established by Subscription in the Year 1807.

1. Hope Fire and Life Insurance Company; capital 2,000,000*l*..

2. County Fire Office, Southampton Street, capital 350,000*l*..

3. Eagle Fire and Life Insurance Company; capital 2,000,000*l*., in shares of 50*l*. each.

4. Rainbow Fire and Life Office, Commercial Road.

5. Atlas Insurance Company, for Fire, Lives, and Annuities.

6. Golden Lane Brewery, Brown and Parry's; capital 300,000*l*., in shares of 50*l*. each.

7. The Old English Ale Brewery, for brewing Ale, Amber, and Table Beer, from Malt and Hops only; capital 75,000*l*., in shares of 25*l*. each.

8. Maiden Lane Brewery.

9. Weston Street Brewery.

10. United Public Brewery, Bankside, shares 52*l*. 10*s*. each.

11. British Ale Brewery, Lambeth—Mainwaring's.

12. Public Brewery, Deptford.

13. The London Genuine Malt Distillery, and Rectifying Company, at Vauxhall; capital 140,000*l*., in shares of 50*l*. each.

14. The Public Distillery for making and rectifying Genuine British Spirits, Cordials, and Compounds; capital 200,000*l*., in shares of 50*l*. each.

15. Another rectifying Distillery, on a smaller scale.

16. Another making and rectifying Distillery, on a large scale; capital 300,000*l*..

17. London Genuine Wine Company, for importing and supplying Vintners and the Public in general with Port, Madeira, and Sherry Wines, free from adulteration; capital 500,000*l*., in shares of 50*l*. each.

18. Britannic and India Wine Company; capital from 250,000*l*. to 500,000*l*., in shares of 100*l*. each.

19. Genuine Wine Company, capital 50,000*l*..

20. London Subscription Wine Company, for supplying the Public with Foreign Wines of the first quality, for ready money; capital 50,000*l*. in shares of 50*l*..

21. Genuine Wine and Foreign Spirit Company.

22. The London British Vinegar Company, capital 100,000*l*., in shares of 50*l*. each, with power to the Committee to increase the capital by the sale of additional shares.

23. Vinegar Manufactory Company; capital 50,000*l*., in shares of 25*l*. each.

greater part before the close of that year.

The Strand Bridge (now Waterloo Bridge) and Vauxhall Bridge were projected, and the subscriptions for them raised in 1808.

---

24. Corn, Flour, and Provision Company, upon a very large scale, with the view of supplying Government, &c.

25. United Public Daily, for the sale of milk.

26. New Medical Laboratory, for the preparation and sale of Genuine Medicines, capital 50, 000*l*., in shares of 50*l*. each.

27. British Coal Company; capital 300, 000*l*., in shares of 50*l*. each, with power to the Committee to increase the capital by the sale of additional shares.

28. Newcastle and Sunderland Coal Company; capital 100, 000*l*., in shares of 50*l*. each.

29. Shields Coal Company.

30. National Light and Heat Company, by F. A. Windsor, 97. Pall Mall; capital 1, 000, 000*l*., in shares of 50*l*. each.

31. London Clothing Company, for supplying the Army, Navy, and Public with Clothes; capital 100, 000*l*., in shares of 25*l*. each.

32. United Woollen Company.

33. Linen Company for Commission Sales, capital 500, 000*l*., in shares of 100*l*. each.

34. London Commission Sale Company, for making advances on Produce and manufactured Goods, and selling them to advantage, capital 1, 000, 000*l*., in shares of 50*l*. each.

35. British Commission Company; capital 1, 000, 000*l*., in shares of 100*l*. each.

36. Albion London Information Office, for Sale or Exchange of Estates, Manors, Livings, &c., the disposal of appointments and practice in the liberal professions, &c..

37. Company for purchasing Canal Shares, and lending Money for completing Canals; shares of 10*l*. each.

38. British Copper Company, J Jones, Lambeth.

39. Cambrian Copper Company; capital 100, 000*l*..

40. Paper Manufacturing Company, by R. Dodd.

41. The London Bank, by Mr. Brown of the Golden Lane Brewery; capital 5, 000, 000*l*., in shares of 100*l*. each, 5*l*. to be paid on subseribing.

42. National Deposit, Interest, and Credit Bank, by F. A. Windsor; capital 5, 000, 000*l*., in 50*l*. shares; to commence business on the 1st of January, 1808.

SECTION 6 *On the state of the circulation from 1804 to 1808*

All the excitement which has just been described, the enormous advance of prices, extending to so many of the most considerable articles of consumption, and the speculations in shares which then prevailed, and a further advance in the wages of labour, occurred during a singularly equable state and moderate amount of the circulation, in as far as depended upon the issues of the Bank of England. This will appear by the following statement. The years 1802 and 1803 are included, for the purpose of showing, that in those two years of low prices, the average circulation of notes of 5*l*. and upwards①, was larger than on the average of the subsequent five years, and the prices of wheat are placed in juxtaposition for the purpose of showing their want of connection with the amount of the circulation: —

Average Price Wheat	31st. Dec.	Bank notes of 5*l*. and upwards.	
57*s*.	1802,	13, 917, 977	Average of two years, 13, 450, 727*l*.
51*s*.	1803,	12, 983, 477	
86s.	1804,	12, 621, 348	Average of five years, 12, 957, 404*l*.
76*s*.	1805②,	12, 697, 352	
76*s*.	1806,	12, 844, 170	
66*s*.	1807,	13, 221, 988	
90*s*.	1808,	13, 402, 160	

① The view would not be much varied, nor the conclusion materially impaired the notes under 5*l*. were taken into the account.

② There was a fall of the exchange, and an efflux of bullion for a few months in 1805, in consequence of subsidies to Austria and Russia, but after the battle of Austerlitz, which led to a peace between Austria and France, the exchanges rallied, and there was a renewed influx of bullion.

And for the purpose of comparison with the circulation anterior to the bank restriction, it may be worth while here to recall to the leader's recollection, that the average amount of the three years ending in December 1795, was 11,975,573*l*.. Thus the average amount of the bank circulation of notes of 5*l*. and upwards, in the five years ending in December 1808, exceeded by less than one million the average amount of the three years ending in 1795!

The position of the Bank, moreover, while all this great disturbance of prices was in progress, and attained nearly its greatest height, was such as it might, and probably would have been, if it had then been paying in cash; for, on the 28th of February, 1808, it stood thus: —

Circulation —	£	Securities —	£
Notes of 5*l*. and upwards,	14, 093, 690	Public	14, 149, 501
Notes under 5*l*.	4, 095, 170	Private	13, 234, 579
	18, 188, 860		27, 384, 080
Deposits	11, 961, 960	Bullion	7, 855, 470[①]
Liabilities	30, 150, 820	Assets	35, 239, 550

The stock of bullion was larger than it had been during the twenty years preceding the bank restriction, with the exception of the short interval from 1789 to 1791. And, if the bank had not fixed the price of gold at 4*l*., by buying at that rate whatever quantity was offered to them, there can be no reasonable doubt, but that the market price would have subsided to the

① There cannot be a stronger presumption than is afforded by this amount of bullion, that the bank had, up to this time, at least, in view, the eventual resumption of cash payments; else, why have bought gold, paying absurdly enough, 4*l*. the ounce for all that was brought to them?

Mint price. ① On the 31st of August, 1808, the circulation was reduced by somewhat more than a million, and the stock of bullion by about a million and a half.

31st of August, 1808.

Circulation	£	Securities —	£
Notes of 5*l.* and upwards	12, 993, 020	Public	14, 956, 394
Notes under 5*l.* –	4, 118, 270	Private	14, 287, 696
	17, 111, 290		29, 244, 090
Deposits –	13, 012, 510	Bullion	6, 015, 940
Liabilities	30, 123, 800	Assets	35, 260, 030

The exchange on Hamburgh, in the mean time, had risen from 34*s.* 4*d.*, in February, to 35*s.* 2*d.* in August. In this state of the exchange, of the stock of bullion, and of the circulation, there was assuredly nothing that could lead to the supposition of any influence by the bank restriction, in raising general prices, and in favouring the speculations in that period, or to the inference, that the depreciation of the currency *caused by that measure*, was greater than the difference between paper and gold.

The very moderate amount, but more especially the equableness of the annual average circulation of the six years from 1803 to 1808, both years included, embracing an interval in which there were such extraordinary fluctuations, and so high a range of prices, and during where such large financial operations were taking place, and such great political changes occurred, are curious facts in the history of our currency.

How it happened, that the Bank, having such powerful motives of

① The price of silver in 1808, although a little above the Mint price, was *lower than it had been during the greater part of last century, and lower than it was at* 1792.

interest, with a view to its dividends, to extend its issues, being no longer under the check of convertibility, the directors having avowed, moreover, that in the regulation of the amount, they disregarded the exchanges, which they held to be uninfluenced by the quantity of bank paper, and that their only guide was, the demand for discount of good bills at 5 per cent? — How it happened, that with such motives to excess, and under the guidance of opinions so unsound, there was so trifling an increase, compared with the amount before the restriction, and so small a variation in the yearly average of the issues?

The bullion committee of 1810, from whose report the foregoing amounts of the annual circulation are extracted, do not advert to this remarkable fact, and much less do they attempt to explain it. They notice only the marked increase, which took place in 1809 and 1810 (and which I shall have occasion to remark upon hereafter), observing, however, as an important principle, that the mere numerical return of the amount of bank notes in circulation cannot be considered as at all deciding the question, whether such paper is or is not excessive.

This is very true, and accounts for some of the phaenomena observed in former periods, as also in subsequent ones, of great alterations in the amount of bank notes, consistently with a state of the exchanges at variance with the indications. But it does not explain how, under the varying but progressive increase of our trade, and under the very extraordinary circumstances of the political and financial state of the country, so equable and so moderate an amount of the bank circulation could be preserved; and how, above all, it could be consistent with so enormous an advance of prices. In order, however, to account in some degree for the comparative smallness of the amount, the committee add,

"But, above all, the same amount of currency will be more or less adequate, in proportion to the skill which the great money dealers possess in managing and economising the use of the circulating medium."

They then refer to the increased use of bankers' drafts, and to the practice of the clearing house among the London bankers, as among the expedients by which the currency is economised, and the same sum rendered adequate to a much greater amount of trade and payments than formerly. But, as we have had before occasion to observe, the improvements in economising the use of the currency have been *progressive*; and yet, a very greatly enlarged circulation of bank notes has been found necessary for carrying on the transactions of the metropolis and the country, consistently with the maintenance of the full value of the paper. This circumstance will, therefore, not go far to account for the very small increase between 1803 and 1808, compared with the amount between 1792 and 1795; and still less to explain the smallness of the variations of the annual amount.

An explanation has already been suggested, with a view to accounting for the general moderation of the issues of the Bank, during the whole period of the restriction; and the solution of the difficulty was stated to be in the circumstance, that the coincidence between the bank rate of discount and the market rate of interest for such bills as came within the bank rules operated in the main, in conjunction with the financial system of the government, as a principle of limitation.

That coincidence seems to have been more uniform in the interval between 1803 and 1808, than in equal periods preceding or subsequent, as may be inferred from the comparatively small variation in the total amount of the securities held by the Bank, which did not during the whole of that interval vary by more than three millions. The most material variation that occurred may here be instanced, as showing the manner in which the two descriptions of securities held by the bank acted upon each other. In February, 1805, the securities were: —

Public -	£ 16, 889, 501
Private - - - -	11, 771, 889
Together - -	28, 661, 390

The government advances, as above, being beyond their usual amount, were soon after reduced by about five millions; and in August, 1805, the securities were: —

Public - -	£ 11, 413, 266[①]
Private - - -	16, 359, 564
Together - -	27, 772, 830

And it may be observed generally, that there has been a tendency to compensation or adjustment between the private and the public securities held by the Bank. It appears, likewise, to have been the policy of the government, not to allow an accumulation of the unfunded debt, as long as the state of the money market admitted of funding without obvious disadvantage.

The amount of discounts, too, bore a nearer and more uniform proportion to the advances to government during this period than before or subsequently.

---

① And during this reduced and low state of the advances to government, the average price of wheat in August, 1805, rose to 100*s*. per quarter.

SECTION 7 *Advances by the bank to government*

With reference to the advances by the bank to government on land and malt, Exchequer bills and other securities, the bullion committee of 1810 remark, —

"That the yearly advances have, upon an average, since the suspension, been considerably lower in amount than the average amount of advances prior to that event, and the amount of those advances in the last two years, though greater in amount than those of some years immediately preceding, is less than it was for any of the six years preceding the restriction of cash payments."

This, of itself, is an important admission, and if the attention of the committee had been sufficiently directed to the inference from the fact, it might have led them to hesitate more than they did, in making the charge of *depreciation by excessive issue.*

But there is one point of view in which the moderation of the advances of the bank to government may be exhibited in a still more striking manner.

From the documents laid before parliament, in consequence of the attention called to the subject by the repeated motions in parliament of Mr. Grenfell, to whose persevering exertions the public are indebted for a considerable abatement, which about that time was made in the charge of the Bank, for the management of the public debt; it appears that the average of the government deposits in the hands of the Bank, in 1806, was 12, 197, 303*l*., and that the amount fluctuated for some years after between eleven and twelve millions. Now, the average of the advances by the bank to government, was in those years somewhat under fourteen million five hundred thousand pounds. *So that the real cash advance, or the medium for the issue of bank notes through the government, as also the real amount available to the government beyond its own cash balance in the hands of the Bank, did not, in the interval now under consideration, much exceed three millions*!

This comparative smallness of the advances to government negatives the supposition so commonly entertained and reasoned upon, as a point beyond doubt, that the bank was rendered by the restriction, a mere engine in the hands of government for facilitating its financial operations, and that the war could not have been carried on without the restriction. In fact, the whole charge of an undue proportion of the issues of the bank in advances to government, will be found to have been confined to the two last years of the war, and *the five years following the peace.* But the comparative smallness of the advances to government, during the period now under consideration, is material in another point of view; for it will be seen hereafter, that the partisans of the doctrine of the paramount influence of the currency upon prices, lay great stress upon the *channel* through which the bank notes are issued, imputing a great superiority of effect to the same amount if issued or withdrawn through the medium of advances to government.

SECTION 8 *General remarks on the state of prices, and of the circulation at the close of 1808*

It is of importance to remark, that this was the state of things after an interval of twelve years from the bank restriction, during which interval there was only one period of a few months in 1801 and 1802, in which the price of gold was above 4*l*. per ounce, or the price of silver higher than it had been during the greater part of last century. And yet at different times in this interval of twelve years, nearly every article of consumption experienced a rise of price fully equal to, if not surpassing, any that it subsequently attained, with the exception of a few articles of colonial produce, which were extravagantly raised, by ill-judged speculations, on the peace in 1814. The price of labour, too, had, by the close of 1808, attained nearly its maximum height, more especially artizan labour.

It has been shown in the case of corn more especially, and of many other articles, and it might be equally shown of the rest of those that had risen, that in every individual instance scarcity, real or apprehended, was the occasion of the advance. It may be true, that in all, or in the greater part, the rise proved to be beyond the occasion. And it is probable, that the rise could not have proceeded to the height which it attained in some of the articles, had it not been for an extension of the country bank issues, and an extension generally of the circulating medium, by bills of exchange, and other forms of credit. But such has been the case, under circumstances favourable to speculation, both before the restriction and since the resumption of cash payments; and it will be seen that the restriction did not exempt over trading in the present instance from its ordinary results.

The question, however, is not, whether the rise was beyond the occasion, but whether it was the scarcity, real or apprehended, of the commodities, or the abundance of money, that was the cause of the advance of prices; and it may be put to any one, who has been at the trouble of examining the facts referred to in the view which has been taken of the period from the restriction to the close of 1808, whether there is the slightest ground to ascribe the rise to an abundance of money, and not to the scarcity, real or apprehended, of the commodities. So palpable, indeed, so clear is the negative of any thing like depreciation, as contradistinguishing abundance of money from scarcity of commodities, that a reference is seldom made by the supporters of the doctrine of depreciation, as arising out of the bank restriction, to the period anterior to 1809. And yet, the mass of high prices of commodities, arising from the circumstances described, have constantly been included in the general impression which the public entertain of great depreciation, caused by excess of money, as characterising the whole period of the bank restriction.

It may be right, however, here to add, that it was only down to the autumn, and not quite to the close, of 1808, that the position of the bank, and the quotations of the foreign exchanges, were in a satisfactory and sound state. In the last three months of 1808, although no increase worth mentioning had taken place in the circulation of the Bank, the exchanges fell rapidly, and there was a considerable reduction of its stock of bullion. But this alteration may be considered as more properly belonging to the next epoch; while, on the other hand, the impulse given to the great advance of prices in 1808, and the anterior period, had not, in some instances, operated to its full extent till the beginning of 1809. The alteration of the exchanges, and of the position of the Bank, in the last quarter of 1808, therefore, will be considered as belonging to the next epoch; while the completion of the rise of prices, originating in, and anterior to, 1808, may be included in the interval which has just been reviewed.

SECTION 9 *Summary of the preceding survey*

As the results of the survey of the period, which has passed under review, it appears —

1. That, during the first year after the renewal of the war with France, the prices of corn were falling, and were, in the early part of 1804, as low as they had been, on an average, in ten years before the war or the bank restriction.

2. That the harvest of 1804 proved greatly deficient, and was the cause of a great rise of the prices of provisions, and the occasion of a fresh rise of wages.

3. That the harvests of 1807 and 1808, although not of so marked a degree of deficiency, were considered to have yielded only scanty crops, which, seeing the *increasing*, and, in the last of those years, the *insurmountable*, *difficulty of obtaining a foreign supply*, rendered a high price the necessary condition, with the aid of the prohibition of distillation from grain, of limiting the consumption to the reduced sources of supply.

4. That the progress of the power of France on the Continent of Europe in 1807 and 1808, and the consequent enforcement of the Berlin and Milan decrees, coincidently with the nonintercourse acts of the United States of America, rendered our actual importations of the most important raw materials for our manufactures deficient in an extraordinary degree, and threatened to cut off all future supply; thus justifying a great rise of prices, on the ground, not only of actual, but of prospective, scarcity.

5. That, while all importable commodities were thus naturally the subject of a great speculative rise, the opening of the trade with the Brazils

and Spanish America afforded great inducements to speculations in exportable commodities.

6. That the state of excitement, usually attendant upon apparently successful speculations, communicated itself to various other objects of enterprise, and occasioned the projection of numerous joint stock companies, and other manifestations of the spirit of adventure.

7. That the great rise of the prices of corn, and of other leading articles of consumption, some of them to a height beyond any which they ever afterwards attained, and the great attendant spirit of speculation and general excitement in 1807 and 1809, *took place under a remarkably restricted and equable state of the bank circulation*, and in a state of the currency which, judging by the exchanges, and the price of bullion, and the position of the Bank, as to its treasure, compared with its liabilities, was such as it might have been in a convertible state of the paper.

8. That this was the state of things, as regarded the position of the Bank, and the value of the currency, after *sixteen years of the war and twelve years of the bank restriction.*

CHAPTER V
STATE OF PRICES AND OF THE CIRCULATION, FROM 1809 TO 1813

The epoch which we are now entering upon, viz., from the close of 1808 to the commencement of 1814, embraces the precise interval which has commonly been fixed upon in proof, as it is alleged, of depreciation of the currency by the bank restriction, greatly beyond the degree indicated by the difference between paper and gold. And what, in a historical point of view, as relates to the commerce of this country, is of much more importance, the interval between the commencement of 1809 and the close of 1813, besides the astounding changes which were wrought in the political condition of the principal states of Europe, embraces events which caused greater revolutions in the principal channels of our foreign trade, and more signal vicissitudes in the fortunes of individuals, than can be found in any other equal portion of our commercial history.

We have seen that, towards the conclusion of the last epoch, the course of political events had been such as tended to the exclusion of this country from commercial intercourse with the Continent of Europe, and with the United States of America. The consequence had been a great falling off of the importation of all European and American produce, and an enormous advance of prices upon the speculation of continued and increasing obstacles to our receiving further supplies. The corn trade, however, as was before observed, had not participated to the full extent of that speculation; for, high as the price was, it does not appear to have been high enough, although the ports were open, to induce adequate efforts to overcome the impediments which then existed to a foreign supply. ①

In the examination of the causes of the great variations of prices observable in the epoch now coming under review, those of corn and other agricultural produce are first to be considered. And, for reasons which will be obvious, the examination will be found to be more conveniently conducted by a subdivision of the epoch into two periods, viz., from the commencement of 1809 to the summer of 1811, and thence to the commencement of 1814.

SECTION 1 *Prices of agricultural produce, from the commencement of 1809 to the summer of 1811*

The strong impression which had prevailed of the insufficiency of the crop of 1808 to meet the consumption till another harvest, without the aid of a foreign supply, *which was not forthcoming*, preserved a high range of the price of wheat through the early part of 1809, and the averages reached 95*s*. in March of that year. But it then became apparent that the stock on hand was not so much reduced as had been apprehended, and that it was likely to suffice for the consumption, restricted as that was by the high price, and by the prohibition of distillation from grain. As, therefore, the harvest approached, and appearances became favourable of the growing crops, the markets gradually gave way, the average price of wheat having,

① The whole importation of wheat from abroad in 1808 had been 81, 466qrs., while our exports to the Peninsula were 77, 567.

in the course of July, got down to 86*s*. 6*d*. : and there is every reason to believe that, if the crop of 1809 had turned out to be productive, and well got in, a great fall of prices would have been the consequence. But the harvest weather proved very adverse. Heavy rains set in in July, and from thenceforward, till the middle of October, the season was exceedingly wet. ① Scarcely any part of the crops was secured in good order; and a very large portion of the wheat suffered from mildew, and from sprouting.

The injury from these causes was more extensive than in any seasons here recorded, excepting only 1799 and 1816. All the crops, including hay, were very much damaged; and the wheat and barley proved to be deficient in quantity, as well as inferior in quality and condition. Prices rose in consequence; and the average for December 1809 were,

Wheat	–	–	102*s*.	6*d*. ②
Barley	–	–	50*s*.	6*d*.
Oats			30*s*.	3*d*.

Previously to any decided indication of mischief to the crops of 1809, the government seems to have been alive to the deficiency of the growth of the preceding year, which had left very little stock on hand, and to have adopted measures for facilitating importation. It appears to have suited the views of the French government, at the same time, to promote an

① It may be sufficient to bring it to the recollection of some readers, if they have been reminded, that it was the season in which the ill-fated expedition to Walcheren took place; for it must be still remembered how much the calamitous sickness which attended it was aggravated by the rains which prevailed, almost incessantly, from its embarkation to its return.

② The very indifferent quality and condition of the wheat of the crop of 1809 kept down the average price: the best samples in Mark Lane were, in December 1809, worth 125*s*.. The price of oats was comparatively low because the quality had been more injured than the quantity; besides that there had been an importation in 1808 of about 500, 000 quarters.

exportation of corn, which happened then (as one of the exceptions to the observation of a general similarity of seasons) to be unusually abundant and cheap in France and the Netherlands. Licenses were accordingly obtained from both governments; and, as a consequence of these measures, about 400,000 quarters of wheat, besides other grain, were imported before the close of 1809.

The spring of 1810 was singularly cold and ungenial: a series of dry east winds prevailed for many weeks together. The hay crops were remarkably deficient.[①] The wheats, at the same time, were generally thin on the ground. This unfavourable appearance of the coming crops, and their general backwardness, combined with the known deficiency of the existing stock, raised the averages in June for wheat to 113*s*. 5*d*.[②]; and the weather having become wet and stormy in July, and the first fortnight of August, prices experienced some further advance, viz., to an average of 116*s*. for wheat.

These high prices, and the speculation on the prospect of a further advance, had stimulated extraordinary efforts to obtain a foreign supply; so that, notwithstanding the enormous expenses of freight, insurance, and licenses, amounting collectively to from 30*s*. to 50*s*. per quarter on wheat, and in proportion for other gram, the importation in 1810 amounted to about 1,500,000 quarters of wheat and flour, and about 600,000 quarters of other grain and meal.

Of the deficiency of the wheat crop of 1809, and of the degree in which

---

① The price of hay rose, in the winter following, to 11*l*. per load.

② Bailey and oats did not participate in the advance; the averages at the close of June, 1810, being 49*s*. 9*d*. and 30*s*. 6*d*.. The prohibition of the distillation from grain might contribute to keep down the price of barley.

we were dependent on a foreign supply for keeping down the prices between that and the harvest of 1810, the following extracts from the Farmer's Magazine will furnish some interesting details: —

"Grain markets, taking all circumstances into consideration, have seldom been worse than for several months past. Three causes may be assigned for the uncommon dulness of the markets from one end of the island to the other. First, the bad weather before and during harvest last year, whereby a large proportion of grain, wheat especially, was in some degree rendered useless as an article to be manufactured into bread. Secondly, the very large, and, for the time, uncommon importation of wheat and oats from France and Holland, and the partial arrivals of wheat from America, — all tended to make a considerable part of British grain absolutely unsaleable, — that imported being in fact generally of superior value, harvested in a better climate, and free of the diseases and accidents which almost ruined the last crop in this country. Thirdly, the prohibition against the use of grain in the distilleries; whereby seven or eight hundred thousand quarters were deprived of a market, at a tune when a considerable part of British grain was fit for no other purpose than distillation." — *Farm. Mag*, vol. xi. p. 100. March, 1810.

"Letter from London, Mark Lane, 5th of March, 1810"

"The character of the crop of 1809 was represented, by the most intelligent agriculturists in every part of Great Britain, as being unproductive, especially in the article of bread corn. The deficient qualities and diminished quantities, and consequent high prices, of wheat which appeared at this market after harvest, attracted the attention of the foreign merchants, and they soon devised means of obtaining supplies from the enemy's coasts. Their activity has already had the effect to introduce into this port, since the date of our last, in the end of November, no less than 220, 348 quarters of wheat, chiefly from the ports of France, Holland, and Flanders; a quantity within 8785 quarters of the whole arrivals of *British wheat* at this market in the year 1809, and equal to more than a half of both the English and foreign wheats entered inwards during the above period."

"These large foreign supplies have certainly checked the tendency to higher prices during winter and have drawn hither buyers from all parts of the island, as well as coasting counties, who require superior qualities to work off their *own* inferior and damp descriptions of wheat."

"State of London markets. Monday, 5th of March.

Wheat.	English white	105*s*.	110*s*.	115*s*. per qr.
—	Ditto, red	94*s*.	96*s*.	102*s*.
—	Dantzic, &c.	108*s*.	115*s*.	117*s*.
—	Brabant and French	92*s*.	98*s*.	105*s*.

Farm. Mag. vol. xi p. 133. March, 1810."

"The value of grain has, in some respects, increased, chiefly owing to the advanced late of freight, and the high price given for wheat at foreign markets. Grain of home produce, except such as is sound and of fine quality, meets, however, with a dull sale, as formerly. The lamentable deficiency of last year's wheat crop, as often mentioned in this work, is now completely ascertained, by the immense importations of the last six months, —importations greatly exceeding those of 1800 or 1801, and by far the largest that ever took place in Britain during such a short period. Without them, it is almost certain that a kind of dearth would have happened."—*Farm. Mag.* vol. xi p. 253. June, 1810.

Letter from London, 2nd of June, 1810.

"The arrivals of wheat from our own coasts, between 3rd of March last and this day, amount only to about 36,000 quarters, while those of foreign growth are 280,000 quarters, forming an aggregate of 316,000 quarters. The sales, dining the same period, are within 1000 of 2000 quarters of this vast quantity. Both accounts are returned to the lord mayor's offices, but, as those of the present week will not be made up till Monday, the exact figures cannot be given. The quantity imported and sold, in these three months, is greater than the total sales of either of the two preceding years, which in 1808 were 276,077 quarters, and, in 1809, 292,205 quarters. The quantity of flour imported has also been extensive." —*Farm. Mag.* vol. xi. p. 277.

Letter from London, 3rd of August, 1810.

"The quantity of English wheat which has appeared at market is quite trifling, not equal in some weeks to one eighth of the consumption; but we continue to receive a full supply of foreign grain, whereby the great deficiency of home produce is amply made up. The arrivals this week, from foreign ports, exceed 25,000 quarters; whereas no more than 980 quarters have been imported coastwise. Good qualities are worth 122*s*. and 128*s*. per quarter; but the average price does not exceed 101*s*. 6*d*.; whence it will appear that a large part is of inferior quality." — *Farm. Mag.* vol. xi. p. 116.

A great turn, however, took place in prices after the middle of August, 1810. The weather, thenceforward, cleared up, and continued uninterruptedly propitious to the progress of the harvest till its completion, insomuch that the whole of the crops was secured in good order. The wheats, although considered to be deficient in quantity[①], were, by their good condition, all available for early use; and from this circumstance,

① Farmer's Magazine, 1810. "Wheat, in almost every case, excellent in grain, but in many districts thin, and by no means an average."

combined with the very large foreign supply, the markets declined thenceforth, the prices by the end of the year being upwards of 20*s*. lower than in August preceding. The averages at the close of 1810 being for

Wheat	–	–	94*s*. 7*d*.
Barley	–	–	41*s*. 7*d*.
Oats	–	–	26*s*. 3*d*.

The corn dealers, who had speculated on the bad weather at the commencement of the harvest, were severe sufferers, and many were ruined; thus swelling the list of bankruptcies, the great extent of which will be noticed more particularly hereafter.

The prices slowly, but progressively, declined till the summer following; the averages for June, 1811, being, for

Wheat	–	–	86*s*.	11*d*.
Barley	–	–	38*s*.	6*d*.
Oats	–	–	27*s*.	5*d*.

It is not a little remarkable, that in the discussions in the House of Commons, in May, 1811, on the bullion report, hardly any reference was made to deficiency of the crops, arising from the seasons, as accounting for the high price of corn, and the large importations in 1809 and 1810. It should seem that the disputants on both sides, with the exception of Mr. George Rose, had no notion of deficiency of crops, as justifying or explaining high prices, except in the peculiar instances of 1794 and 1795, and 1799 and 1800.

Mr. Horner must have been under an inexplicable misconception of the facts of the case, if the report of his speech, when bringing forward his resolutions on the 6th of May, 1811, be correct. According to that report, page 812. vol. xix. Parliamentary Debates, he is stated to have said, —

"It is allowed, that the principal article of import in the last year was grain, and that import was enormous. Now it appears to me, that the House should most seriously consider what could be the reason that produced a necessity for about 2, 000, 000 of quarters in one year, which was not a year of famine. When we consider the great part of our population which is employed in manufactures, and the great and increasing portion of that population which is on the list of paupers, no man can look to the possibility of another year of dearth, without feeling the most painful and serious alarm. I look upon this increase of the price of corn as a very strong argument in support of the opinions which I have taken the liberty to state to the committee."

It is here perfectly clear, that Mr. Horner either denied the scarcity as the cause of the high price, or that he confounded dearth with depreciation. Now dearth means dearness, arising from scarcity of the commodity, while depreciation supposes no scarcity of the commodity, but simply an increase of money raising prices.

Mr. George. Rose replied,

"The honourable gentleman complains of the large importation of corn lately as a great evil, and threatens inquiry respecting it. My defence will be short, but, I hope, satisfactory, — had the importation not been permitted, the distress for bread would have been extreme. With the aid of two millions of quarters of foreign corn, the quartern loaf was at fifteen pence, and, without such aid, it would probably have been at half-a-crown. The consequences which must arise, from paying foreigners for so large a quantity of corn as would probably be imported, were too obvious not to have been foreseen, but in such a dilemma there was no hesitation between submitting to the inconvenience of the nature apprehended, and to the want of bread to the necessitous part of our population."

The retort was complete, but produced no impression. The attention of the house and of the public was absorbed in the question of principle; and the utter untenableness in argument of the principles for which Mr. Rose and his colleagues in the ministry, with the bank directors, contended, cast into the shade, as irrelevant and inconclusive, all mere matter of fact. The truth is, that if it had not been for the very large importations of corn between the harvests of 1809 and 1810, the scarcity would have been most severely felt; and when Mr. Horner asked, what could be the reason that produced a necessity for about two millions of quarters of corn in one year, which was *not a year of famine*, the simple answer was, that, *but for that importation, it would have been a year of famine.*

SECTION 2 *Fall of prices of commodities, and commercial distress, from 1809 to 1811*

But while the price of corn had undergone this fluctuation of a rise of nearly 30*s*. the quarter, and again a fall to the same extent, between the summer of 1809 and that of 1811, and while some descriptions of agricultural produce, such as hay, for instance, and other provender, were still scarce and dear, all other productions, whether raw materials or manufactured articles, experienced a very great fall of price, between the commencement of 1809, and different periods in 1810 and 1811.

The great advance, and the enormously high range, of prices in this country, in 1808, while on the Continent they were low, (by the operation of the same causes as made them high here), induced the merchants on both sides to make great efforts to overcome or elude the obstacles to importation, opposed by our own orders in council, as well as by the continental system. Accordingly, measures were taken, by means of licenses from the government of this country, and of simulated papers, which were calculated to lull the vigilance, or satisfy the scruples, of those foreign governments which were the unwilling tools of the overbearing power of France at that period, for the purpose of importing, on a large scale, the commodities which had experienced so great a rise.

The measures so taken were effectual; and the importations, accordingly, in 1809 and 1810, were, independently of corn, which has already been noticed, of overwhelming magnitude, as will appear by the following comparison with the imports of the preceding year: —

Years	Wool	Silk		Tallow	Hemp	Flax	Linseed
		Raw	Thrown				
	lbs.	lbs.	lbs.	cwts.	cwts.	cwts.	Bush
1808	2, 353, 725	637, 102	139, 312	148, 282	259, 687	237, 722	506, 332
1809	6, 845, 933	698, 189	501, 746	353, 177	858, 875	533, 367	1, 119, 763
1810	10, 936, 224	1, 341, 475	450, 731	479, 440	955, 799	511, 970	1, 645, 598

But not only was there this enormous increase of importations of raw materials from the Continent of Europe. Of cotton the imports were, in

1808 – – 43, 605, 989 lbs.
1809 – – 92, 812, 282
1810 – – 136, 488, 935

Even of West India produce, the prices of which had not presented so great an inducement, there was a considerable increase, thus Sugar, imported in

1808 – – – 3, 753, 485 cwts.
1809 – – – 4, 001, 198
1810 – – – 4, 808, 663

And of Coffee, the quantity imported in 1810 was double of what it had been in 1807, viz.,

1807 – – – 417, 642 cwts.

1810 – – – 828, 683

The following Table will present, at one view, the fluctuations in the price of some of the most considerable imported articles, betweeen 1807 *and the summer of* 1811.

	1807.		1808 – 1809.		1810 – 1811.	
	Lowest.	Highest	Lowest.	Highest.	Highest	Lowest.
	l. *s.* *d.*	*l.* *s.* *d.*	*l.* *s.* *d.*	*l.* *s.* *d.*	*l.* *s.* *d.*	*l.* *s.* *d.*
Cotton, Georgia – – per lb.	0 0 10	0 1 2	0 0 9	0 2 6	0 1 7	0 0 7
—Pernambuco	0 1 9	0 1 11	0 1 8	0 2 11	0 2 3	0 1 2
—Bengal and Surat	0 0 10	0 1 3	0 0 9	0 1 9	0 1 6	0 0 4
Tobacco, Virginia	0 0 4	0 0 8	0 0 4$\frac{1}{2}$	0 2 0	0 1 1	0 0 3
Sllk, Piedmont, thrown	1 10 0	2 2 0	1 19 0	5 12 0	2 14 0	2 4 0
Wool, Leonessa	0 6 7	0 6 9	0 6 7	1 6 0	0 14 0	0 7 0
—Seville	0 2 6	0 5 3	0 2 6	0 18 0	0 9 0	0 2 6
Hemp – – per ton.	57 0 0	66 0 0	67 0 0	118 0 0	76 0 0	57 0 0
Flax	65 0 0	80 0 0	75 0 0	142 0 0	100 0 0	68 0 0
Tallow, Russian – per cwt.	2 13 0	3 12 0	3 10 0	5 12 0	4 4 0	3 1 0
Linseed – – per quarter	2 3 0	3 5 0	2 19 0	7 10 0	5 2 0	2 10 0
Oil, Galipoli – – per ton.	64 0 0	70 0 0	68 0 0	85 0 0	73 0 0	57 0 0
Ashes, American – per cwt.	2 4 0	3 9 0	2 17 0	4 9 0	3 1 0	1 0 0
Rice, Carolina	1 3 0	1 6 0	1 10 0	3 8 0	2 0 0	1 1 0
Tar, American – per barrel	1 1 0	1 8 0	1 8 0	2 6 0	2 4 0	1 3 0
Sugar, Muscov. Gaz. Average per cwt. ①	1 10 9	1 17 10	1 15 8	2 10 6	2 13 11	1 14 11
—White Havannah	2 0 0	2 6 0	1 16 0	3 5 0	3 15 0	1 10 0
Coffee, Jamaica	5 12 0	8 0 0	4 15 0	6 10 0	7 6 0	2 14 0
—St. Domingo	——	none	4 0 0	5 10 0	5 12 0	1 16 0

① It is to be observed with reference to sugar and coffee, that they had not participated in the great speculative rise in 1808-1809. They rose a little in the spring of 1810, in consequence of shipments to the Baltic, which were mostly confiscated when they reached their destination; and the quotations are here introduced to show the extreme depression which these articles underwent in 1810, 1811.

As in the short importations in 1808, combined with the apprehension of failure of future supply, there was substantial cause for a great advance of price, so, in the superabundant supplies of the two following years, there was a sufficient cause for the great fall which, in *many instances*, left to the importer, after paying for the enormous charges of importation, *nothing whatever for the prime cost.*

While this great fall was taking place in the price of the bulk of imported commodities, a total stop was put to our exports to the Baltic, by the extensive confiscations which had occurred in the summer of 1810 in the ports of Germany, and Prussia. The returns, too, from South America were now coming round; and these left a ruinous loss to the exporters, many of whom had bought the goods on credits maintained by the circulation of accommodation paper.

From the close, therefore, of 1809, through 1810, there was a complete exemplification of the circumstances which are conducive to a reduction of private paper, and to a diminution of transactions on credit, viz., stagnation and despondency, as succeeding to a state of speculation and overtrading. And so many circumstances, on so large a scale, combining in the same direction, the fall of prices, the reduction of private paper, and the destruction of credit, were greater and more rapid than were ever before, or have since, been known to have occurred within so short a space of time. A general dismay prevailed throughout nearly all branches of trade, during the last six months of 1810, and the first few months of the following year, when the depressing causes had produced their greatest effect. The following extracts, from the commercial reports inserted at the end of each number of the Monthly Magazine, convey the best and, according to my recollection, the most accurate description that I have met with of the state of distress which then prevailed: —

"Monthly Commercial Report, 1st of August, 1810."

"The failures of several houses of the very first respectability, both at London and in different provincial towns of Great Britain, have, within the last month, been unprecedented in number and importance. A West India broker, who has long been considered the first in his line, was, we are told, the prime cause of the stoppage of a banking house, whose credit was previously unimpeached. The several banks in the country, connected with the London house, of course shared its fate; and from them the evil spread to merchants, manufacturers, traders, and, in short, to the very servants and dependents of these, numbers of whom are thrown out of employment, and their families deprived of bread. Speculations in Spanish wool, an article which has fallen about fifty per cent, are considered as the origin of those unlooked for disasters. Five Manchester houses have stopped payment in the city, and, we are sorry to add, have involved numerous industrious persons, both in town and country, in their ruin. The demands upon the five houses are said to amount to *two millions*; but it is supposed that their real property will ultimately cover all deficiencies. Speculative exports to South America are the rock upon which these houses have split, in consequence of these unexpected events, public credit is at the present moment as low as ever it has been in the memory of man: the fluctuation of prices in the money market is unprecedented, and the depression so considerable, that, omnium is fallen to two and a half per cent discount. We understand that some respectable merchants have waited upon the bank directors, in order to solicit their aid towards the alleviation of the burdens with which our internal commerce is at present borne down. The result of this application is not as yet publicly known; we trust it will prove favourable. The renewal of our intercourse with the United States of America has, in some sort, benefited the manufacturing interest: but this felicitous effect is almost swallowed up in the vortex of those calamities, which it has been our painful duty to record."

"Holland. — All trade between Great Britain and this devoted country is completely put a stop to by the rigorous execution of the French emperor's anticommercial decrees. It is even reported that the captains and part of the crews of two vessels were shot for violating the prohibition."

"Prussia. — Money is so extremely scarce in the Prussian ports, that the merchants can with difficulty collect sufficient to defray the import duties; and interest is represented to be at the extravagant rate of two and a half per cent, per month."

1st of December, 1810.

"A numerical evidence of the present state of trade may be deduced from the number of bankruptcies in the London Gazette. inserted in this magazine: —

They amounted this month, in	1810, to	273
The same month, —	1809, —	130
Ditto - - —	1808, —	100
Ditto - - —	1807, —	97
Ditto - - —	1806, —	65
Ditto - - —	1805, —	87
Ditto - - —	1804, —	60

Besides stoppages and compositions, equal in number to half the traders in the kingdom! These failures throughout the kingdom have wonderfully affected the manufacture of every description of goods; and a general want of confidence exists between the manufacturer and the export merchant. The speculators at Liverpool have completly overstocked the different markets of

South America, where, at present, English manufactured articles can be purchased at a loss of twenty per cent to the exporter, with the exception of a few articles, on which little or no credit could be obtained here."

1st of January, 1811.

"In our last report we stated the vast increase of bankruptcies within the last month, compared with similar months for seven years back; and we regret to say that they still continue to increase in number, and that confidence in the mercantile world seems nearly at an end.

Discount, unless bills, &c., of a few of the first houses in the city, can only be done through the medium of bill-brokers, at an extra commission, exclusive of the regular interest.

In Lancashire the cotton manufacturers appear, by the late Gazettes, as well as by private information, to be greatly distressed, and business quite at a stand. In Manchester, and other places, houses stop not only every day, but every hour. Cotton wool is in no demand at any price, and no export of the manufactured goods, except a few fine sorts to Rio, &c. The trade of Birmingham, Sheffield, &c. quite at a stand, and no orders for execution there, except a few for our home consumption. At London, Liverpool, and Bristol, the king's stores are full of all kinds of colonial produce, as coffee, sugar, rum, &c., for security of their duties, and the proprietors in the greatest possible distress, not being able to force sales of these articles."

To prove that these are not exaggerated descriptions of the commercial distress which prevailed in this country at that period, I need only refer to the parliamentary debates in the spring of 1811, from which I have made as many extracts as my limits will permit."

Extracts from the Report of the Select Committee of the House of

Commons on the State of Commercial Credit, 7th of March, 1811.

"Your committee found that memorials had been presented to his Majesty's treasury, towards the latter end of the last and the beginning of the present year, stating the great embarrassments and distress which were felt amongst the manufacturers in the cotton trade in Glasgow and Paisley, and their vicinity, and praying for public assistance; that the same were confirmed by the representation of a meeting held in the city of London on the 12th of February, which sent a deputation to wait upon the Chancellor of the Exchequer with a copy of the resolutions adopted at that meeting. These resolutions your committee have inserted in the appendix to this report.

Your committee found, by the evidence of the witnesses they examined, that those statements and representations were founded on fact.

It appeared to your committee that the principal part of the distress winch was complained of had arisen out of great and extensive speculations, which commenced upon the opening of the South American markets in the Brazils, and elsewhere, to the adventures of British merchants.

Your committee also found that great distress was felt in a quarter which was much connected with this trade, namely, amongst the importers of produce from the foreign West India islands, and from South America.

That great part of the returns for the manufactures which were exported to those parts of the world came home in sugars and coffee, which, not being entitled to sale in the home market, there were no immediate means of realizing their value.

These representations of the distress experienced in the trade of the cotton manufacturer and exporter, and from the want of market for foreign colonial produce, were also confirmed by respectable merchants and traders in

London; who also stated that the embarrassments were felt in other branches of trade, not connected with foreign commerce or colonial produce."

Extract from the Speech of the Chancellor of the Exchequer, in the Debate on the Commercial Credit Bill.

"The consideration of this important subject, he observed, divided itself into three heads: — first, the nature and extent of the evils which the manufactures and commerce of the country were enduring; — secondly, what were the causes of those evils; —and, thirdly, the measures by which the evils might, with the greatest probability, be removed. With respect to the first of these considerations, he apprehended there could be no different of opinion whatever, but that the nature and extent of the distress, described in the report of the select committee, rendered it advisable that parliament should, if possible, adopt some measure by winch that evil might at least be diminished. It appeared distinctly by the report, that the distress, originating with the merchant, and disabling him from paying the manufacturer, was felt most severely by the manufacturer and those employed by him. All the principal manufacturers had been compelled to contract, and some wholly to suspend, their works. It appeared by the report that there was scarcely a cotton manufacturer in the kingdom who had not diminished, by one half, the number of persons employed in his mills, and that many of the smaller manufacturers had discharged their people altogether. It appeared, also, that those who were retained by the first description of manufacturers were retained at a reduced rate of wages. The consequences must necessarily be, as they were represented to be in the report of the select committee, that the most calamitous distress prevailed throughout many of the manufacturing districts. The report also stated that the merchants who traded with the western world, not being able to find an adequate market for their produce, this circumstance aggravated the distress of the manufacturers, and the whole operating upon the other branches of trade, although not immediately connected with those to which he had referred, produced a general want of confidence, and suspension of credit, which requited the prompt and effectual application of some adequate remedy."

The commercial distress of that period was not confined to the United Kingdom. It prevailed on the Continent of Europe, as may be observed by the foregoing extracts: and that the same description of distress applied to the commerce of the United States will appear from the following extract of a letter from New York, dated 11th of February, 1811, communicated to me by a friend, largely interested at that time, as well as at the present, in the trade with that country.

"Such times for money were never known, and all confidence among merchants is totally, and, indeed, very justly, destroyed. Since the middle of December we have bad between sixty and seventy failures in this city, and many more are expected to fail in the course of this and the following month."

I am indebted to the same friend for the following extract of a letter from his Liverpool house, to a mercantile correspondent.

Liverpool, Nov. 22. 1810.

"The effects of a vast import of colonial and American produce, far above the scale of our consumption at the most prosperous periods of our commerce, and attaining a magnitude hitherto unknown to us, have, in the present cramped state of our intercourse with the Continent, developed themselves in numerous bankruptcies, widely spreading in their influence, and unprecedented in extent of embarrassment. It is but fair, however, to ascribe a portion of these evils to the consequences of a sanguine indulgence of enterprise, in extensive shipments of our manufactures to South America, which so confidently followed the expedition to La Plata, and the removal of the government of Portugal to Brazil: they are further aided by the speculations which prevailed during the various stages of the American nonintercourse, and which, unfortunately, were not confined to the duration of the circumstances which excited them. In the struggle to support themselves, the speculators have had recourse to new and extensive engagements, in the face of probabilities and facts too incontrovertible to have been slighted, until the united action of the accumulating imports, and the want of an adequate vent, have overwhelmed them. The event only can enable us fully to appreciate the effects of this imprudence, which, more than any preceding defalcations, have involved the mercantile character of our country, and destroyed confidence in a degree that will require a long period of prosperous circumstances to retrieve."

Great as was the fall of prices, and severe as was the commercial distress, which prevailed in the early part of 1811, these circumstances, calculated as they were to modify the practical application of the principles, for the most part correctly laid down, by the Bullion report of 1810, were not at all adverted to in that report, nor were suffered to occupy any prominent part in the discussions in the House of Commons, to which that report gave occasion, in May, 1811. Indeed, the Bullion Committee, in their report, and their supporters in the House of Commons, seem equally to have proceeded on the assumption that all commodities had risen; and the inference held out was that they had risen in consequence of the increase of bank notes, and in common with the rise in the price of gold. No evidence whatever had been taken by the Bullion Committee respecting the prices of commodities; and the only allusion to these is in the passage wherein it is said, "the prices of all commodities have risen, and gold appears to have risen in price only in common with them. If this common effect is to be ascribed to one and the same cause, that cause can only be found in the state of the currency of this country." This observation was made at a time when all commodities, provisions alone excepted, which were scarce, from the season, *were falling rapidly in price, and had been falling when gold was rising*. But at the time when the discussions in parliament took place, namely, in May, 1811, even corn had fallen considerably in price, as we have seen; and nearly all other commodities were at a ruinously low late, compared with the cost of production, which had been so greatly increased by the extravagantly high freights and premiums of insurance to which the importations were then subject. ①

① The following are specimens of the charges of importation, to which commodities that we stood most in need of were subject, between 1809 and 1812, compared with the charges of importation in 1837, and the reader will thence judge whether the high prices of those articles are attributable to war, as increasing the demand, or to war, as obstructing the supply.

The freight and premium of insurance* from the Baltic to London, on the average of the seasons, were as follows: —

			1809 – 1812.			1837.		
On Hemp	– –	per ton	£	*s.*	*d.*	£	*s.*	*d.*
			30	0	0	2	10	0
Tallow	– –	—	20	0	0	1	10	0
Wheat	– –	per quarter	2	10	0	0	4	6
Timber	– –	per load	10	0	0	1	0	0

The charges of importation in those two years on all other commodities from the Baltic were in the same proportion.

* In 1809 there were instances when 30*l* per ton was paid for the *freight alone* of hemp; and the insurance varied from 20 to 40 per cent, making these two items of charge amount to between 40*l*. and 50*l*. per ton on hemp, and in a similar proportion on other articles of impertation from the Baltic. But I have rather taken the medium late which prevailed through the season. There was no very material reduction in those charges till 1813.

The strange misconception under which Mr. Horner laboured, as to the

---

The expenses attending the importation of silk, which was brought by a circuitous route * from Italy, through the north of Europe, were enormous Some came likewise through France; and the charges of conveyance from Italy to Havre and duty of transit, amounted to nearly 100*l*. per bale of 240*lb*., net weight, exclusive of freight and insurance from Havre hither. The whole expense of freight and insurance from Italy does not at present amount to more than 6*l*. per bale.

But, while the cost of articles imported from the Continent of Europe was thus enhanced by the difficulty of communication, the same cause raised the price of colonial produce, and of some kinds of British manufactures, to a still greater proportionate height on the Continent, inasmuch as the vigilance and severity of the decrees of the enemy were exercised more directly against imports from, than against exports to, this country. One or two instances may serve to show the degree in which these obstructions were calculated to raise the prices of such commodities abroad.

The charges of freight and French license, on a vessel of little more than 100 tons burden, have been known to amount to 50, 000*l*. for the voyage merely from Calais to London and back: this made the proportion of freight on indigo amount to 4*s*. 6*d*. per pound: the height at present is about 1*d*. per pound!

A ship, of which the whole cost and outfit did not amount to 4000*l*., earned a gross freight of 80, 000*l*. on a voyage from Bourdeaux to London and back.

Among the means devised by the ingenuity and enterprise of adventurers to elude or overcome the obstacles presented by the decrees of the enemy, one in particular, which was resorted to on an extensive scale, deserves mention, as illustrating, in a striking manner, the degree in which those obstacles were calculated to increase the cost to the consumer. Several vessels laden with sugar, coffee, tobacco, cotton – twist, and other valuable commodities, were despatched ** from hence at very high rates of freight and insurance to Salomca, where the goods were landed, and thence conveyed on horses and mules through Servia and Hungary to Vienna, for the purpose of being distributed over Germany, and, possibly, into France. Thus it might happen, that the inhabitants of that part of the Continent of Europe most contiguous to this country could not receive their supplies from hence, without an expense of conveyance equivalent to what it would be if they were removed to a distance of a seavoyage twice round the globe, but not subject to fiscal and political obstructions. It is not to be wondered at that the articles subject to such expenses should be sold at enormously high prices, viz, 5*s*. and 6*s*. per *lb*. for sugar, 7*s*. per *lb*. for coffee, 18*s*. for indigo, and 7*s*. and 8*s*. for cotton, for these prices were the condition requisite to overcome the obstacles to supply.

With just as much reason might the high prices on the Continent, of articles subject to such obstructions, be resorted to in proof of the effects of war demand, or of the state of their currency, as the high prices in this country, of timber, hemp, flax, silk, &c., and of the manufactured articles into the composition of which these raw materials entered, be considered to prove the extra demand and consumption arising out of the war, or to indicate the depreciation of paper beyond the difference between the market price and the mint price of gold.

* On one occasion, two parcels of silk were despatched from Bergamo to this country at the same time, *one by the way of Smyrna and the other by the way of Archangel*: the former was a twelvemonth and the latter two years, on its passage.

** The refined sugar was packed here in small boxes, made at a considerable additional expense, for the express purpose, to contain not more than about 2*cwt*. each, so as to admit of being slung one on each side of a horse or mule for conveyance overland.

facts of the case in regard to corn, has already been noticed; and Mr. Henry Thornton, following on the same side, seems to have been under an equally erroneous impression as to facts relating to commodities generally; for, in the debate of the 6th of May, 1811, he is reported to have said,

"It was material to observe, that there had, since the beginning of the war, been a continual fall in the value of money; he meant of money commonly so called, whether consisting of cash or paper. This had by some been estimated at 60 or 70 per cent, and certainly was not less than 40 or 50 per cent, which was, on the average, 2 or 3 per cent, per annum: it followed from hence, that if, for example, a man borrowed of the bank 1000*l*. in 1800, and paid it back in 1810, having detained it, by means of successive loans, through that period, he paid back that which had become worth less by 20 or 30 per cent than it was worth when be first received it. He would have paid an interest of 50*l*. per annum for the use of this money; but, if from this interest were deducted the 20*l*. or 30*l*. per annum which he had gained by the fall in the value of the money, he would find that he had borrowed at 2 or 3 per cent, and not at 5 per cent, as he appeared to do. By investing his money either in land or in successive commercial undertakings, in the year 1800, and then finally selling his land or his commodities in the year 1810, he would find the produce amount to 200*l*. or 300*l*. above the 1000*l*. which be had borrowed; which 200*l*. or 300*l*., being deducted from the 500*l*. interest which he had paid, would make the neat sum paid by him to be only 200*l*. or 300*l*.."①

① I have been induced to notice and comment upon this opinion of Mr. Henry Thornton, not only because of his deservedly high authority on the subject of the currency, but because the particular opinion here quoted was referred to by Lord Ashburton, in his evidence before the Agricultural Committee of the House of Commons in 1836, as confirmatory of his belief that the depreciation of the currency at that time was greatly beyond the difference between paper and gold.

It is clear that the meaning of the speaker is that the rise of prices here supposed was caused by the bank restriction; and the date assigned to the first operation of this cause is the year 1800, being that in which there first occurred any difference between paper and gold. Viewing it in this light, the hypothetical case here put involves a total misconception of the state of facts; for there were very few commodities in which, If 1000*l*. had been laid out in 1800, a loss would not have been sustained of 20 and 30 per cent, and upwards, in addition to the interest upon finally selling the commodities in 1810. The money, indeed, if laid out in land, or in houses, or in shipping, in 1800, would have produced a profit upon selling in 1810 and 1811. But this exception is easily accounted for. The frequent recurrence of deficient harvests, when, by the obstacles to importation, the rise of the prices of agricultural produce was in a greatly increased ratio to the deficiency, had given a character of permanence to the range of high prices, which enabled the landlords to obtain increased rents upon every termination of a lease. In several instances the rents were raised to treble of what they had been in 1792, and speculations in purchases of land were almost certain to render a profit. In the case of houses, the increasing taxes upon building materials, and the great rise in the price of timber, in consequence, not only of the heavy duty, but of the high freight and charges on importation, when combined with an increasing population, operated as a premium on all existing buildings, and necessarily caused a great rise in that description of property. And as to shipping, there was not only the increased and increasing cost of the materials, which raised the building price, but the employment was extended by the demands for the transport service, which required tonnage on a greatly enlarged scale for the war in the Peninsula. These descriptions of property were doubtless higher in 1810 than in 1800; and the price of labour having been slowly but progressively advanced, in consequence of the frequent recurrence of periods of dearth, the increased wages had acquired the character of permanence. But with these exceptions, which, so explained, afford no ground for ascribing their comparatively high price to depreciation of money, nearly all other objects of exchange were *lower in price in* 1810 and 1811 *than in* 1800; *in few instances less than* 20 *per cent*, *and*, *in some instances*, *upwards of* 50 *per cent*, *as measured in paper*, *while gold had risen* 25 *per cent.* It may be matter of surprise that Mr. Henry Thornton, who, in his excellent work on paper credit, in 1802, had so well exposed the hasty conclusions of Mr. Boyd, as to the influence of the bank issues in causing the high prices of corn in 1799 and 1800, should, in 1811, have laboured under such a misconception of the actual state of markets as to be led into an error so similar to that which he had some time before animadverted upon. The fact is, that Mr. Thornton, who was profoundly and accurately acquainted with the principles and details of banking, had not necessarily, from his occupation as a banker, any knowledge of markets; and nothing can more strongly prove how little aware he was of the actual state of them, and of the fluctuations to which they had been subject, or of the causes of those fluctuations, than the passage here quoted from his speech. His exposition, at the same time, of the general principles of currency was full and clear, and, indeed, the best that had then been given; and his exposure of the inconsistencies and fallacies involved in the maxims avowed by the bank directors, and supported by the government, was unanswered and unanswerable.

Mr. Vansittart, in his speech on the same occasion, presents a curious and somewhat amusing contrast. While his arguments in support of the views of the government, and of the doctrine of the bank directors, and of the proposition embodied in his unfortunate resolution, form a model of ingeniously perplexed, and elaborately unintelligible, general reasoning, his statements of facts indicate extensive and accurate information as to the nature and extent of the disturbing causes which were operating upon the exchanges and upon prices, and which accounted for them independently of any supposed influence upon them by the state of the circulation.

"The general scale of prices, he observed, had been progressively but slowly advancing for many years previous to the bank restriction, and does not appear to have been affected by that event. But the scarcity in 1800 and 1801 produced a great and permanent effect, particularly on the price of labour; and it has been so far from being remarkable in the last two years, that though the price of provisions has been high, from causes sufficiently notorious, that of most articles of merchandize is considerably reduced. The last period of three or four years is, indeed, remarkable for great and sudden fluctuations of the prices of merchandize, corresponding with the extraordinary and violent changes which have taken place in commercial policy; but the present state of prices is so far from justifying the opinion of a currency depreciated from its excess, that it would rather lead to a contrary inference, if it were not easy to be accounted for by obvious causes."

In a subsequent speech, on the 13th of May, 1811, Mr. Vansittart pointed out how, in some instances, taxation perpetuated prices which, in their origin, and temporarily, had been those of dearth.

"But the principal reason," he said, "which produced that remarkable increase of prices, which has subsisted from that time without any extraordinary variation, was the great additional mass of taxes imposed, while the effects of the scarcity were passing away, and prices returning to the former level. It may serve by way of illustration to mention a particular instance. The price of beer had, among other articles, been considerably advanced during the scarcity. In the spring of 1802, the price of malt having fallen that of beer was reduced; but a tax was soon after imposed by parliament to the exact amount of the reduction. The price was, accordingly, raised again, and remained the same to the consumer as during the scarcity."

Lord Castlereagh, who equally failed in rendering his general principles intelligible, observed, however, justly enough, "that, if the Bullion Committee could have traced any advance of price in the leading articles of consumption, which could be fairly shown to connect itself with the alleged excess of notes, they would have annexed to their report tables of the prices current during the period which has elapsed since the restriction bill took place. So far from prices having advanced in the two or three last years, since exchanges became unfavourable, and bank notes are assumed to be depreciated, he believed the fact to be the reverse."

And in the House of Lords, in the course of the debates on that most anomalous measure, lord Stanhope's gold coin bill, lord Bathurst, in his reply to Lord King, asked, "Was there a general advance in the price of commodities? Let the noble lord compare the current prices at present with those in 1808, and he would find that a large proportion of commodities, and those by no means inconsiderable commodities, had fallen in price. He would find that iron and wool, unfortunately for the noble lord adduced as instances of a rise in price, tallow, cotton, and a great number of other commodities, had experienced a great fall. When there was a depreciation in the currency, there would be a general advance in the price of commodities; but, if there was a general advance, it did not follow that there was depreciation."

In neither of the two houses, however, did the principal speakers on the side of the Bullion Committee seem to think it incumbent upon them to explain this anomaly of prices according to their doctrine. They were intent only on exposing the outrageous absurdity and inconsistency of the proposition involved in Mr. Vansittart's third resolution.① In that object they so far succeeded, that, although the resolution was carried by a large majority of the House of Commons, the public has assented to the general principles for which the Committee and its supporters contended.

SECTION 3 *Revival of credit, and improved prospects of trade, in the summer of 1811*

The suffering state of commerce, which has been described as the consequence of the great fall of prices in 1809 and 1810, and of the disastrous result of the speculative exports, did not continue, however, in the same degree of intensity beyond the spring of 1811, when it seems to have reached its height.

At that time, as we have seen, it attracted the notice and interference of Parliament. An act was passed, in April, 1811, granting a sum, not exceeding six millions of Exchequer bills, to be advanced by commissioners to the distressed merchants and manufacturers, by way of loan on adequate security. This measure, in consequence of which, however, not more than two millions were eventually advanced, was then,

① Mr. Vansittart had said, "I wish the house *to pledge itself to the belief* that bank notes still are, as they have always been, equivalent to legal coin, for the internal purposes of the country, the only purposes to which they ever have been applicable."

as it probably is still, supposed to have arrested the tendency to depression, and to have contributed to the subsequent revival of trade. In that opinion I did not and do not participate. If the causes of abundance of commodities at home, and our exclusion from foreign ports, had continued, there would have been no ground for a rise of prices: and, if prices had not risen, the parties who borrowed the Exchequer bills would have been injured instead of benefited by the facility of holding their goods so much longer; as they would thereby have incurred loss of interest, warehouse-rent, and other expenses, and must at last have submitted to the same, if not to lower, prices than they might originally have obtained. But whether the measure was or was not calculated to do the good intended, there is reason to believe that it did not come into operation at all till circumstances had occurred favourable to a revival of the activity of trade, and, consequently, to a removal of the causes of the then existing distress.

Those circumstances were, the complete expulsion of the French from Portugal, and the progress of the British army in Spain, which opened nearly the whole Peninsula to a commercial intercourse with this country. The glut of our exports to South America and the West Indies had been carried off by low prices, and a brisk demand had succeeded. The intention of Russia to resist the French was becoming manifest; and an anticipation was confidently entertained of a relaxation of the prohibitions against imports into the Russian ports.

The progress of improvement, is described in the following extracts from the periodical work which I have before quoted: —

Monthly Commercial Report, 1st of June, 1811.

"The expulsion of the French out of Portugal has once more opened a trade with that country, and, in consequence of it, vast quantities of goods of the manufacture of Great Britain are now shipping for Lisbon and Oporto; among which the manufactures of Manchester, &c., will not be the least in quantity. Linens, calicos, and woollen cloths are in great demand in Portugal.

South America.— In our last we stated the trade of this country to he rather brisk, and have the pleasure now to say that every mail from the Brazils confirms it."

1st of July, 1811.

"Since our last report, the manufactories have revived in a great degree, chiefly owing to large orders for all kinds of woollen, linen, and cotton goods having arrived here for the markets of Portugal and of South America. The goods of Birmingham and Sheffield are also in great demand at these markets. Credit and confidence, we are happy to say, revive, and the towns of Manchester, Nottingham, &c. feel vast benefit from the happy change that has taken place.

The West India Islands ate now in want of all kinds of British manufactured goods, as the stock in hand in these islands has been purchased up with avidity for the Spanish settlements. Irish linen, sheeting, &c., render a full profit of twenty per cent, more than the usual profit attached to such speculations."

This improvement, however, as it so immediately succeeded to a period of great distress, was not yet marked by such eagerness of speculative shipment as had distinguished 1808 and 1809.

While our export trade was slowly recovering, there appealed, towards the autumn of that year, a more marked tendency to a general advance in the prices of agricultural produce, and of imported raw materials.

SECTION 4 *Rise of the prices of agricultural produce, and high range of them, between the harvest of 1811 and the harvest of 1813*

The scanty crops of corn of 1810 had been eked out by the aid of the large foreign supply, at rather declining prices, till the approach of the harvest of 1811, when, in consequence of the bareness of the stock on hand, and the unfavourable appearance of the crops, combined with unsettled weather, prices began to rise in August, and thenceforward advanced steadily and considerably till the eve of the following harvest, when, as will be seen, they attained their greatest height.

As it was the deficiency of the crops of the harvest of 1811 which, with little stock remaining from the preceding year, and without the means of obtaining a foreign supply, occasioned the high prices of 1812, and as those high prices form the standard a decline from which has been ascribed to the operation of Peel's bill, it is necessary to notice in some detail the circumstances connected with it. The more especially because the fact itself of any deficiency at all, as resulting from that year's crops, appears not to have been contemplated, or, at any rate, has not been admitted, or even adverted to, by the supporters of the several theories of depreciation or of war demand. The further presumptive proofs of the negative of those theories will be pointed out hereafter. In the mean time, the following extracts from contemporaneous publications must be considered as forming a mass of the best evidence, of which the nature of the subject is susceptible, of the deficiency of the crops of corn in this country. A deficiency quite sufficient, when considered with its attendant circumstances, to account for the high prices which have been so gratuitously ascribed to the currency or to war demand. The following is an account of it, from one of the circular monthly reports of that period (Oct. 1811).

"The state of the wheat crops seems now to be ascertained with probable accuracy throughout the island, as somewhat below an average quantity, and far inferior to that of last year in point of quality. Reckoning both quantity and quality, persons of the most general information decide upon a deficiency of a full third. There will be a considerable quantity of black wheat, and in many parts of the north the barley is *strongly* smutted."

This estimate was fully confirmed; for, in another monthly report in December, 1811, it is said,

"The former statements respecting the defects of the crops of wheat, both in quantity and quality, are fully and unfortunately confirmed. The autumnal price of wheat, is indeed, at an enormous height, although the farmers have been universally liberal in supplying the markets, considering the season, and, as there are various impediments to foreign supplies in times like the present, the real state of things cannot be too widely promulgated, with a view to timely economy in expenditure."

A corroboration of the general estimate of the defective state of the crops of that year will be found in the following extract from the Farmer's Magazine, more minutely descriptive of the deficiency: —

"December, 1811. — The wheat crop is less or more a defective one in every district, but more so in some districts than in others. According to our accounts it can rarely be estimated above five eighths of an average crop, though, what is surprising, the quality of the grain is generally good, a circumstance which seldom happens when the crop is a failing one. Indeed, as the failure this season was not, in many instances, occasioned by mildew (at least in Scotland), the grain that was in the ear arrived at complete maturity, without being stinted of nourishment. The deficiency evidently proceeded from wetness in May — from cold frosty nights in June — from boisterous winds when the plant was under the blossom process — and from want of sun and heat when the grain was formed in the ear of the plant. Wheat is a grain always comparatively unproductive in a cold season such, as the last one, and the same remark is applicable to bailey, the crop of which, generally speaking, is below an average. Oats, and peas, and beans, may, however, be considered as fair crops, though, according to our accounts, many of these grains, upon thin soils, suffered so much from the wetness in May and June as not to prosper afterwards.

From all these circumstances a rise of corn markets was the necessary consequence, though at this time it would be lather rash to speculate or prognosticate upon their state at a more advanced period of the season, when prices may be supposed to have gained their proper level. The present rate of markets will be seen from the accounts which follow. Hitherto there has been little or no importation from foreign countries, and it is understood that the crops upon the Continent are scantier this season than usual."

And the following copy of a petition from Liverpool will place beyond a doubt the fact of the general impression of the great deficiency of the crop of 1811.

"At a public meeting of the inhabitants of Liverpool, held on the 4th of November, 1811, John Bourne, Esq. Major, in the chair, it was unanimously resolved, upon the motion of John Gladstone, Esq, seconded by Thomas Rodie, Esq., that a petition should be presented to the Prince Regent, praying that he would suspend the further distillation of spirits from grain until the meeting of Parliament.

"THE HUMBLE PETITION, &c. &c."

"Showeth,

That your petitioners being deeply interested in the welfare of this populous town, and this great manufacturing county, cannot but view with great anxiety the progressive and alarming advance in the prices of corn, in connection with the fact now ascertained, that the produce of the late harvest is very deficient, and that the weather for gathering it in, in the northern parts of Great Britain, and for preparing the wheat lands generally for the next crops, has been extremely unfavourable.

That your petitioners are well informed the potato crop in Ireland has so materially failed, that this important necessary of life now sells in the Dublin market at the excessive price of 6*s*. per cwt., from which circumstance your petitioner apprehend that the usual supplies of corn from Ireland, upon which the numerous population of this town and the county of Lancaster are known in a great degree to depend for subsistence, are likely to be much curtailed.

That, in times like the present, when no dependence can be placed on receiving supplies of foreign coin, it becomes of the first importance to husband to the utmost the crops of this country.

That the average weekly prices of coin in England and Wales, according to the returns received in the week ending the 26th of October, as published in the London Gazette of the 2nd of November, are as follows:—

	s.	*d*.
Wheat	101	6 per quarter.
Barley	47	4
Oats	29	10

Which equal, and, in several instances, exceed the prices at the different periods when the legislature, in their wisdom, thought fit to interpose to prevent the distillation of spirits from grain (the year of extraordinary scarcity only excepted), as will appeal from the following comparative statement taken from the official returns.

Average price of wheat, barley, and oats, in England and Wales, according to the weekly returns nearest to the following periods.

Nearest Weekly Returns.

Date.	Distillation.	Wheat.		Barley.		Oats.	
		s.	*d.*	*s.*	*d.*	*s.*	*d.*
1795	Prohibited.	93	10	46	0	29	2
1797	Removed.	52	3	28	4	15	10
1800	Prohibition.	133	0	76	7	41	8
1802	Removed.	76	9	41	1	23	4
1808	Prohibition.	81	6	44	3	38	10
1808	Continued.	92	7	45	10	33	8
1809	Prohibition.	95	7	46	6	34	4
1809	Prohibition.	101	9	50	7	31	11
1810	Prohibition.	101	7	46	5	27	5
1811	The last return.	101	6	47	4	29	10

That on these grounds your petitioners humbly conceive there exists an urgent necessity for the interposition of the loyal prerogative before the meeting of Parliament, more especially as, should the measure he deferred till that period, the distillers will have laid in their stocks of grain for the season, a large proportion of which will either be distilled or converted into a slate unfitting it for the food of man.

In the spring of 1812, the general impression was, that the stock in hand was very defective. The following is an extract from a printed report, dated in May, 1812: —

"The stock of wheat on hand in the most productive eastern counties, is alarmingly deficient according to the best accounts that can be obtained."

Whether that impression, which was very general, had been well or ill founded, it was equally calculated to affect prices. This deficiency, real or supposed, of the stock of grain in the country, and the absence of any prospect of effectual relief by importation, became more alarming as the summer advanced, in consequence of apprehensions which were entertained of the result of the approaching harvest.

The whole of July, and part of August, 1812, proved cold and wet, and the harvest commenced under very unfavourable appearances. From a combination of these circumstances, there was a great excitement and spirit of speculation among all persons in the corn trade; and as the range of high prices (with an interval of depression between the harvests of 1810 and 1811, so short as not to have been felt at all by the landlord, and very little by the farmer) had been of an unusually long continuance, it was hastily concluded, as it unfortunately but too often is upon such occasions, that the causes of that high range were permanent. This accordingly was the period in which rents experienced their greatest rise, and speculations in land became most general. And there is reason to believe that, under these circumstances, the country circulation must have recovered from its shock of 1810, and have acquired a renewed extension.

In August, 1812, the average prices were, for England and Wales, per Gazette average—

	s.	*d.*
Wheat,	155	0
Barley,	79	10
Oats,	56	2

In Mark Lane, the finest Danzig Wheat fetched 180s. , and Oats, in one or two instances, were sold at the enormous price of 84*s*. .

The corn markets have on no occasion since attained the same elevation.

Meat in Smithfield reached the following quotations: —

	s.	*d*.		*s*.	*d*.
Beef,	5	2	to	6	2
Mutton,	5	2	—	6	4
Veal,	5	6	—	7	6
Pork,	5	4	—	6	10

The weather during the harvest of 1812 was unsettled, but not so decidedly wet as materially to injure the crops. There were conflicting opinions as to the yield. The following are extracts from some of the reports of the time; making all due allowance, the crops of grain generally, and of potatoes in that year, appear to have been under an average.

Farmer's Magazine, August, 1812.

"There has seldom, or perhaps never, been a period when the new crop was a subject of greater and more general interest than the present; and it was our particular wish to obtain the best and fullest information of its appearance. We feel very grateful to our correspondents who have enabled us to present reports of it, and of the condition of the industrious pool for the last quarter; and then communications will certainly be perused with that attention which their peculiar importance must command.

Though appearances are different, as might be expected, from the diversity of soil and culture, the general character of the ensuing crop, as far as an opinion can be formed of it at this period of the season, must be represented, we fear, as rather unfavourable. The impression, after a very careful examination of the reports, is, that unless we have two months at least of singularly warm, clear, and dry weather, the grain crops will not leach an average; that common oats, particularly in many situations, and peas and beans generally, must be very late indeed. From recent and afflicting experience of partial failure in the crops of wheat, it is not a matter of surprise if a few of the intelligent writers are a little alarmed at the indications of disease which that crop already exhibits in some districts, and which there was but too much reason to expect from the late cold, humid, and ungenial state of the atmosphere."

Agricultural Report. Monthly Magazine.

"Wheat harvest has been protracted and extremely tedious in the distant counties; the farmers being obliged to wait an unusual length of time for the grain to ripen, which, in the interval, has taken considerable damage from wet. This unfavourable circumstance will add to the stock of unsound and light corn. The last year's stock is literally exhausted in all quarters, and markets in consequence have continued to use for several weeks. The early speculators, who hurried their wheat to market, to the great deterioration of its quality, have failed generally in their object, as the subsequent rise in prices has proved. The favourable opinion of the potato crop has not been realised; they yield but indifferently, probably in the proportion of a defect of one fourth of the variable quantity of last year. In the mean time, certain ill informed newspapers teem with the usual deplorable nonsense about monopoly, forestalling, and hoarding farmers and dealers!"—*Middlesex*, *October* 27. 1812.

There was still no prospect of a foreign supply, for, high as the price here was, it was insufficient to cover the great expenses of importation, added to a relatively high price at the shipping ports.

The deficiency of our own crops in 1811 and 1812 does not appear to have been so great as it had been in 1794 and 1795; or, again in 1799 and 1800. It is clear, therefore, that the prices of 1811 and 1812 would not have been so high if there had not been a virtual exclusion of foreign supply, which rendered it necessary to eke out our own produce by economy; and this could only be effected through the medium of a relatively high range of prices.

It must be obvious that, the effect of a succession of crops, such as have been described, more or less deficient, in raising prices so much beyond the degree of defect, must have been to afford a great amount of gain to be distributed among the agricultural classes. Independently of the encouragement arising from these profits, continued through so great a length of time, there was now a confidence, which had not before existed, in the prospect of the continuance of them. The average produce of five seasons was supposed to represent what would be the utmost that any five succeeding seasons were likely to vield; and as there was not, till the close of 1812, any appearance of a relaxation of the continental system of exclusion directed against the trade of this country, a continued absence of foreign competition was fully anticipated.

Under these circumstances, rents, upon the expiration of leases, were advanced in full proportion to the high range of the prices of produce; and, in several instances, they were raised threefold or upwards of what they had been in 1792. Every purchase of land previous to 1811, whether made with or without judgment, turned out favourably according to the market rates, and it was supposed, in consequence, that money could in no way be so profitably employed as in buying land. Speculations, therefore, in land, or, as it is termed, land jobbing, became general, and credit came in aid of capital for that purpose. A staking, but not, I believe, a singular instance of that description of speculation, was exhibited in the case of a petition presented to parliament some years after, representing that the petitioner had, in the years 1811 and 1812, laid out 150,000*l*. partly his own and partly borrowed, in the purchase of land, which had since fallen so much in value, that he was ruined by the loss; praying, therefore, to be relieved, by what it has been the fashion to term an equitable adjustment of contracts, but which means, in reality, an indemnification for bad speculations.

The extension of tillage, and the application of fresh capital to land alicady in cultivation, proceeded in full proportion to the great gains derived from the produce at such high prices. The number of inclosure bills was —

In 1805	–	71	1800	–	122
1806	–	76	1810	–	107
1807	–	91	1811	–	133
1808	–	92	1812	–	119

It is not easy to imagine, that any person, not biassed by a preconceived theory, who will have been at the trouble of going through the evidence which has been here adduced, can resist the conclusion, that the produce of the seasons from 1808 to 1812, both years included, was more or less deficient. And seeing, according to that evidence, that of the five seasons embraced in that interval, the first was partially deficient, and the four following decidedly so; seeing, moreover, that relief by importation was attainable only in two of them, viz. 1809 and 1810, and then only on the condition of being subject to expenses of licence from our own and from the foreign hostile governments, and of freight and insurance amounting collectively to, at least, 30*s*., and in many instances to 50*s*. the quarter on wheat; while in 1811 and 1812[①], hardly any foreign supply at all could be obtained, there being an equal dearth on the Continent of Europe, and especially in France, the wonder is rather, not that prices were so high, but that they were not higher. Of this, at least, I feel persuaded, that were a succession of five such seasons to occur again, *subject to an equal difficulty and expense of obtaining a foreign supply*, or to a duty on importation equivalent to the difference of freight and insurance at that time compared with the present, and if, moreover, an alarm were superadded, by the prospect of not getting any aid at all by importation, we should witness, a range of prices, *at least*, as high as then prevailed.

SECTION 5 *On wages and salaries as connected with the prices of necessaries*

It may be, as indeed it has been, observed as a ground for questioning,

---

① The only instance that I have met with in the evidence, appended to the several parliamentary agricultural reports, of any witness who appears to have had a distinct recollection of the state of things connected with the corn markets at this period, is Mr. Joseph Sandars of Liverpool. In his evidence before the committee of 1833, he observed, page 218: —

"I have never known any but one year, in which there was any prospect whatever of famine, of the people not being able to get sufficient, and that was in the year 1812, resulting from the crop of 1811, when we were shut out from the rest of the world; wheat gradually advanced from 10*s*. a bushel, to 21*s*. or 25*s*.. That year we were on the very verge of famine, and I can give a remarkable proof of it; in ten days after the crop of oats had begun to be cut in Lancashire, the price of oatmeal, notwithstanding it was at three times its present price, that is, at 3*l*. a load, notwithstanding the crop was within the reach of consumption, in one week it advanced 1*l*. from absolute scarcity. That year, I recollect, at the termination of it, we never showed a sample of corn at all; it was always bespoken."

And yet it is with reference to this period of severe dearth that it has been said by one of the principal authorities for the doctrine of depreciation, "Those were not the prices of dear corn, but of cheap money; not of scarcity, but abundance." *Letter to Lord Archibald Hamilton.*

whether there was a scarcity in these seasons justifying the high prices, that although the prices of corn were as high as they had been in 1795, and 1796, and in 1800, and 1801, there was nothing like the same importance attached to them. No committees of parliament to inquire into the causes of the deficiency and to suggest remedies. ① The answer is that the high prices of 1795, and 1796, and of 1800, and 1801, came abruptly, combining dearth from failure of produce with the effects of heavy taxation, which fell directly or indirectly on consumable commodities, while wages and salaries had been adjusted to the scale of prices resulting from a state of peace and plenty. It has already been observed, in treating of those earlier periods of dearth, that they presented the alternative of the actual starvation of considerable numbers of the working population, or of a rise of wages, whether permanent, or temporary and variable. A great rise of wages, but still far short of the rise in the price of necessaries did take place, partly permanent, and partly temporary and variable, including under the latter description parish allowances and individual contributions. And not only

① In the Letter to Lord Archibald Hamilton before referred to, the writer, after adverting to the years 1795 and 1800, and admitting them to have been years of real scarcity, goes on to say, page 29., "shortly afterwards ensured years not of scarcity but abundance, years of increasing revenue, and increasing prosperity among the poor, whilst they paid year after year prices for wheat of 87*s*. 9*d*., 95*s*. 7*d*., 106*s*. 2*d*., 94*s*. 6*d*., 125*s*. 5*d*, and 108*s*. 9*d*., which last five prices quoted are the average prices of five successive years, ending with 1813. No committees sat in these years to consider of the high price of corn, and of distress arising therefrom." It is hardly possible to imagine a more egregious misapprehension of facts, than is contained in the above passage. Upon the perversion of years of scarcity into years of abundance I have already remarked. With regard to the assertion of an increasing revenue, the fact, on the contrary, is, that the produce of the permanent taxes fell off in each of the years 1811 and 1812. And it is well known that this circumstance, indicating an approach to the limits of the power of further taxation, induced the resort in 1813 to an appropriation of the nominal sinking fund for the interest on the further loans.

did a rise of wages take place on the occasion of those memorable scarcities, but there was a further use when, after a short intermediate subsidence of the price of provisions, between 1801 and 1808, a recurrence of defective crops and increasing taxation, and consequent high prices of food and other necessaries, gave occasion to further claims for advance of wages: in most occupations these had reached their maximum before 1812.

The wages of agicultural labourers and artisans had been doubled, or nearly so. Salaries from the lowest clerks up to the highest functionaries, as well as professional fees, had been considerably raised on the plea of the greatly increased expenses of living, the expense of living having been increased, not only by the increased price of necessaries, but by a higher scale of general expenditure, or style of living, incidental to the progress of wealth and civilisation. Thus, upon the recurrence of the seasons of dearth between 1808 and 1812, there was more of an adjustment, although still inadequate, of the pecuniary means of a huge part of the different classes, which prevented so great a degree of the pressure of distress as had been observable in the previous scarcity.

But while the wages of agricultural labourers and of artisans had been raised in a considerable, although still inadequate proportion to the increased price of necessaries, this was not the case, or only partially so, as regarded the wages of the working people in manufactories. Considerable numbers of these had no advance of wages; or if they had, the advance was more than compensated by reduced hours of work. In the branches of trade which were affected by the state of stagnation and discredit in 1810 and 1811, and in those which depended upon a demand for export, many workmen were thrown wholly out of employ. The distress accordingly among these classes was very severe, and was the cause of considerable disturbances in the manufacturing districts. ①

SECTION 6 *Advance of prices on the continent of Europe in 1811 and 1812*

It may be objected by persons who may still profess to be sceptical, as to the fact of scarcity, in explaining the advance of prices of provisions and of labour in the period referred to, that these prices were purely artificial; and were the result, according to the theory of one set of reasoners, of the alteration of the system of our currency, and according to another, of the influence of war demand, arising out of our large expenditure defrayed by loans. Upon either hypothesis the rise of prices and of wages is supposed to be from a cause operating locally, either by an increase of paper money, or by the large loans raised, in this country.

It so happens, however, that a similar rise of the prices of provisions and of other necessaries, and of labour, took place in 1811 and 1812 on the Continent of Europe generally as well as in this country, during the period referred to, with only an allowance for the difference of the ordinary level of their prices, compared with ours.

---

① The Prince Regent, in a message to the House of Commons, in June 1812, referred to the violent and dangerous proceedings carried on in several counties of England. In further proof of the distressed state of the working classes at that time, it may be observed, that the poor rates, which in 1803, a period of low prices and agricultural distress, had amounted to 5, 318, 204*l*., rose in 1812 and 1813 to 8, 640, 842*l*.. And it was stated in the House of Commons (Parliamentary Debates, vol. xxi. p. 1004.), that a committee, appointed at Liverpool, to examine into the condition of the poor, reported that, there had been in one month, namely, January, 1812, an increase of numbers from 8000 to 15, 350.

Never was there a greater delusion than that which prevails under the influence of the currency theory, representing this period as one of great and increasing prosperity.

It has before been observed, that some similarity of seasons, in point of marked preponderance of drought or wetness, and of inclemency or propitiousness, and consequent productiveness or otherwise, has been found to apply generally to parts of the Continent of Europe, but more especially to the principal parts of France and Germany. This observation, however, is subject to considerable exceptions; for instance, the seasons of 1808 and 1809 appear to have been more productive on the Continent of Europe, and in France especially, than in this country; the prices there were consequently low, and induced the large exports to this country, notwithstanding the enormous expenses of freight, insurance, and licences in 1809 and 1810. But 1810, 1811, and 1812, on the Continent of Europe, participated of the character of the seasons in this country, and the rise of prices there was fully *in the same proportion* as took place here in those years. That the scarcity in France, consequent upon the unproductiveness of those seasons, was great and real, admits of being proved by irrefragable evidence. The fact is alluded to by all the writers of authority on the subject of the corn trade and of the corn laws of that country, and is described as entailing a state bordering on famine. Mons. J. B. Say, the justly celebrated writer on political economy[①], so characterises those seasons, and gives the following quotations, as those of the important market of Roye in Picardy, for the measure equal to fifty-two litres two centimes: —

① In a letter addressed to Mr. James, which appeared in the Morning Chronicle on the 21st of August, 1822.

			liv.	so.	der.
1808	–	–	5	18	0
1809	–	–	6	16	3
1810	–	–	9	4	3
1811	–	–	16	5	6
1812	–	–	13	9	9

The average prices in all France were —

		Per Hectol		Per Winchester qr.	
		fr.	cnt.	*s.*	*d.*
1809	–	14	90	38	$0\frac{1}{2}$
1810	–	19	63	49	$7\frac{1}{4}$
1811	–	26	17	67	$1\frac{1}{2}$
1812	–	34	33	87	$11\frac{1}{4}$

Returns from Consuls abroad, *7th of December*, 1826.

But these averages give no adequate idea of the extent of the real rise of prices in an extensive portion of that country, as independently of the imperfect mode in which they are taken, having reference only to the prices, and not to the quantities in the districts making the returns; and their embracing districts which might casually have been better provided, but could not by reason of the intercourse by sea between their distant maritime provinces being intercepted by our fleets, equalise their produce with those most deficient; the government made great sacrifices of money to keep down prices, by importing from abroad and selling at prices below the cost. From the consular returns of prices in some of the departments in France the rise appears to have been greater; thus, at Nantes, the quotations were, in

		fr.	cnt.
1809	–	12	4 per hectol.
1812	–	37	72
And at Bourdeaux		14	85 in 1809,
		38	65 in 1812. ①

In an elaborate work on the corn trade and corn laws in France, published at Paris by P. Laboulinière, entitled "De la Disette et de la Surabon-dance," vol. ii. p. 417., is the following passage: referring to the year 1812, he says —

"La récotle fut mauvaisc, la cherté devint excessive; le septier de blé Cut vendu dans plusieurs provinces jusqu' à 100 francs (150*s*. the quarter), et la misère fut tiès grande. Les sacrifices faits par le gouvernement Impérial pour ies subsistences peuvent être évalués à 80 millions (upwards of three millions sterling). Les mers à cette éepoque n' etoient pas libres, il fallut done établir par terre le transport des grains

---

① "In Germany and in Italy, Spain and Portugal, nearly a corresponding rise of prices occurred. The following are among other numerous instances of the great rise of the prices of wheat. —

		1808-1809			1811-1812	
Louvain	–	31*s*.	7*d*.	to	68*s*.	8*d*.
Rotterdam	–	44*s*.	4*d*.	—	81*s*.	9*d*.
Christiania	–	24*s*.	5*d*.	—	73*s*.	6*d*.
Alicante		61*s*.	8*d*.	—	141*s*.	10*d*.
Bilboa	–	53*s*.	0*d*.	—	98*s*.	6*d*.
Lisbon	–	96*s*.	3*d*.	—	152*s*.	6*d*.

Tables by the Statistical Department of the Board of Trade. vol. v. p. 450.

Of none of these places can it be said, that the rise was produced by a demand from this country; for, in point of fact, we imported next to none from the North of Europe in 1811 and 1812, while shipments were actually made from this country to the South of Europe.

depurs Hambourg jusqu' à Paris; quand momentanément on put profiter des rivieres, il y eut des frais de chargement considérables."

Here most assuredly there is nothing of paper circulation or of war demand defrayed by loans, to account for the rise of prices: credit was nearly annihilated in France in those times; and it is well known, that the expenses of the war were not defrayed by loans. As little can the scarcity in France be accounted for by extra consumption occasioned by the war. The armies of France, at that time, were far beyond her own territories. The greater part were in the North of Europe, among the cheapest of the corn-growing countries; and, most assuredly, in the supplies sent from France for the troops, there would hardly be included any large proportion of mere articles of food; nor at any rate of the more cumbersome ones, such as corn.

In 1809, when the war in Germany was carried on upon a very large scale, the prices of provisions were comparatively low both in Germany and in France. This low price on the Continent in 1809 negatives not only the hypothesis of extra war consumption, but it negatives also the opinion of the influence on continental prices of the addition to the stock of the precious metals abroad, by the disengagment of them from this country; for, in 1809, all the bullion that could be spared from hence was sent for the purpose of defraying our then immense foreign expenditure. And with reference to this supposed operation of the bank restriction in depreciating the precious metals, how would it account for the circumstance that France *exported corn in* 1809, and *imported largely*, and at an enormous expense to the government, in 1811 and 1812. The export of wheat from France, in 1809 and 1810, was 637,273 quarters; while the imports, in 1811 and 1812, and the early part of 1813, amounted to 1,337,219 quarters.

The fact of the scarcity and high prices of corn in France in 1811 and 1812 is important in a twofold point of view.

1. It favours the presumption of a cause common to the two countries, of which none more probable than the influence of the seasons; inasmuch as these, in the majority of instances, are known to have some similarity of character, at the same time that there is direct evidence of dearth from those two seasons in the present instance.

2. It accounts for our prices having risen higher than with a similar deficiency of our own produce they would have done, by the circumstance, that the purchases of corn in Germany by the French government, combined with the enormous charges of freight and insurance, to this country, prevented our getting a foreign supply, of which we stood in need in those years.

It is not, however, the price of corn only in France at the period here referred to, that affords the strongest presumption, if not an irresistible proof, in the negative of the theories of currency and war demand. A rise of prices of other commodities and of labour took place in Fiance, and generally in other countries, from a period anterior to the bank restriction till 1811 and 1812, nearly corresponding with that which occurred in this country.

The corresponding rise of prices, and the rate of living abroad, was referred to by Mr. Rose in the course of the discussions, in 1811, on the Bullion Report.

"Let it not (he said) be imagined that a rise in the articles of life has been confined to this kingdom alone. A most attentive inquiry bus satisfied me, that the expense of living has gone on in a ratio of increase throughout various parts of the Continent, as well when the precious metals have been the sole circulation, as when paper has been abundant; and all this without any connection with the price of gold. In France, where no paper circulates except in the capital, and there only a very limited amount, we have the following evidence to that effect. In a report to the Agricultural Society at Paris, in 1805, M. Silvestre observes, that 'in most of the departments the price of labour is increased since 1789, by one third at least, and in some by one half; in a few it is doubled: and this rise is more general with respect to workmen than to servants at yearly wages. The society has ascertained that all the instruments of cultivation are raised in price in a proportion nearly similar; that building materials have also risen from a third to a fourth; beasts of burden about one half; and all other articles requisite for the maintenance of a farmer's family in the same proportion.' In a speech of Mons Daru to the legislative body in 1810, he observed that the revenue which was appointed for Louis the XVIth, in 1791, and continued to Napoleon, was no doubt considerable, but if attention be paid to the difference between the real value of money at that time and at present, it will not be thought an extravagant assertion, that the same income does not now represent more than two thirds of what it did then."

The following statement, however, extracted from M. J. B. Say's work, entitled, "Cours complet d'Economie politique," (tom. 3. pp. 27, 28. *note*), will exhibit more in detail the great rise of prices in France of labour, and of implements of husbandry, and of several other articles in 1811, as compared with 1789.

"I extract" (he observes) "the following document from an official paper:—'Comparative prices of objects for the use of a farmer in the township (Arrondissement) of Saint Denis, before 1789, and under Napoleon.'

(From a report made to Napoleon by the Minister of the Interior, in 1811.)

N. B. Wages by the year, and task work are reduced into wages for a day."

(French money reduced into Sterling, at the exchange of 25f.)

	Before the Revolution			Under Napoleon			Observations
	£	*s.*	*d.*	£	*s.*	*d.*	
Journeyman catwright	0	0	$5\frac{3}{4}$	0	0	$11\frac{1}{2}$	Besides board.
farrier	0	0	$5\frac{1}{4}$	0	0	$9\frac{1}{2}$	
harness-maker	0	0	$4\frac{1}{2}$	0	0	$7\frac{3}{4}$	
mason - -	0	1	$9\frac{1}{2}$	0	2	$9\frac{1}{2}$	Including board, but not his labourer or assistant
locksmith -	0	1	$7\frac{1}{4}$	0	2	$4\frac{3}{4}$	Including board, and they find their tools.
carpenter -	0	1	$7\frac{1}{4}$	0	3	$2\frac{1}{2}$	
tiler, slater, or thatcher	0	2	$4\frac{3}{4}$	0	4	$9\frac{1}{2}$	
Head carter - - -	0	0	$4\frac{3}{4}$	0	0	$7\frac{3}{4}$	Besides board.
Under ditto - -	0	0	$4\frac{1}{2}$	0	0	$6\frac{1}{4}$	
Head shepherd - -	0	1	2	0	2	$1\frac{1}{2}$	
Under ditto - -	0	0	$7\frac{3}{4}$	0	1	4	
Farm-yard boy - -	0	0	3	0	0	$7\frac{3}{4}$	Besides board.
Pourtry-yard maid	0	0	$2\frac{1}{2}$	0	0	3	
Thresher - - -	0	1	$0\frac{1}{2}$	0	2	0	Is paid by measure.
Reaper and mower -	0	2	0	0	4	$9\frac{1}{2}$	
Day laboarer (man) -	0	0	$11\frac{1}{2}$	0	1	$9\frac{1}{2}$	In summer.
(woman) -	0	0	$5\frac{3}{4}$	0	0	$8\frac{1}{2}$	
A plough - - - -	2	8	0	4	0	0	With 1st iron work.
A cart - - - -	9	0	0	17	0	0	

	Before the Revolution			Under Napoleon			Observations
	£	s.	d.	£	s.	d.	
A cart harness – –	2	8	0	5	12	0	For the shape horse.
Ropeslthe quintal 108th. avoirdupois – –	2	8	0	4	0	0	
A spade or a hoe – –	0	2	$4\frac{3}{4}$	0	4	0	
A horse shoe – – –	0	0	$3\frac{1}{4}$	0	0	$7\frac{1}{4}$	Nailed on.
Rough building stones	1	2	$4\frac{3}{4}$	1	12	0	The cubic *toise* (about 261 cubic feel Eng).
Plaster(of Paris) – –	0	12	$9\frac{1}{2}$	0	17	$7\frac{1}{4}$	The *muid* of 36 sacks (about 22 bushels).
Lime – – – –	2	1	$7\frac{1}{4}$	3	1	$7\frac{1}{4}$	The *setier* (about $4\frac{1}{3}$ old bushels).
Tiles (the 100)	0	12	0	1	4	0	Made in the neighbourhood.
Bar iron – – –	0	14	$4\frac{3}{4}$	0	17	$7\frac{1}{4}$	The *cent*.
A plough horse – –	13	8	0	24	0	0	
A fat pig – – –	3	4	0	6	0	0	Weighing about 216 lbs. avoirdupois.
A sheep(of that country)	0	9	$7\frac{1}{4}$	0	14	$4\frac{3}{4}$	
Chickens(the pair) –	0	1	0	0	1	$5\frac{1}{4}$	
A cloth coat – – –	2	12	0	4	0	0	
A pair of leather breeches	0	19	$2\frac{1}{2}$	2	8	0	
A pair of shoes – –	0	3	$7\frac{1}{4}$	0	5	$7\frac{1}{4}$	
A hat – – –	0	9	$7\frac{1}{4}$	0	14	$4\frac{3}{4}$	
Fire-wood – – –	0	16	$9\frac{1}{2}$	1	8	$9\frac{1}{2}$	The double Hère ou voie (2 cubic metres, about 66 cabic feet English).
Char coal – – –	0	2	$9\frac{1}{2}$	0	5	$7\frac{1}{4}$	The sac of Paris.

"Napoleon had re-established and increased all the taxes of the *ancien régime*. It may be supposed that the farmers who were consulted as to the above prices, may, from discontent, have slightly exaggerated the difference; for it does not appear that prices have increased since."

It is probable that there may be inaccuracies in the reduction into English measure, in the foregoing translation; but they do not affect the main fact of the *proportionate advance* of prices.

The rise of the prices of provisions and labour (and of most other objects of exchange) abroad, corresponding so nearly dining the period of the restriction with those in this country, has always been a point of difficulty with the partisans of the doctrine of depreciation, by increase of money, as resulting distinctly from that measure. Accordingly, in the debates in 1811, on the bullion report, and again on the gold coin and bank note bill, the topic was either wholly evaded, or very slightly touched upon, by those who argued from the high prices of commodities in this country, the depreciating effect of the bank restriction on the value of the currency. A vague reference was made in one or two instances to the operation of the metals disengaged from this country, as tending to raise bullion prices, as if it were possible for a rise of prices of from 50 to 100 per cent, to have been produced by the addition of about 12 or 15 millions of gold and silver, to the circulation previously existing in the commercial world.

In the course of those debates, Sir George Shuckburgh's table was adverted to, as showing that a general cause of depreciation of the value of money had been in steady progress from the time of the Norman conquest. Mr. George Rose referred to that table for the purpose of inferring that the rise of prices was from a cause which had been in operation anterior to, and was in progress independently of, the bank restriction. And, so far as that incorrect and absurdly constructed table[①] could be considered as an authority, it served to favour the argument against the imputed effect of the restriction. But it was likewise referred to by some of those who were most strenuous in contending for the depreciating effect of the restriction. Although how it could strengthen *their* argument, it is not easy to see. For surely the restriction act ought in fairness to be absolved from so much of the rise of prices as could be referred to a law which was supposed to be in steady and progressive operation independently of that measure.

The evidence which has thus been adduced of the prevalence of scarcity of corn, not only in this country but on the Continent of Europe, cannot, if fairly followed out, fail of establishing the sufficiency of that cause, combined as it was with extraordinary, and as it proved, insurmountable impediments to importation into this country, to account for the great rise and high range of prices which prevailed till the harvest of 1813. The effects of that harvest, both in this country and abroad, will be noticed presently; in the mean time a brief view may be taken of the coincident state of prices of other articles.

SECTION 7 *Prices of commodities from the summer of 1811 to the summer of 1813*

During the same interval as that in which we have had occasion to observe upon the rise of the prices of provisions, viz. from the summer of 1811 to that of 1813, there occurred a renewed scarcity, partly actual and

① For an exposure of the incorrectness of the details, and the absurdity of the princple upon which that table has been constructed, see Arthur Young "On the progressive Value of Money," and the 3rd volume of the *Edinburgh Review*, in an article headed "Wheatley on the Currency."

partly apprehended, of many leading articles of importation.

In consequence of the discouragement arising from the low prices in this country in 1810 and the beginning of 1811, there was little inducement to import in the face of enormous charges; heights and insurances from the Continent of Europe continuing so high that, without an advance of prices here, little or nothing would, in some instances, have been left for prime cost. The stocks, therefore, of wool, silk, cotton①, hemp, flax, tallow, timber, &c. became scanty towards the end of 1811; and there were grounds at the same time for apprehending a further scarcity. The preparations by the French for the invasion of Russia gave reason to fear that, however disastrous to the former it might eventually prove, the intermediate consequence would be a cutting off of the supplies of naval stores and of other produce from thence; and as the French armies spread over Prussia, all shipments from that country became more difficult and hazardous. Our differences with America were then rapidly tending to an open rupture, and the produce of that country naturally participated in the causes of advance.

Thus by far the majority, in point of importance, of imported commodities, requisite as raw materials for the supply of our manufactories, and essential for the support of our navy, became, from real and anticipated scarcity, objects of speculation; these naturally gave

---

① This will appear from the following comparison of the imports into Great Britain: —

Year	Wool	Silk	Cotton	Tallow	Hemp	Flax	Linseed
	lbs.	lbs.	lbs.	cwt.	cwt.	cwt.	bush
1810-1811	10, 936, 224	1, 792, 206	136, 488, 935	479, 440	955, 799	511, 970	1, 645, 998
	4, 739, 972	622, 383	91, 662, 344	292, 530	458, 547	243, 899	594, 016

And these articles, in consequence experienced a considerable rise, although not to the elevation which they had attained in 1808 and 1809.

rise to an extension of mercantile transactions on credit, both with and without the intervention of paper; and this state of actual and anticipated scarcity, and consequent expectation of higher prices, which formed the basis of the extension of credit and of the circulation of private paper, continued, with only a few variations incidental to peculiarities of demand, till different periods in 1812 and 1813.

SECTION 8 *Fall of the prices of corn, and of other European produce, in 1813*

The prices of provisions, and of European produce generally, having attained their greatest height at different periods in 1812, began thenceforward to fall. The decline in the prices of corn commenced in the autumn of that year, and was at first rapid, having been between August and November 1812, upwards of 40*s*.; viz. from 155*s*. to 113*s*. 6*d*., but thenceforward there was not much variation till August, 1813.

The prices gave way, however, rapidly after the harvest of 1813①, which proved to be very abundant.

It was this decidedly favourable season which developed the full effects

① The fact of a great fall in the price of agricultural produce having preceded both the termination of the war and any supposed preparation for cash payments, testing as it does on most incontrovertible evidence, it may appear strange that it should not have been more generally adverted to in the discussions to which the questions respecting the currency, and the transitions from war to peace, have given rise. The wonder will cease, however, when it is observed that the customary mode of referring to the prices of corn in treating of subjects connected with them, has been to take the average of the year ending with December. This mode involves the fallacy which has already been pointed out, and is calculated to convey the impression that the high price of corn continued till the return of peace, which is supposed to have induced preparations for cash payments.

of the encouragement that had been held out by the long previous range of high prices to the application of great additional capital to the land. The extent to which that encouragement had operated is stated by the Committee on the Corn Laws, in 1814 (Report, p. 3.), in the following terms: —

"It appears to your committee to be established by all the evidence, that, within the last twenty years, a very rapid and extensive progress has been made in the agriculture of the United Kingdom: that great additional capitals have been skilfully and successfully applied, not only to the improved management of lands already in tillage, but also to the converting of large tracts of inferior pasture into productive arable, and the reclaiming and inclosing of fens, commons, and wastes, which have been brought into a state of regular cultivation."

There had not only, thus, been an increased breadth of land in improved cultivation, but the produce per acre was unusually large. The whole fall, resulting from these causes, will clearly appear by the following statement of the average prices: —

		Wheat.	Barley.	Oats.
August,	1812,	155*s*. 0*d*.	79*s*. 10*d*.	50*s*. 2*d*.
Dec.,	—	121*s*. 0*d*.	64*s*. 0*d*.	44*s*. 1*d*.
August,	1813,	112*s*. 0*d*.	55*s*. 7*d*.	40*s*. 4*d*.
Dec.,	—	73*s*. 6*d*.	42*s*. 11*d*.	27*s*. 7*d*. ①

① The price of oats fluctuated in an extraordinary degree, the average price had been, in

January, 1812,		31*s*. 9*d*.
June,	—	69*s*. 0*d*.

Here is a *fall exceeding fifty per cent* within two years, during which the price of gold had been rising, and attained the greatest height that it ever reached, and was, on an average, higher than at any preceding or succeeding period. Moreover, *while the decline in corn was most rapid, the price of gold was actually rising*; viz. from June 1813, when gold was at 5*l*. 2*s*. 6*d*. to the close of that year, when it got up to 5*l*. 10*s*..

The fall in the prices of commodities imported from the Continent of Europe was taking place in proportion as the opening of the ports from whence they were shipped diminished some of the expenses of importation; but the decline of prices was at first slow, because the continued hostility of Denmark, and the war with the United States of America, kept freights and insurances at a high rate. Still it was actual or prospective abundance that occasioned the tendency to a fall at the close of 1813.

It appears, then, that the occurrence of a single good harvest, and the removal of some part of the political obstructions to a foreign supply, had the effect of producing a great fall in the prices of corn, and of other articles of European produce; or, in other words, that immediately upon the cessation of what one might have thought had been obviously enough the cause of advance, prices tended to a subsidence to the level from which they had risen. And if abundant proof had not already been adduced of the absence of the causes commonly assigned, viz. of the bank restriction or war demand, it would be found in the fact, that the bank issues, and the war demand continuing on as large a scale as ever, or rather on a greatly increased scale, prices of corn, and of all the other articles that had risen with corn, were falling rapidly in 1813. But were it possible that the conclusion to that effect could be made stronger, it would be so by reference to the circumstance of an equal fall of prices of corn in France, consequent upon the harvest of 1813, and this while the war was still carried on, on a gigantic scale, and nearer to her own frontiers. In truth, the prices continued to fall there while the war was waged within her own territory. The fall in the price of wheat in France, between 1812 and 1814, was from 34 fr. 33 cents, the hectolitre, to 17 fr. 73 cents. ; being nearly 50 per cent, or the same as occurred coincidently in this country. Now, according to the theory that the gold disengaged from this country diminished the value of the precious metals on the Continent, and was the sole or the main cause of the rise of prices there during the restriction, how is this fall of the price between 1812 and 1814 in France, and on the Continent of Europe generally, to be accounted for consistently with such hypothesis; this fall of prices having occurred when the stock of gold spared from this country, and added to the circulation of the commercial world, was precisely at its maximum? This instance, however, is only one among many, that not only was the amount of the metals disengaged from this country, totally inadequate to produce any perceptible effect on prices, but that the facts are in the order of time of their occurrence, at variance with the hypothesis.

SECTION 9 *Rise of prices of exportable commodities in 1813*

As a still further illustration of the manner in which the anti-commercial character of the war and of the Continental system had operated on prices, it may be observed, that while corn and other European raw produce were falling, all articles of export, viz. West India, and generally all transatlantic, produce began to rise coincidently with the first tendency of the former to fall. The lowest point of depression of West India produce, and of other commodities, including manufactures, calculated for the markets of the Continent of Europe, and the United States, occurred at the close of 1811, and in the early part of 1812. All these articles experienced a moderate degree of improvement towards the close of 1812, with the exception of such descriptions as were exclusively or chiefly calculated for export to the United States, and these of course were much depressed by the war which then broke out. By the retreat of the French from Moscow, not only the ports of Russia were seemed from the danger of being again shut against us, but daily tidings were received of other ports in the north of Europe being opened to a trade with this country; and sanguine expectations were beginning to be entertained that the ports of France itself would at no remote period be open to us. The new markets — for such they might then be called — which were thus presented, and the prospect of more, gave rise to a speculative demand for all the articles really wanted, and for many others which it was anticipated would probably be wanted, by the countries with which we had then suddenly come into communication. Colonial produce, as it had been most depressed by our previous exclusion from those markets, experienced the greatest and most rapid advance, but many other articles of export participated in the demand, which prevailed thenceforward till the close of 1813, and the early part of 1814, with greater or less intensity according as the events of the war seemed to hasten or retard a general peace. The conclusion of the war was then hailed as holding out the prospect of an unlimited demand on the part of the inhabitants of the Continent, for the articles from the use of which they had been so long debarred.

The earliest shipments of such exportable commodities as had been bought at the low prices answered of course, and the profits thence arising naturally encouraged the subsequent speculation. This speculation, and the consequent over trading, proceeded to a most extravagant length till the spring of 1814. It began, as has already been noticed, with the great reverses of the French in 1812, and went on, with fluctuations, according to the vicissitudes of the subsequent military operations, till the peace of Paris, which was the consummation of the views of the speculators; the ports of France, as well as those of all the rest of Europe, being then opened to a direct commercial intercourse with this country.

It had been usual, in former periods, to consider that colonial produce should rise in war and fall in peace, in consequence of the difference of the charges of importation; but the period in question was supposed to form an exception to this general rule: it was calculated that the inhabitants of the Continent, having been so long debarred by the anti-commercial decrees of their governments from the enjoyment of sugar and coffee, and of various other descriptions of commodities would, now that commercial intercourse with this country was restored, require a supply, at almost any price, of most of the articles that had been accumulated here during the absence of foreign demand. Proceeding on this supposition, a great number of adventurers, departing from their ordinary pursuits, entered into speculations in exports with the greatest avidity. Many retail tradesmen who failed in 1814 and 1815 were, upon a disclosure of their accounts, found to have been concerned in shipments of sugar and coffee to the Continent. The contagion spread to the outports (of these, Leith and Hull were most prominent); and it was said that a large proportion of the shopkeepers residing in them, who failed at that time, owed their ruin to having been tempted into speculations of the kind which I have described.

	1811-1812.		1813-1814.	
Coffee, Jamaica, per cwt. – –	54*s*.	73*s*.	118*s*.	142*s*.
St. Domingo, – –	36*s*.	42*s*.	116*s*.	126*s*.
Sugar, Gazette average, – –	34*s*.	11*d*.	97*s*.	2*d*.
Havannah, white, – –	30*s*.	46*s*.	110*s*.	134*s*.
Cotton, bowed Georgia, per lb. – –	7*d*.	9*d*.	2*s*. 4*d*.	2*s*. 6*d*.
Cochineal, – – – – –	29*s*.	31*s*.	47*s*.	52*s*.
Indigo, E. I. superior, – –	8*s*.	9*s*. 6*d*.	12*s*.	16*s*.
Pepper, black, – – – –	7*d*.	$7\frac{1}{2}d$.	20*d*.	21*d*.
Tobacco, Virginia, – – – –	2*d*.	7*d*.	1*s*. 10*d*.	5*s*. 6*d*.
Logwood, per ton – – – –	10*l*. to	11*l*.	22*l*. to	23*l*.

This extraordinary rise of all exportable produce which took place only in consequence of the approaching peace, and reached its greatest height when the peace was concluded, and when, according to the received doctrine, preparations were begun by the bank with a view to cash payments, attended by a reduction of the quantity of money, is commonly blended with the state of prices of agricultural and generally of European produce, which had begun to fall when exportable articles had begun to rise, and which had fallen upwards of 50 per cent, *before* 1814, which is the earliest date assigned for the supposed preparations for cash payments, and consequent reduction of the quantity of money. And thus a mass of high prices of all commodities is erroneously assumed to have coincidently prevailed, until according to one theory the war demand had ceased, and according to the other theory, until preparations for cash payments had commenced, and the quantity of money had been reduced. The facts already stated are obviously decisive as to the theory of war demand; and if the circumstances which have been detailed in connection with the fluctuations of prices in the whole interval between 1808 and 1814, should appear to be sufficient to account in every instance for the most marked variations, it will follow that alterations in the quantity of money cannot have had any considerable share in producing those fluctuations. Not to mention the incorrect use of the term depreciation from excess of money to designate the rise of one great class of objects of exchange, when another equally important class is undergoing a proportionate fall.

This is the argument à priori against the presumption that the effect of the bank restriction had been that of raising prices by increasing the quantity of money in the period now under consideration. And a reference to the state of the circulation will serve to show that there was no such increase of the quantity of money arising out of the bank restriction as would account for those effects.

SECTION 10 *State of the circulation from 1809 to 1813, both years included*

It has been seen that in the earlier part of 1808, the bank was in such a position with respect to the state of its treasure, compared with its liabilities, as would have been perfectly consistent with a convertible state of its paper. It has further been seen, that while such was the position of the Bank, a spirit of speculation had arisen from a view of the great falling off of imported commodities, and that an enormous rise of prices had been the consequence, without any preceding increase of bank issues. That great rise of prices held out the strongest inducement for efforts on the part of the merchants to import largely in the coming season. It was necessary for this purpose either to transmit considerable funds abroad, or to lodge extensive credits for drafts on this country. The war carried on by this country in the Peninsula against France, had commenced, and required large sums in specie to be sent thither for the pay and subsistence of the allied armies; and treaties for a subsidy to Austria were on foot, with a view to her declaration of war with France, which took place in the spring of 1809.

These circumstances were calculated to operate powerfully on the exchanges, and a considerable depression of them accordingly took place, without being preceded by any increase of the circulation of the bank of England. ① The average amount of bank notes of 5*l.* and upwards had been for the quarter ending.

		Exchange on Hamburgh	
30 June, 1808,	£ 13, 189, 270	1 July,	35*s.* 3*d.*
30 Sept. , —	13, 060, 650	30 Sept. ,	33*s.* 9*d.*
31 Dec. , —	13, 259, 780	30 Dec. ,	31*s.* 3*d.*

And this fall of the exchanges had taken place, notwithstanding that the bank had in the mean time parted with bullion to the amount of upwards of three millions. There was no price of gold quoted at the close of 1808; but, in proportion to the exchanges, it should have been about 4*l.* 7*s.* 6*d.*.

① It is more fair, with a view to a practical conclusion, to take the average amount for a quarter, than to take particular days. But the same conclusion of the negative of any increase of bank notes, to account for the first great depression of the exchanges, will be manifest if we take, as points of comparison, corresponding days, thus: —

		Exchange on Hamburgh.
29 Feb. , 1808	11, 093, 690	34*s.* 6*d.*
29 Feb. , 1809	14, 241, 360	31*s.* 0*d.*

Here then is a sudden divergence between the value of the paper and that of gold, to the extent of about 12 per cent, without any such increase of the amount of the bank issues as could by possibility be assigned as the moving cause of that divergence. Thus far, therefore, there can be no difficulty in concluding that in this divergence it was the gold that by an extraordinary and sudden demand for it, for purposes of foreign payments, had become of increased value, and not that the paper (being stationary in amount), had become of diminished value. And if the bank had thenceforth continued to keep down the amount of its issues, although the probability is, that under the increasing pressure of the great additional expenditure which we shall have occasion to notice, the exchanges might still have fallen, the grounds of presumption that the depression of the exchanges, and the high price of gold, were not caused by the increase of bank notes, would have been irresistible. The inference, too, would have been inevitable, that it was the gold that had diverged from the paper, and not the paper from the gold. Not but that the amount of the paper might, consistently with the rule which ought to govern the bank issues, be considered to have been excessive, inasmuch as it was the duty of the directors to have contracted their issues, in order to have preserved the value of their paper on a level with that of gold; but the question immediately under consideration is, whether there is presumptive evidence of an increase of money having been the moving cause of the fall of the exchanges and the rise of the price of gold. It is possible — so increased, apparently, were the functions of bank of England notes — that if the amount had been merely kept down in 1809, at what it had been in 1808, the further depression of the exchanges might at least have been stopped, and they might even have rallied. But, notwithstanding the rapid fall of the exchanges at the close of 1808, the bank issues, instead of being reduced or simply limited to what they had been, were for sometime thenceforward increased in amount.

As it was at this period that the great divergence between paper and gold ocurred, and gave rise to the bullion controversy which has in various forms ever since subsisted, it may be worth while, previously to examining the connection between the bank circulation, as it actually existed, with the state of the exchanges, and of the price of gold and of commodities, to consider hypothetically what might have been the effect in a commercial and financial point of view, if such a regulation of the amount of bank paper had been adopted, as might have been effectual in preserving the value of it on a level with that of gold.

In considering what might in this case have been the state of things compared with what it was, we are not to suppose such a system of management of the bank as prevailed before the restriction, and has prevailed since the resumption of cash payments; because being, in 1808, fully in a position that would, under ordinary circumstances, have admitted of paying in cash, the directors would, according to their former, and according to their more recent practice, have delayed taking the measures of precaution which the extraordinary circumstances that then arose imperiously prescribed. They would, as they had formerly, and have since done, neglecting the early indications by the fall of the Exchanges, and the consequent drain on their coffers, of the necessity of contracting, and at any rate of not enlarging the circulation, have yielded to the increased and urgent applications, whether of government for advances, or of the mercantile community for discounts, and so have allowed the further pressure on the exchanges, and the drain on their coffers, to acquire such force as no subsequent effort would be sufficient to counteract. It is therefore perfectly clear that if the restriction had not taken place in 1797, and if the convertibility had proceeded as it might subsequently have done (subject to some effort under the pressure of 1800 and 1801), till the close of 1808, the bank would, under its ordinary mode of management, have inevitably been brought to a stand in 1809. For the disturbing circumstances which have already been noticed as coming into operation, in depressing the exchanges, were acquiring an enormously increased force; and the amount of the payments abroad, for which it had become necessary to provide, in fulfilment of engagements *already entered into*, had, in 1809, risen to an amount much beyond that which could be met by exports of commodities in sufficient time, or upon points directly applicable for those payments, supposing even that there existed no political obstacles to exportation.

The government expenditure abroad amounted, in 1808, 1809, and 1810, to upwards of thirty-two millions, and the importations of grain to upwards of ten millions①, making together, extra foreign payments, to the

① Government expenditure abroad: —

1808	–	–	–	£ 9, 552, 000
1809	–	–	–	10, 235, 000
1810	–	–	–	12, 372, 000
				32, 159, 000

Value of grain imported: —

1808 –	–	–	£ 336, 460	
1809 –	–	–	2, 705, 496	
1810 –			7, 077, 865	10, 119, 821 42, 278, 821

Appendix to Mr. Vansittart's Speech on the Bullion Question, 1811.

amount of forty-two millions. But, in addition to these great payments to be made abroad, there was, in the two latter years, an unusually large importation of other goods besides corn; and these goods, as well as the grain, being imported wholly in foreign ships, and being of a very bulky description, the freights, which were extravagantly high, constituted a very important addition to the other items of foreign payments. Mr. George Rose staled, in his speech on the Bullion Report, in 1811, that not less than five millions and a half had been paid in the preceding year for foreign freights, from the impracticability of employing British shipping to the ports in the North of Europe. And while the payments to be made by this country were swelled to this enormous magnitude, the rigours of the Continental system, aided in their operation by the effect of our own orders in council, tended more and more to circumscribe the means of export of commodities to meet those payments. So effectual was the system of exclusion from the Continent of Europe, of the principal articles of usual export from this country thither, that while coffee here was under 4*d*. the pound, it was worth 4*s*. to 5*s*. the pound in France.

And it has been argued[①], and justly argued, that as the prices of our exportable commodities were already so low here, and so high on the Continent of Europe, as to hold out all possible inducement to overcome the obstacles which then existed to the introduction of them into the

① This point has been urged with remarkable force and clearness by the writer of a series of letters under the signature of H. B. T., which appealed in the Morning Chronicle in December, 1833, and January, 1834, and have since been published in a collected form. The same line of argument against the received doctrine of depreciation from excess of money consequent on the bank restriction, has been followed, and very clearly stated, in a publication, entitled, "Observations on the Report of the Bullion Committee of 1810, in a Letter addressed to the Members of the Political Economy Club, by A. G. Stapleton, Esq." 1837.

Continental markets, no additional reduction of prices of those articles in this country, that could have been effected by the utmost contraction of the circulation, would have forced the export of an additional cask of sugar or coffee, or an additional bale of our manufactures. The vast accumulation of colonial produce and of manufactured exportable commodities which took place in this country in 1810 and 1811, and which contributed greatly to the distress prevailing at that period, is referred to in proof of the insurmountable impediments then existing to exportation. ①

This argument is correct as far as it goes②, but it takes in only one of the points of view in which the influence of a different regulation of the bank issues is to be considered. It may be admitted, that a contraction of the circulation would not, or at least might not, have been effectual in inducing any additional exports of commodities. But it would, if *timely* applied, have had a very great effect in reducing the amount of the imports, and in reducing also the amount of the sums to be transmitted abroad by a saving of the difference of exchange. If, seeing the enormous speculations which were on foot between the close of 1807 and the summer of 1808, and becoming aware of the political circumstances which inevitably led to a very large government expenditure abroad; feeling,

① In the letters of H. T. B., already referred to, the writer says, "If 60,000 tons of coffee, held here unsaleable at. 6*d*. the pound, while coffee was 4*s*. or 5*s*. the pound on the Continent, is not evidence that the impediment was more than all the subtlety of mercantile men could overcome, it is in vain to look for proof of such a fact."

② It applies, perhaps, more distinctly to 1810 and 1811, than to 1808 and 1809; as it was not till the actual burning and confiscation in the Prussian ports, in 1810, of goods shipped to a vast amount from this country, that the system of exclusion became so effectual.

indeed, the effect of those circumstances by the demand for bullion①, of which the stock in the bank was rapidly decreasing; and seeing, moreover, the strong tendency which, early in the autumn of 1808 was manifested to a fall of the exchanges, the bank had contracted its issues, it is fairly to be presumed that a contraction *so timed* would, although carried only to a moderate extent, have had a considerable influence upon the amount of the imports in the following season. If the merchants had become apprized, by a notice similar to that which the bank had given in December, 1795, of a limitation somewhat below the usual or the expected amount of accommodation by discount, and by a generally diminished facility in the money market, which would have followed from such a limitation by the Bank, in the autumn of 1808, that they were not to rely, in entering into further engagements, upon the accustomed facilities, there is every reason to believe that their orders would have been under lower limits of price; or, if they sought consignments, they would not, indeed, they could not, have offered such large advances upon them. The consequence of such lower limits, or, of lower offers of advance, or, in other words, of greater prudence in mercantile engagements for importation, would have been most important in its influence on the exchanges. The whole of the imports in 1809 and 1810② would have been less, and the cost of the smaller quantity

① Not, indeed, on the part of the public, as the paper was not convertible, but on the part of Government, which was the same in effect, as regards the present argument.

② The comparison of the official value of the total of imports stands thus: —

		£
1808	–	– 29, 629, 353
1809	–	– 33, 772, 409
1810	–	– 41, 136, 135

would have been less, not only in the ratio of the lesser quantity, but also of the lower price. But if the whole quantity imported had been less, there would have been a considerable reduction of the sums to be paid to foreigners for freight, not only by the diminished quantity, but by a lower rate, in consequence of the less demand for foreign shiproom. From the difference under these two heads alone, there would have been a great abatement of the pressure for foreign payment; and, considering the very circumscribed sphere of exchange operations which then exibted, it can hardly be doubted that this saving of the sums to be transmitted from hence or drawn for from abroad, would have had a sensible effect on the exchanges. And in whatever degree the exchanges had been higher, their improved state would have caused a further saving of the sums to be transmitted for our government expenditure abroad, inasmuch as it would have diminished the amount to be paid by the government here for a given amount of foreign currency required.

It is hazardous to form computations reduced to precise figures, on data so vague, but, speaking in general terms, it may be assumed to be highly probable that the saving in the balance of foreign payments, which would have been effected by a timely and systematic contraction by the bank of its issues in the autumn of 1808, would have been sufficient to have prevented the exchanges from falling so low as to have put it out of the power of the bank to continue to pay in specie, if it had not been restricted from so doing.

It may be objected to this view, that although, by an early and somewhat forcible contraction, the value of the paper might have been preserved on a level with that of gold, the object would have been too dearly purchased by the inconvenience to commercial interests, from a forced limitation of discounts, and by the financial difficulty which it would have occasioned.

This was the ground taken by ministers in defending the conduct of the Bank. The answer is, that the inconveniences which the merchants might have experienced from disappointment as to the extent of discounts, and from a diminution of the facilities, generally, on which they may have relied, would, taking them as a body, have been much more than compensated by a saving of a great part of the enormous losses which the importations of those two years entailed upon them, —losses which, in point of fall of markets embracing such a variety and extent of articles, have most assuredly *no parallel*, within the same period, in our commercial history. The state of commercial distress and discredit consequent upon these losses has already been described; the number of bankruptcies in 1810, 1811, and 1812, namely, 7042 in the three years, having been unparalleled before or since. ① The system, therefore, upon which the bank acted, and which, upon principle, the directors justified in their evidence before the Bullion Committee, viz. that they could not issue too much paper by the way of discount on good bills of limited date, at 5 per cent per annum, was, besides the depreciation of bank paper which it entailed, productive of much more loss than benefit to the mercantile interests. And

① With reference to the state of commercial distress and discredit which prevailed in 1810, it may here be observed, that little notice has ever been taken of it by the supporters of the currency doctrine, and still less has any plausible reason been given for it, consistently with that doctrine. The discredit and distress were clearly the consequence of the great fall of prices. Now if, as according to that theory is supposed, the rise of prices had been caused by an increase of bank of England paper, how happened it, that, with a further increased issue, they should have fallen? and if that increased issue had not been enough, why should there have not been a still further issue, for the express purpose of supporting prices, and thus preventing the loss and discredit attending the fall? It may be said, that the increased issue by the bank in 1809 and 1810 was not more than sufficient to compensate for the failures of the country banks. True: but why did not the Bank, as by that theory it is supposed that it could, make an issue so much greater as to prevent those failures.

as to the financial difficulty which a contraction of the circulation might have entailed, it may be doubted whether the increased rate of interest at which the loans would have been raised, would not have been more than compensated by the smaller amount which would have been required, in consequence of the great saving which an exchange at or near par would have made, not only on the enormous sums which the government had to transmit for payments abroad, but also on all the contracts for naval and military stores, the cost of which was increased by the depression of the exchanges.

Upon the whole, if the grounds for computation of the saving in the government expenditure on the one hand, and the higher interest that might have been payable by government on the other, were carefully gone over, there would, perhaps, be found reason to conclude that the one would have gone a great way to balance the other. At any rate, it may be of use to suggest this point of view for consideration, so as to make it at least a question whether, on the one hand, there is sufficient ground for the opinion so generally and so implicitly received, that the manner in which the bank did regulate its issues, afforded a facility uncompensated by disadvantages at least equivalent, arising out of the same system; and whether, on the other hand, the public did not, in the lower rate of interest on the loans, receive a compensation for the larger sums raised. So much, however, may with confidence be asserted, that, according to any legitimate conclusion from facts that are generally accessible, the mercantile classes were great sufferers, and the government were not gainers, by the deviation on the part of the Bank, at the close of 1808 and throughout 1809, from the course which it would have been compelled to pursue, if it had then been under the obligation of paying in cash. Or, in other words, the mercantile interests certainly, and the public finances probably, would have been gainers, if the bank directors, disregarding the applications for increased discounts or advances, had steadily adhered to their duty of preserving their paper in a sound state; that is of maintaining the equivalence of their promise of pay to an actual payment. Anyone that would follow out step by step what they did, and compare it with what it was their duty to have attempted, must be satisfied that they might have succeeded, with less advantage indeed to their proprietors, but more creditably to themselves, and more beneficially to the public. For this purpose, however, it was requisite that they should have been vigilantly alive to the premonitory symptoms, which were observable for some time before the fall of the exchanges in 1808, and then to have instantly taken measures for contracting the circulation.

Instead, however, of attending to the premonitory symptoms of the earlier part of 1808, or to the more decisive indications at the close of that year, which should have led them to reduce the circulation, they extended it; thus committing the fault of which they had been guilty in 1782 and in 1795, and which they repeated in 1824; and rendering it more difficult, if not impracticable, to restore the value of the paper to its standard as long as the pressure of foreign payments continued. The increased issues were as follows: —

Last quarter of 1808,	Notes of 5*l*. and upwards. £ 13, 259, 780	Under 5*l*. £ 4, 163, 380
1st — 1809,	13, 504, 510	4, 335, 880
2nd — —	13, 978, 370	4, 555, 880
3rd — —	14, 144, 960	5, 195, 830
4th — —	14, 464, 730	5, 477, 730

The circulation having been enlarged continuously throughout 1809, while the exchanges were falling, afforded a strong presumption of the relation of cause and effect between the increase and the fall, and, at all events, removed all plea of attempt on the part of the bank to preserve the value of its paper. It was this coincident increase of bank notes with the fall of the exchanges, and the rise of the price of bullion, that gave occasion to Mr. Ricardo's first pamphlet, entitled, "The High Price of Bullion a Proof of the Depreciation of bank Notes," and, subsequently, to the appointment of the Bullion Committee of the House of Commons early in the session of 1810. And, doubtless, there was a fair *primafacie* ground for the inference, that the divergence, then so strikingly observable between the gold and the paper, was caused by a diminished value in consequence of an increased quantity of the latter, and not by an increased value of gold in consequence of the greater demand for it for pusposes abroad. But although it was the duty of the bank directors to contract, and at any rate not to extend the circulation, under the circumstances stated, there are very strong grounds for believing that, increased as it was in 1809, it did not exceed the amount that would have been compatible, but for the extraordinary state of things arising out of the war, with a maintenance of the paper at its full value in gold.

The whole increase, it is to be observed, of notes of 5*l*. and upwards, in the first quarter of 1809, was very trifling, and left the amount to be still very much below the lowest point to which the circulation has been at any subsequent time reduced; while the increase of notes under 5*l*. can hardly have been adequate to replace the progressive disappearance of guineas, which must have been hastened by the great and sudden fall of the exchange. For that fall of the exchange, the immense amount of our foreign payments fully accounts; and there were coincident with the demand for bullion for that purpose, circumstances in operation, which conferred a still further value on the precious metals on the Continent of Europe.

In consequence of the cessation of all commercial credit and confidence, and of security of property throughout the extended seat of war, there was necessarily a great absorption of the metals, not only for the purposes of interchange, which would no ordinary times have been performed by bills of exchange, or simple credit, but also for the purposes of hoarding, which in times of such insecurity must have been practised to a very great extent. From these causes alone, gold and silver must have acquired a greatly increased value. But if to these causes be superadded the absorption of specie in the military chests of the great contending powers, both in the North and South of Europe, the wonder should rather be, that, without a greater diminution of our circulating medium than had then taken place, there was not a still stronger manifestation of the increased value of the metals, or rather of foreign currencies as measured in ours. In truth, the circumstances here adverted to may be considered as having operated in a great contraction, and consequently in an increased value, of the currencies of the Continental States of Europe.

These causes of increased value of the metals were in operation on an extending scale till nearly the termination of the war. And the effect of them would have been still more marked in the depression of our exchanges, if it had not been that there was, from 1809 to 1811, coincidently with that contraction of the Continental currencies, a great diminution of the credit part of the circulation in this country, as a consequence of the great fall of prices. For, although the small increase of the amount of the bank circulation, in the early part of 1809, might seem to afford a presumption of an increase of the quantity of money; that presumption is countervailed by the consideration, that, notwithstanding a further increase of bank notes, *the prices of nearly all commodities fell coincidently with such increase.*

The greater part of the commodities which had been the subject of speculation on the extraordinary political events of 1807 and 1808, and the consequent short importations, had reached their greatest height before the close of 1808: but after the spring of 1809. the fall was general. ① There can be no doubt that the fall of prices, and the great revulsion of credit, attested by the numerous failures between 1809 and 1812, had the effect of contracting the country bank and credit circulation, and thus virtually reducing the quantity of money in a greater degree than could be compensated by the contemporaneous increase of the bank of England issues. As the rise of prices in 1807 and 1808 bad been accompanied by an increase of the country bank and credit circulation, so the great fall of prices in 1809 and 1810 was attended with a great reduction of it: the increase and diminution being in each case obviously the effect, and not the cause, of the alteration in prices.

The extensive failures of commercial and banking establishments in 1810 have already been adverted to; the commissions in that single year were no fewer than 2314, of which 26 were against bankers. And a strong presumption that the increased issues of the Bank of England in 1810, amounting to about 2, 500, 000*l*. in notes of 5*l*. and upwards, and 2, 000, 000*l*. in notes under 5*l*. , did not fully supply the vacuum of the

---

① Wheat participated, as we have seen, in the general fall of prices, viz. from 95*s*. in March, to 86*s*. 6*d*. in July following; and it was not till the bad harvest of 1809 that the prices of corn rose again.

circulation so created, is afforded by the circumstance, that the foreign expenditure being on an increasing scale, the exchanges rose, that on Hamburg from 28*s*. 4*d*. to 31*s*. 9*d*., and the price of gold fell from 4*l*. 11*s*. to 4*l*. 4*s*. 6*d*. The rise of the exchange would probably have been greater, if returns could have been received for the large exports which were made to the Baltic, and particularly to the Prussian ports, in the summer of that year. The whole of the goods so shipped, however, were seized, burnt, or confiscated, in pursuance of the decrees of the French government.

The enlargement of the Bank circulation in 1810 had been entirely the consequence of an increase of discounts. And we may here notice one of many misconceptions which prevail with reference to the influence ascribed to the regulation of the bank issues during the restriction. It has been supposed that the rule, as explained by the directors, must have operated not only in a constant tendency to excess, but that the readiness of a resort to the bank for discounts afforded a constant facility, and consequent *motive*, for speculations. But the fact is, that the variations in the amount of the private securities held by the Bank, were indicative only of variations in the market rate of interest, as compared with the bank rate. And so far from the truth is the supposition, so commonly entertained, that an increase of the bank issues, through the medium of discounts, afforded not only a facility, but an inducement, to the speculations which occurred during the restriction; that, on the contrary, while the most memorable of the speculations took place without any such increase, the most striking instances of enlargement of the amount of discounts *followed* a recoil from the great speculations, and was coincident with the greatest depression of markets, and with consequent commercial distress. Thus, in 1808[①], when the utmost extravagance of speculation prevailed, the amount of private securities held by the bank ranged at between 13 and 14 millions, —being no perceptible increase upon what it had been during the three or four years preceding. But the fall of prices thenceforward, was followed by a progressive increase of issues, through the medium of discounts, which in

① It is not here meant to contend that it was not in the power of the Bank, by a refusal of applications for discount, in 1808, to have forcibly reduced the circulation, and thus to have repressed much of the spirit of speculation, especially of that which extended to prospective engagements. The observation in the text simply applies to the fact, that no material increase of discount at the bank had preceded or accompanied the great rise of prices, and the general spirit of speculation which prevailed in 1807 and 1808, so as to admit of the assignment of such increase as an exciting cause, this being the sense in which the charge is commonly made. And the great enlargement of the issues through that medium in 1810 has not unfrequently been referred to as being the supposed cause of raising prices, — the hypothesis involving an error of fact as to the time in which the rise and fall of prices took place.

There is one point of view in which there might be a question whether, if the bank had, in 1808, forcibly limited its issues through the medium of discounts, and not only not have enlarged, but contracted, them in 1809 and 1810, the ultimate effect might not have been a higher range of the prices of corn and of other European produce in 1811 and 1812, than actually prevailed. The immediate effect of such violent contraction would have been a more rapid fall of prices in 1809, and there would thus have been both diminished inducement, and diminished means for endeavouring to overcome the great obstacles which then existed to obtaining supplies from the Continent of Europe. Now, it was the magnitude of the importations in 1809 and 1810, which contributed to mitigate the scarcities in 1811 and 1812, of corn and other European produce. On the supposition, therefore, that the circulation had been forcibly contracted at the close of 1808, and through 1809 and 1810, prices, low as they were with reference to the cost of production, would have been still lower in 1810; but they would, from increased scarcity, have been higher in 1811 and 1812. Lord Castlereagh seems to have had a glimpse of this view, when he said, in the course of the debates in 1811, "But the effect of a full circulation upon prices at home, I conceive to be the reverse of what is supposed. I admit that the first effect of a reduction of the circulating medium would be to lower prices, — the value of the circulating medium itself being enhanced in proportion to its scarcity: but it would soon operate in a corresponding degree to check reproduction; and although the produce on hand would sell cheaper, less being produced, the prices must speedily rise again, the demand continuing the same from the scarcity of the article." This reasoning is admissible only under the peculiar circumstances of those extraordinary times; and if he had used the term importation, instead of reproduction, the expression would more clearly have designated the supposed consequences.

August, 1810, reached the enormous and unprecedented amount of 23,775,093*l*.. This greatly increased amount of discounts, and the consequent enlargement of the bank circulation, were coincident, as we have seen, with the most depressed state of markets, and with the greatest commercial distress. In proportion as markets and commercial credit tended to a revival, the private securities held by the bank underwent a progressive diminution; and the amount in February 1813, — a period which was precisely that in which the prices of both imported and exportable commodities, and of labour, were in the aggregate higher than in any former or subsequent period, — was reduced to 12,894,324*l*., being a reduction of upwards of 10 millions; and the amount of the bank circulation, which in August, 1810, had been 17,570,780*l*. of 5*l*. notes and upwards, was, in February, 1813, 15,497,320*l*., being a reduction of upwards of 2 millions.

The diminution of discounts, and of the bank circulation, after August, 1810[①], till the commencement of 1813, is still further remarkable, as

① Of the enlarged issues by the bank in 1810, it appears that a considerable part remained unemployed by the bankers, and was returned by them to the bank within six months after, without having been in circulation.

Mr. Manning, a director of the Bank, and member of parliament, when replying to some observation in the House of Commons, on the bank circulation, 8th of December, 1812, said, "In July or August, 1810, it would be remembered that the number of notes in circulation was about 25 millions, but this excess was occasioned by the failure of two large houses in London, which produced a considerable sensation in the country. Bankers in the various principal towns then made demands upon the Bank, to insure themselves against a run upon their firms; but, within six months, the greater part of three millions was returned to the Bank of England, without having been employed." The fact that so large a proportion of the increased issues had been returned to the bank unemployed, proves that there was a principle of resistance in the channels of calculation to receive beyond a limited amount, or, in other words, that there was in the system, irregularly as it worked, and imperfectly as it was explained, a principle of limitation which operated in counter action of all the supposed motives and tendencies to constant excess.

being illustrative of the principle of limitation, which has been noticed as arising out of the rules, or rather the routine, by which the bank was guided in its issues; for it should seem that the bank was as passive in the reduction of its discounts and of its issues between 1810 and 1813, as it bad been in the enlargement of them between 1808 and 1810. The reduction between 1810 and 1813, moreover, shows, accompanied as it was by a great fall of the exchanges, and a rise in the price of gold, how great and violent a contraction below that reduced amount would have been requisite to counteract the increased pressure on the exchanges, arising from the enormously increased, and progressively increasing, foreign expenditure of the government.

If the bank directors had, at the close of 1808, acted resolutely upon the principle of regulating the issues by the exchanges, instead of being passive under a demand for discounts, there is reason to believe, as we have had occasion to observe, that, by a systematic and sustained effort, they might have succeeded in maintaining the value of their paper on a level with that of the gold in which it professed to be payable; and that, by regulating their issues, the trade of the country would have been preserved in a sounder state, while the government, if liable to pay a higher interest on the loans, would have had at least an equivalent, and perhaps a greater saving in the exchange. This, however, could only have been effected by early and precautionary measures adopted upon the first manifestation of the tendency to a great decline of the exchanges: for when the fall of the exchanges had proceeded to the length which it had done between 1808 and 1811; and when, notwithstanding the enlargement of the bank issues, the revulsion of prices and of credit had been so great as it was in 1810 and 1811; and when the foreign expenditure was proceeding on an increasing scale; an attempt on the part of the bank directors to retrace their steps, with a view to raise the value of their paper to that of the gold, for which there was an increasing demand, would have entailed the necessity of so violent a contraction, as, without insuring its object, would have aggravated in an extraordinary degree the commercial distress which then prevailed.

But it is of importance to remark, that whereas, during the very considerable enlargement of the issues in 1810, when they reached an amount beyond the average of what they were subsequently until 1813, prices generally fell, so, with *diminished circulation* of Bank of England notes in 1811 and 1812, the prices of corn and other European produce rose considerably: and again, with an increased circulation in 1813, those same articles which had so risen, fell most rapidly. The negative of the so often imputed connection between the issues of the bank and the prices of wheat, will strikingly appear from the following comparison: —

Average Circulation of Bank Notes of 5*l*. and upwards in the three Months ending			Average Price of Wheat in the Weeks ending		*s.*	*d.*
31 Dec. 1809	–	14,464,730	31 Dec. 1809	–	102	6
Do. 1810	–	16,873,760	Do. 1810	–	97	1
Do. 1811	–	15,413,310	Do. 1811	–	106	8
30 June 1812	–	15,458,660	30 June 1812	–	133	10
30 Sept. 1812	–	15,833,770	31 Aug. 1812	–	155	0
			30 Sept. 1812	–	131	0
31 Dec. 1812	–	15,647,350	31 Dec. 1812	–	121	0
Do. 1813	–	16,092,590	Do. 1813	–	73	0

The reduction of bank issues between 1810 and 1813 is remarkable, not only as accompanying a rise, and an extraordinarily high range of prices of

European produce, but as being followed by a renewed fall of the exchanges, and a great rise in the price of gold. Thus, at the close of 1811, the exchange on Hamburg, although the circulation was less by near a million and a half than at the close of 1810, fell from 31*s*. 9*d*. to 24*s*., and the price of gold rose from 4*l*. 4*s*. 6*d*. to 4*l*. 19*s*. 6*d*.[①]

Notwithstanding this great fall of the exchanges, and the rise of the price of gold, there is every reason to believe that the quantity of money, relatively to the transactions of the country, was less in 1811, than it had been before or has been since.[②] The amount of the bank circulation was

---

① In order to show how much of the fluctuation of the exchanges was dependent upon the greater or less obstruction of the channels of intercourse, it may be observed, that the quotation on Hamburgh, in the early part of 1813, rose to 30*s*. 6*d*., being an advance of near 25 per cent, while the price of gold *coincidently rose* to 5*l*. 5*s*., or upwards of 5 per cent.

② In an article of the Edinburgh Review for 1811, containing a critique on several publications of that period on the currency, the writer, while agreeing to consider the divergence between the paper and its standard as constituting a depreciation of the paper, calls in question the peremptoriness of the conclusions of Mr. Ricardo and Mr. Huskisson, that the fall of the exchanges necessarily implied an increase and excess in the amount of the currency of this country, and illustrates his own view by the following hypothetical cases, of which the last represents the state of things as, it appears to me, it actually existed, with reference to the currency, in 1811: — "In the case of a diminished supply from the mines, or a greater consumption of the precious metals in some of the principal states of Europe, an immediate demand would be felt in the rest for bullion to be exported; the market price of bullion would be raised for a time above the Mint price, the notes of the different banks would return upon them to be exchanged for corn, which would be sent abroad. The consequence would be, that the whole currency, consisting still of the same proportion of paper to coin, would be diminished in quantity and raised in value; the market price of bullion would soon sink to the Mint price; the exchanges, which had been unusually unfavourable, would be restored to their accustomed state; and no other effect would be felt, than a general fall of prices throughout the commercial world.

"Now if, in the case last supposed, the paper of one of these countries were not convertible into coin, and very little specie remained in calculation, it is quite clear that the currency would not have the means of assimilating itself to the currencies of the nations with which it was connected; the market price of bullion would rise very greatly above its mint price; all the gold which could readily he collected, would be exported, but as this would be inconsiderable, and as the great mass of paper would remain undiminished, or perhaps slightly increased to supply the vacancies occasioned by the gold exported, the

lower than it had been in the year preceding, or has since been. And the country bank and the general credit circulation must have been greatly reduced by the extraordinary number of failures, and the general state of discredit then prevailing.

Mr. George Rose remarked, and dwelt at some length, on the presumptive evidence of there being a reduced amount of circulating medium in 1811, as compared with the period anterior to the restriction. And if he was right in his computation, by which he made out that the quantity of gold in circulation bad been, in 1798, forty millions, it must have been beyond question, that the total of the circulating medium, in 1811, must have been less than in 1798. Mr. Rose, after stating the grounds for his computation of the quantity of gold, went on to say,

"If, then, in estimating the coin in 1798, we rate it,	instead of
40,000,000*l*., at - - - - - - -	£ 35,000,000
The Bank of England notes then in circulation were -	11,278,000
	£ 46,278,000
Coin in circulation now (perhaps a high estimate) -	3,000,000
Bank of England notes in circulation - - -	23,000,000
	26,000,000
	£ 20,278,000

"Here, then, is a sum of 20,000,000*l*. in the whole less than in 1798, notwithstanding the immense increase of our revenue, commerce, and manufactures; from which, however, should be taken the amount in

---

great excess of the market price of bullion above the mint price, and the very unfavourable exchanges, would become permanent(subject, however, still to variations occasioned by the balance of trade and payments), and the currency of such a country would be, to all intents and purposes, depreciated, when compared with gold and silver and the currencies of other countries, just as it would be from an original excess of paper issues, *although, on the whole, taking paper and guineas together, the amount of the currency might not be increased by a single pound.*"

deposit in the Bank, whatever that may be."

There is no doubt that the amount of gold above stated is an exaggerated estimate; and the country bank circulation is wholly omitted. At the same time it is doubtful whether the country circulation, reduced as it had been by failures and general discredit in 1811, was then, except by the amount of small notes, which may be taken to have been at the utmost from four to five millions, larger than it had been immediately previous to the commercial revulsion in 1792-1793.[①] While, on the other hand, it is hardly possible to conceive that the enormously increased pecuniary transactions of the country did not, notwithstanding the continued

---

① In the Report of the Lords' Committee on cash payments in 1819, (p. 12.) a reference is made to the estimates formed of the amount of the country bank circulation from the stamps issued.

"From these materials" (the committee observe), these calculations have been drawn. The committee are inclined to think, that of these two approximating estimates, the second is best adapted to their view of the subject; but they submit them both to the House, with a full sense of the imperfection to which they are necessarily liable.

F7.				F8.
21, 374, 000	–	1810	–	21, 819, 000
20, 977, 000	–	1811	–	21, 453, 000
20, 047, 000	–	1812	–	19, 944, 000
22, 342, 000	–	1813	–	22, 597, 000

The computations are then given for the five years following, which will be noticed hereafter. And the committee very judiciously add, "These estimates must not only be very far removed from accuracy, respecting any particular year, but many causes of uncertainty attach to them, even if they were considered merely as affording data for calculating the relative circulation of different years." There is, indeed, every reason to believe, that these estimates are *very far* removed from accuracy respecting any particular year, the amount being obviously overrated; and if they were to be considered as affording data for calculating the relative circulation of different years, the inference to be drawn from them would be strangely incongruous with the currency theory. According to one of these estimates, the amount of country bank notes was less by 1, 300, 000*l*., and in the other, by nearly two millions, in 1812 than in 1810. And we have already had occasion to observe, that the circulation of the Bank of England notes of 5*l*. and upwards was also less in 1812.

improvements in economising the use of bank notes, require, in 1811, an increased circulating medium, as compared with the period preceding the restriction.

But although in the state of discredit and distress, which prevailed in 1811 any attempt at forced contraction by the bank of its issues, would have been in the highest degree unadvisable, the case was very different in 1813. Commercial credit and general confidence had been restored. The country circulation was evidently experiencing a renewed extension. And although corn and other European produce was falling, a general spirit of speculation was manifesting itself upon the prospect of peace, in a great rise of prices of all colonial produce, the eventual extravagance of which has been described (p. 347.).

Under these circumstances, combined with the prospect then in view of an approaching termination of the war, an effort might and ought to have been made by the Bank, to counteract the increasing pressure of foreign payments, and the increasing depreciation of its paper compared with its standard, by a reduction of its circulation. Such a measure would have involved a departure, by the Bank, from the system which the directors avowed and defended; and it was, therefore, not to be expected. But it would have been in every point of view beneficial. It would have repressed, in some degree, the extravagance of speculation, on the prospect of a peace, in exportable commodities, and thus have prevented some of the great losses of the two following years. It would, indeed, at the same time, have accelerated the fall of agricultural produce, which was already in progress; but an accelerated fall, instead of being injurious, would, in 1813, have been beneficial to the agricultural interests. If, instead of the lingering fall between the harvest of 1813 and the close of

1815, the price of wheat had fallen, as, but for the resistance of the farmers (aided by the facility with which, being in good credit, they could obtain advances), it ought, by at least 10*s*. per quarter more than it did in the autumn of 1813, the ports would have been shut, under the corn law of 1804, and a great part, of the importation of 1813, and the whole of that of 1814, would have been kept out, and the markets would not have been so much depressed as they were in 1815. The foreign payments would have been diminished by that amount, and by a reduced scale of importation of other European produce; but in a much more important degree would they have been diminished by the less unfavourable exchanges which would have been the consequence of a forcible contraction of the circulation.

But although the circulation was not contracted in 1813, as it ought to have been, there was very little extension of it — indeed, hardly any worth mentioning, the whole increase of that year, or of the last six months of it, being only from two to three hundred thousand pounds, in notes of 5*l*., and upwards, beyond what it had been in 1812: and the entire amount, namely, sixteen millions, was considerably below that which was soon after found to be compatible with a rise of the exchanges and a fall of the price of gold to par: thus affording the strongest possible presumption, that the quantity of money was not greater in 1813, than might, but for the great and increasing pressure of the enormous foreign expenditure, have been maintained in a convertible state of the currency.

SECTION 11 *Summary of the preceding survey*

As the result of the view thus presented of the great variation of prices, in connection with the state of the circulation, during the interval here under consideration, it appears —

1. That there were four deficient harvests in succession; viz. 1809, 1810, 1811, and 1812. The scarcity arising from the deficiency of the two first, was relieved by a large importation, chiefly from France, and from ports under the dominion of France; but in the two last years, there being a severe dearth also in France, and the charges of importation being nearly 50*s*. per quarter, the deficiency of our own crops was unrelieved by any foreign supplies worth mentioning.

2. That immediately after the harvest of 1813, of which the crops were abundant, and after the opening of the ports of the Continent, while the charges of importation, although still high, were greatly reduced, the prices of corn fell rapidly, and before the end of that year were more than 50 per cent, lower than they had been in 1812.

3. That in the great fluctuation of prices observable in this interval, while corn and other European produce, of which, from the seasons, combined with obstructions to importation, there was a great scarcity, rose very considerably, all other descriptions of produce and manufactures (except in as far as these were raised in value by the high price of the raw materials) experienced a great fall of prices, and were, in the great majority of cases, lower in 1811 and 1812, than they have been on an average since 1819: on the other hand, when corn and other European produce began to fall, all other produce, which had previously been low, began to rise; and the further progress of the fall of the former, and of the rise of the latter, proceeded almost simultaneously, and with nearly equal rapidity in opposite directions: thus proving that they were under the influence of opposite causes; whereas it is the character of depreciation arising from increased quantity of money, to raise all prices, although some

more and some less, according to the nature of the articles.

4. That the great fall in the prices of corn and other European produce, in 1813, occurred while the expenditure of government in the prosecution of the war, defrayed by loans, was proceeding on a scale of greater magnitude than in any former period of the war, or, indeed, than in any former period of our history: thus negativing the theory of war demand in accounting for the previous rise of prices; because, if war demand raised the prices, why did it, when on an increased scale of expenditure, suffer them to fall?

5. That the rise of prices on the Continent of Europe, and in France especially, between 1809 and 1812, had been as great, relatively to their usual rate, as in this country; and the rise was more general, inasmuch as while sugar and coffee, and all articles of transatlantic produce, were extremely low in this country, they were on the Continent extravagantly high. Thus, coffee and sugar in bond, which would not fetch 6*d.* the pound in this country, were worth from 5*s.* to 6*s.* the pound in France; and all other transatlantic produce was high there in the same proportion.

6. That a fall in the prices of corn and other European produce, took place in France, and on the Continent of Europe, in 1813, fully equal to, or rather exceeding, the fall in this country. And as that fall was coincident with the lowest state, in point of quantity, of the precious metals in this country, and consequently with the largest addition that was at any time made from hence to the stock of bullion on the Continent, a fresh proof is afforded of the absence of the influence ascribed to the disengagement from, and the reabsorption by, this country, of the quantity of gold requisite to sustain a convertible state of the paper.

7. That, according to all the means accessible for forming a computation

of the amount of the circulating medium, there was no such increase of it, taking into consideration the greatly extended pecuniary transactions of the country on the one hand, and the tendency to an economised use of the currency on the other, as would not have been compatible with a maintenance of the value of the paper on a level with that of gold, had it not been for the enormous foreign expenditure, which, under the extraordinary impediments that existed to the export of, commodities to the Continent of Europe, operated as a violently depressing cause upon the exchanges, and conferred a great temporary increase of value on gold.

8. That there were causes in operation, arising out of the circumstances affecting the cost of production, and the supply of, and the demand for each commodity, which account fully for the great variations of prices during the period under consideration, without having recourse to the supposition of alterations in the quantity of money as having been calculated to produce those effects. And that, as far as presumptive evidence goes, there were no such alterations of the quantity of money occurring in such order of time as to justify the assignment of them, in the relation of cause and effect, with the great variations of prices which are observable in the period that has passed under consideration.

END OF THE FIRST VOLUME.